D0595024

Many thanks to
Michael H. Cranford
For the fine cover art

The Artist

Michael H. Cranford is a successful artist living on the Osa Peninsula, where he has taken up residence since 1999. Michael works primarily in acrylic paints and air brush. His distinctive style can encompass both realistic and surrealistic perspectives. He shows his work all over Southern Costa Rica, and does many commissioned murals throughout the area. He offers art classes to the children of Puerto Jimenez on the Osa Peninsula, and also provides private instruction at his studio/home in Agujas.

The Artist's Personal Statement

"As an artist living in the rain forest of the Osa Peninsula, I am inspired by the richness of the biodiversity and by the vivid colors that influence my life every day. Through my art, I learn about myself, about my life and about my time on this magnificent planet. Our environment is truly precious and I hope that my artwork will inspire everyone to take notice of our surroundings, the trees, the birds, the marine life, and to act in a manner that blends with and compliments Nature versus affecting Nature in a negative way. We are this planet's caretakers, and I hope that my artwork will inspire everyone who has chance to view it."

Michael's work can be seen at both Juanita's Mexican Bar and Grille and the NatureAir office in Puerto Jimenez on the Osa Peninsula. You may also see some of his work in Playa Tortuga at Hotel Posada Playa Tortuga, and at The Café de Artistas in Escazu near San José. For more images of Michael's work, see his web site at www.michaelincostarica.com. The cover images on this book are available in both T-Shirts and Posters. You may contact Michael directly at miguelincr@hotmail.com, or by calling him at 011-506-378-3013.

THE SOUTHERN COSTA RICA HANDBOOK

ALEXANDER DEL SOL

Printed in Costa Rica by:
Imprenta Elimar
San Isidro, Costa Rica
771-0714

Alexander del Sol
Rincón   8203
Pto. Jiménez, Costa Rica
Central America
alex@southerncostaricahandbook.com
alexdelsol@yahoo.com
www.southerncostaricahandbook.com

National Library of Costa Rica Cataloguing in Publication Data

917.286
A376s

    Alexander del Sol, seud.
    The southern Costa Rica handbook
    Alexander del Sol – 3 ed. – Puntarenas,
    C.R.: B.R.A., 2002, 2004

    ISBN 9977-12-483-3

    1. Costa Rica - Descripciones y viajes.
    2. Turismo
    Costa Rica. I. Título.

READERS' COMMENTS / TESTIMONIALS

What do experienced travelers and tourists have to say about this handy guidebook? Keep on reading to find out . . . .

"Excellent. I recommend this book to anyone who likes to get off the beaten path."
— *Mike Hayes, Clearwater, Florida, USA*

"As a mountain bike tour operator here in Costa Rica, accurate and timely information regarding hotels, restaurants, and attractions is very important. Alexander del Sol's "The Southern Costa Rica [Handbook]" is by far my best source of info for Costa Rica's 'Last Frontier'. My only regret is that he has not written one for the rest of the country!"
— *Kevin Hill, Bi-Costa Rica Bike Tour*
<bicostarica@bruncas.com>

"Mr. Alexander del Sol, it was a pleasure to read your book. . . . . The guide is a valuable, informative synopsis of what the southern portion of Costa Rica has to offer. Having been to Costa Rica several times before I read your guide, I can state unequivocally: the guide is very accurate and current."
— *Barry Nolan, Whitby, Ontario, Canada,*
<B.Nolan@dnd.ca>

"If you are traveling to the Southern Zone of Costa Rica and looking to get the inside scoop, I highly recommned this handbook. I read all of the major Costa Rica handbooks, but none of those books provided the detail and insights found in this handbook."
— *A reader from Long Beach, California, USA*
(www.Amazon.com)

"Having once lived in southern Costa Rica I thought I wouldn't find a use for Mr. Alex del Sol's *The Southern Costa Rica Handbook*— how wrong I was! This up to date book kept me informed of many fun places and adventures I would have otherwise missed"
— *Andrea Karns Guzinski, Waxhaw, North Carolina*

ABOUT THE AUTHOR

Alexander del Sol lives, plays and works all year round in one of the most beautiful and magical places on Earth: the southern zone of Costa Rica. He resides in the magnificent Osa Peninsula, straddled by the Golfo Dulce ('Sweet Gulf') on one side and the Pacific Ocean on the other, and home to one of the last great stands of virgin lowland rainforest in Central America, the Corcovado National Park. Backed by lust forest and looking out over the Sweet Gulf above the town of Rincón, he encourages the visitation and exploration of this blossoming region before more of its pristine beauty departs us on the trailers of lumber trucks. A surfer, diver, entrepreneur and writer originally from California in the United States, Alexander traveled to Australia, Mexico, Hawaii and other sun drenched locales before deciding to make the tropics his permanent home. He finally emigrated to Costa Rica after tiring of the maddening rat race and modern city life. Once you see where he and his family are living the *pura vida* in southern Costa Rica, you will definitely understand why he made the momentous decision to settle there. If you believe that this may also be a possibility for you, feel free to contact him directly for inside information on the region.

__Author's Message:__ Thank you for purchasing this handbook. I truly hope it enhances your enjoyment of this pristine and beloved region of our beautiful planet. I would deeply appreciate your feedback on any and all subjects regarding this work. Please e-mail me with your comments, suggestions, or even crazy stories of your adventures down here. Really. Thanks again, and may your travels through the Southern Pacific zone of Costa Rica create indelible memories of joy and pleasure that last a lifetime – or longer.

Pura Vida,

SIMPLE TRAVELER

Why do we come?
Simple travelers. Perhaps to feed our souls
The sights,the sounds, the smells
The feel of a different time,
A different place.

Maybe to escape the constant struggle
to hide who we really are.
The confusing tapestry of emotions and desires
Long hurried, long unfulfilled.

To trade the jungle
For the ever-present fear of loss
Of all we have and crave.

To swap the endless pulsing
Of the waves upon the shore
For the speed with which time wears
Tattered and torn the garment of our Being.

The tropical air and humidity
For the stifling consistency of our
Ordinary lives.

To escape for a few brief days
The life we've long outgrown,
That serves us poorly now, in which
Duty and fear keep us
Firmly in our place.

We let our souls the freedom to be
So that when we return to
All that we seek to posess
We can remember
Who we really Are and
Who we dream to be.

--Composed by Hugh Jewell, an inspired traveler, and gifted to
the author in Drake Bay, the Osa Peninsula, Costa Rica

TABLE OF CONTENTS

FORWARD

This book was originally created to fill an informational void. In 1997, there was a dire need for more complete and accurate information on the pristine southern zone of Costa Rica, which the vast majority of the general guide books on this beautiful country almost completely lacked. Tourists arrived disoriented and confused, and their informational resources were part of the cause, and not the solution. The original editions of this book (in its former life as *The Southern Costa Rica Guide*) fulfilled this need fairly well, and somewhat more completely with each new edition. After evolving over the last several years, this publication now strives to serve an even greater purpose.

As our beloved planet goes through massive changes on both the physical and non-physical planes, and our species experiences social and spiritual upheaval as it edges closer and closer to a major evolutionary shift, people need places to go where they can reenergize their minds, rejuvenate their bodies, and reconnect with both Nature and themselves in a lasting and meaningful way. We all need to recapture that sense of life as adventure, a perpetual journey of joyful discovery, that we all used to have as young children but somehow lost along the way. In the modern post-industrial world, with all its violence and madness seemingly run amok, this can be quite a challenge. But here in southern Costa Rica, these aspects of life in the 21st century are much more a matter of personal *choice*, versus the fact of day-to-day life that they are in most places in the world today, including my country of origin. Sanctuary is something one can truly find in this peaceful country, and the magical process of healing can begin.

Another aspect of a vacation in southern Costa Rica is that one can literally create one's own adventure, custom tailor one's experience from a virtually limitless panorama of choices. You won't find a more picturesque, colorful or stimulating canvas with which to play. Your brush strokes can be wide or thin, deep or shallow, sharp and linear or wildly chaotic — like life itself, it's completely up to you.

This handbook, besides simply providing detailed information on places to stay, some attractive dining options, and scores of tours to experience, now anticipates going beyond these relatively modest goals. With this humble work I hope to assist travelers to fulfill even deeper needs in their personal lives, by guiding them into and through one of the most fascinating and spiritually refreshing places on our troubled planet. I am grateful for the opportunity to do this, and hope that I can make a positive difference in at least some of your lives. May it be so. Enjoy!

INTRODUCTION

The southern zone of Costa Rica[1] has been claimed by many to be the most beautiful spot on this planet. With one of the last great stands of unspoiled primary rain forest in Central America, its deep, sweet gulf teeming with abundant aquatic life, scenic cascading rivers and waterfalls, the highest mountain peak in Central America, and one of the highest levels of biodiversity in the entire world, this often overlooked region of the country is a treasure trove of experiences for both the ecotourist and adventure traveler alike. This is where 'the rubber meets the road' in regards to issues such as biodiversity, sustainable development, and conservation of natural resources, and where individuals such as yourself can really make an impact, even just as a visitor. Verdant mountain peaks rise up out of forested valleys as clear sparkling streams tumble down from the highlands. Farmland, pasture and rain forest blend with giant mangrove swamps, where both the fishing and bird watching are unparalleled anywhere. Over 60% of the land is covered by rain forest, and this region is home to the largest concentrations of indigenous peoples in the country. This particular area is by far the most biodiverse in the country, and Costa Rica is one of the most biodiverse countries on the planet, with over 5% of the known species of life forms on Earth. We have four national parks and a national reserve, plus dozens of private reserves and wildlife refuges. Situated between the Talamanca Mountain Range and the Pacific Ocean, and stretching from San Isidro and Dominical in the north to Punta Burica and San Vito in the south, it covers a vast array of complex tropical ecosystems from lowland wet forests and mangrove swamps to ridge top cloud forests and rocky highlands. It's all here, and always ready for you to enjoy.

Before we continue, let me clear something up. The southern zone of Costa Rica, though not networked with high-speed trains or perfectly maintained superhighways (Thank God!), is *EASY TO GET TO*. This area is absolutely accessible, is a relatively short drive from San José (only about 3

---

[1]Technically this is known as the 'Southern Pacific Zone', as the Atlantic coastal areas of Costa Rica (far to the northeast and geographically isolated) are not considered part of this region. Most people — including myself — simply call it the 'Southern Zone'.

hours to San Isidro de El General), and has no more potholes or landslides along its roads than any other area of Costa Rica. In addition, there are hundreds of places to stay, eat and play in, for travelers on every budget, in every significant area of interest. Period. It is <u>no problem</u> to get down here, any time of year. As a matter of fact, the southern zone has had significantly *less* problems with flooding, landslides and other storm damage than our neighbors to the north (Guanacaste, the Central Valley, the Atlantic coast) since hurricanes began regularly hitting Costa Rica in 1996. With the completion and paving of the bulk of the Pacific Coast Highway (PCH) in 2000, and the current paving of the last unfinished stretch of coastal highway between Quepos and Dominical, the coastal areas and extreme southern zones are even more accessible, and comfortably so. The road from the Inter-American Highway (IAH) into the Osa Peninsula was also patched up again in 2003 (I live here – it's really true), making this particularly pristine and captivating area even more attractive as a travel destination.

Another fact about the southern zone of Costa Rica: it's relatively crime-free. If you have heard any alarmist stories about the purportedly "high" level of crime anywhere in Costa Rica, you will find that the vast majority of it occurs in the Central Valley, specifically in San José and its suburbs. Sure, there are a few scattered thefts and break-ins and such here and there throughout the rest of the country — this *is* planet Earth, you know — but anything more than that is very rare and almost negligible statistically, though *extremely* overpublicized in the ethnocentric and propagandistic international media. Compare this country to New York, Los Angeles, Miami, any significant city in Europe, or any other countries in Central America in regards to real crime statistics, especially violent crime, and all your concerns will simply fade away. You are much safer here than you would be almost anywhere else in the world. And *that* is a fact! The natives, though maybe a bit hard to communicate with if you don't speak Spanish, are overwhelmingly friendly, and always ready to help if the need arises. Many tourists have related their personal experiences with the local Ticos to me, and how eager they have been to lend a hand if the need arises.

Regarding the subject matter of this book — the southern Pacific zone — you'll have plenty of opportunity to read about it on the following pages. Just let me say here that, according to both myself and the majority of visitors I have talked to after their trips around the area, this region of Costa Rica is definitely the most pristine and beautiful. The three other areas most commented on as being the 'highlights' of this country are Arenal Volcano, the central Pacific coast, and Monteverde Cloud Forest, in that order. Some have given me positive feedback about the Guanacaste and Atlantic Coast areas, and I'm sure they are wonderful, too. The surfers sure think so. But most people have given the southern zone even higher marks.

HOW TO USE THIS GUIDE

In regards to the information contained in this guide, it is assumed that (1) you have already done some research into Costa Rica and what you are hoping to experience here, (2) you have at least one of the major guide books with you — *Costa Rica Handbook* (highly recommended), *The New Key To Costa Rica, Frommer's, Lonely Planet*, etc. — and (3) you read English. It is also assumed that you have a general road map of Costa Rica. If you don't, you should definitely pick one up in San José whether you are driving or not, as this book includes maps of most of the major tourist towns of the southern zone, but only a general map of the region. Almost all the bookstores in the country carry at least one type of road map of the country, and detailed bus schedules can be picked up in San José (7th Street Books below the Morazan Park near the Hotel Del Rey is a good source for both). This book is meant primarily to supplement your other sources of traveling information, as it only covers the southern zone of Costa Rica. However, especially if you are visiting the southern zone exclusively, it can definitely fill the bill by itself. The low cost alone makes it worth the investment even if you have a couple of general guide books already (especially since they are usually way out of date and often inaccurate – the first moment they hit the bookshelves of stores their information is already at least six months old!) I also recommend the additional resource of the internet. This magical medium has opened up the world to all of us in a way that is unparalleled in the past. Take advantage of it. For the surfers among you, one site that has lots of current info and photos are www.crsurf.com (based in Dominical). Check it out.

Using this book is easy. Just find the section describing the area where you're heading, and read about it. Maps of the town or area you are reading about, if one is included, will be found at the end of that particular section. If you are not yet in the area, I have included web sites and e-mails for those businesses that have them (which is most of them now, especially the lodgings). This is by far the best way to get more detailed information on each place, and even book your stay in advance. I highly recommend this route if it is available to you. Also, the official tourism board of the southern zone, CIPROTUR, has an extensive web site with many southern zone businesses in it. Their internet address is www.ecotourism.co.cr. It's all in English. By the way, according to this organization, this book is the official guide book for the region.

Finally, many of the details that usually accompany a general guide book of Costa Rica (history, culture, geography, politics, economics, etc.) will not be found here, due to the above cited assumptions, and also the smaller scope of this publication. For the average traveler, that type of information is something more appropriate for a sociology class, anyway. Hey, you're on vacation! Don't sweat the details — just relax, enjoy yourself, and dive in . . . . to the southern zone, that is.

GENERAL INFORMATION

Throughout the book, I will be mixing in some Spanish words so that you can more easily orient yourself to both your environment and the language here. In addition to the mini-dictionary and phrase section at the end of this book, I will often put the local Spanish word or phrase for something in italics immediately after the English word (*palabra*), like that. Later I will simply put the Spanish word in italics, especially if the English translation is not quite appropriate in its literal sense. I hope this helps you.

Shopping in the south is great, especially for basic items.

For supplies and groceries, there are plenty of small general stores (*pulpería*) around. Every town with more than 30 people will have one. There are also some fairly large supermarkets (*supermercado*).

The people are typically very friendly and helpful. Although it might not be a good idea to stop somewhere in the middle of downtown San José to ask for directions in broken Spanish or exchange money on the street, it is not only perfectly safe to do this in the southern zone, but quite often recommendable. As was mentioned earlier, street crime down here is almost nonexistent, and the people, both Ticos and foreign expatriates living here, are overwhelmingly outgoing, helpful, and friendly. Don't be surprised if you get invited to someone's home for a cold drink (*refresco*), or to their ranch or farm (*finca*) to visit a private waterfall. It happens!

Whatever your background, a rudimentary knowledge of Spanish will prove to be VERY helpful. Despite what any person or book may tell you, most Ticos do NOT speak English or any other foreign language, and even their Spanish is not what you would call textbook perfect. If you don't speak Spanish already, you would be well advised to invest in a good phrase book and study it thoroughly *before* you get here. I have included in this edition a short section with helpful words and phrases, and a few more words here and there to help you out as I mentioned earlier (*italics*), but there is no substitute for conversational skill in the native language. Good luck.

As far as telecommunications go, the phone system here in Costa Rica is getting better all the time. The new 'chip' public phones are pretty reliable, as are the 197 phones (*colibrí*), and they have them in all cities and most towns. Internet cafes have multiplied like lemmings, and almost every tourist town has at least one. Now if we could just get the government internet monopoly broken up . . . .

Speaking of the internet, I again strongly encourage you to get on the Net before you come here. Most of the businesses in this book, especially the lodgings, now have decent to excellent web sites describing their area and services, some with extensive photo galleries. I've included their addresses at the end of their individual reviews. Sure, the descriptions in this book are about the best you will find anywhere of these areas and services. But a picture is worth a thousand words, as they say, and the internet is the quickest, easiest and cheapest way to check out all your options before you head down here. In addition, things change fast (especially around here), and you should check the current prices of lodgings before booking your stay. Besides, it's fun.

SOME NOTES ON LODGINGS

There are almost as many styles and types of lodgings in the southern zone of Costa Rica as there are people who run them. The selection is excellent, from basic budget to rustic luxury, though the emphasis is definitely on simple comfort suited for this environment and climate.

To save us all a little bit of time and effort, I will give you here the most common, basic features of all the hotels, *cabinas*, and other types of lodgings listed here in this book. The following items and conditions will be found in every place included here, and the occasional exceptions will be noted when necessary.

Cleanliness is the rule. In fact, the standards of both the Tico and foreign owned businesses here is positively exceptional. Even the lowest budget, rinky-dink motels are usually kept nearly spotless, even if the tiles are chipped and the light bulbs are hanging by a wire. All guests are typically provided with soap, toilet paper, a sheet and pillow with case, a bath towel (sometimes only if you ask, though), and any extras of these items upon request, within reason. Of course, the middle and upper range hotels are even more accommodating. Fans are always provided in the lowland areas (of varying type), though a few lodges in the more 'outback' areas without public electricity may not have them. Check-in times are basically whenever you arrive, and check-out is generally at 2:00pm. The *colón* is the official currency here, though U.S. dollars are universally accepted, and usually travelers checks with a passport as ID. All phone numbers listed are Costa Rican unless otherwise indicated (all calls within the country are considered 'local', and there are no internal area codes). To call from the U.S.A. or

Canada, dial 011-506 before the number (the area code for the entire country is 506).

I have found the accommodations here in the southern zone to be clean, safe and comfortable during my extensive personal travels in the region. I am confident that you will find the same to be true for you, too. Due to both inflation (the programmed devaluation of the colón) and to avoid confusion, all prices in this edition are given in U.S. dollars, unless otherwise indicated. IMPORTANT NOTE: All room rates given are for the 2004 high season, which ended on April 31, 2004. During the low or 'green' season, rates are almost always lower, sometimes dramatically so. I have noted both rates in many instances, but be aware that these rates are the sole responsibility of the business owners, as that is where I got my information. Management and ownership change frequently in these parts, for better or for worse, but the combination of your 'heads up' attitude and this handy, informative handbook should give you the maximum advantage in securing what you want at the best possible price. I also encourage you (one more time . . .) to check out their web sites if you get the chance, as they'll provide you with much more updated information and visuals than I could possibly get across here, and occasionally offer discounts if you book your stay directly. It's all just a mouse click away . . . .

CAMPING IN THE SOUTHERN ZONE

The southern Pacific zone of Costa Rica is ideal for the camping adventurer. It has it all: mountains, forest, beaches, mangroves, farmlands, pastures, etc., all of it breathtaking and still pretty wild. In each section I have included some pertinent information for those of you interested in this manner of travel. Here I will just give you some basics on what to expect.

The locals down here are overwhelmingly accepting of your chosen style of accommodations. Of course, the local hotel, *cabina*, and lodge owners would prefer you spend some time in their establishments — and I recommend that, too, at least for a break now and then — but their attitudes are not at all hostile, and often very accommodating. Many places offer camping areas and/or facilities for a very minimal fee ($5-$10 per tent is the typical range). Camping along the beaches within 50 meters of the average high tide level is always free in Costa Rica, since this is public land not ownable by any individual or non-government entity. However, be aware that even if you camp within this public zone, an adjacent business is <u>not</u> required to offer you any of its facilities, even if they have some of their structures within the same 50-meter zone (the zoning enforcement here is still pretty lax). By far the best policy is to maintain a warm, friendly and open-minded attitude with the local landowners, and they will reciprocate in kind nine times out of ten. The current fee to enter the national parks is $6, and reservations are necessary to camp at the stations within their borders. If you speak decent Spanish, you can really make this trip an adventure of a lifetime, as many thousands of hectares of secluded primary rain forest, 'private' beaches, isolated waterfalls, etc. can be opened up to you for exploration and private enjoyment if you are willing to communicate with the local Ticos and compensate them a little for letting you camp and hike on their land. Just don't forget: *they* are the locals, and *you* are the foreigner. Respect the land, the beaches, and especially each other, and always remember to <u>pack your trash</u>. What comes around, goes around . . . . Happy trails!

GETTING DOWN SOUTH

If you are traveling by car, the best route, according to the many rent-a-car travelers we've talked to, is to drive down the Pacific coast. This is by far the most interesting and scenic route, and will bring you to Dominical almost as quickly, but infinitely more pleasurably, than the trip over the mountains. From San José the road has now been completely paved and resurfaced all the way to Quepos on the central Pacific coast, with the last unpaved portion between Quepos and Dominical being finished in 2004-2005. More and more people are using it as an alternative to the **Inter-American Highway** (abbreviated from here on as the **IAH**). The hard-packed gravel road which forms the '**Costanera Sur**' or **Pacific Coast Highway (PCH)** south of Quepos has been much improved over the last two years, and they completed paving it from Dominical all the way down to Palmar several years ago (see the Southern Pacific Coast section), where it hooks up again with Central America's main terrestrial artery, the IAH, which is the other major land route to the southern zone. If you choose the mountain alternative, you will cross over the Cerro de La Muerte (Mountain of Death) at an altitude of about 3,500 meters (11,500 feet). This way is a bit faster, especially if you are going to San Isidro de El General and Mt. Chirripó, though there are frequent delays during the rainy season due to work with heavy machinery to clear landslides. From San Isidro on the other side of the mountains, it's less than an hour on a nice paved road to Dominical on the Pacific Coast.

By bus: **TRACOPA** has several runs daily to the southern zone, both direct (*directo*) and regular (*corriente*), with destinations including San Isidro, Palmar Norte, Golfito, Ciudad Neily, San Vito and Paso Canoas. They leave from the Alfaro terminal in San José at 14th Street and 5th Avenue. The bus company **MUSOC** also runs buses almost hourly from their San José terminal on the south side of the city to San Isidro every day, and their buses are generally much nicer than TRACOPA's. **Transportes Blanco** runs two buses a day to Puerto Jiménez from downtown San José just a block away from the Atlántico Norte terminal (6:00am and 12 noon). All the Pto. Jiménez-bound buses go down the IAH through the mountains, and pass through San Isidro, as do the TRACOPA buses. One other bus line -- based at the Coca Cola terminal -- has a daily run directly down to Uvita on the Pacific coast, passing first through Jaco Beach, Quepos, and Dominical. This one runs two trips daily on weekends during the low season and every day during our summer or high season. You can also catch any of several buses a day to the southern Pacific coast and Quepos via the Transportes Blanco terminal in San Isidro, which also has additional daily buses to and from Pto. Jiménez during the high season. I have included detailed bus schedules for several areas in this book, but be forewarned: these schedules can change! I highly recommend that (1) you confirm departure times in advance whenever possible, and (2) you get to the bus stop early, especially in areas under development like the Pacific Coast.

By plane: both **SANSA** (the government's domestic airline) and **NatureAir** (formerly TravelAir) have daily flights to Palmar Sur, Puerto Jiménez, Drake Bay and Golfito. Charter flights can be booked also, and some of the nicer lodges and hotels in the south will arrange this as part of your package if you call ahead.

IMPORTANT NOTES

For the most up-to-date information on the subject of this book, the southern zone of Costa Rica, please see my web site: **www.SouthernCostaRicaHandbook.com**. I will be posting new information, adding inside tips, correcting any errors in the printed edtion, and expanding my site with both text and photos as time goes on. Take a few minutes to check it out.

This publication is made possible in part by a minimal financial sponsorship of the businesses described herein. However, these businesses are only provided *space* in this handbook in exchange for their contribution, while the *content* is almost exclusively created by me. In other words, what you read is truth (at the time I reviewed the business), and not just 'advertising'. Some people think that guidebook authors should never write upbeat, complimentary descriptions of hotels, restaurants, etc., and completely trash at least a few. As a positive thinker, I personally hold the opposite view. This area is so incredibly beautiful, and has so many wonderful places to experience, I can't help but be positive. You'll see what I mean when you get here. I call it as I see it and experience it -- that's my job, after all. And in those very few cases where I haven't actually eaten the food or done the tour or walked the hotel property, I edit the information I get as objectively as possible. I do my best. I hope it helps you.

With the above in mind, if you find after touring the southern zone of Costa Rica with this book that any information on these pages is not accurate, I would deeply appreciate it if you e-mailed me right away to let me know. After properly investigating your report(s), I will make the needed corrections as soon as humanly possible, including posting them with other updates on my web site. Thank you.

THE CAPITAL AND THE MOUNTAINS

The region around San Isidro de El General is a rural-agricultural area with many small *finca* owners who grow coffee, sugarcane, basic grains like corn and beans, tobacco, fruits and vegetables. It consists of the long and fertile Valle de El General bordered to the east by the Talamanca mountain range where Mount Chirripó — the highest mountain in Costa Rica at 3,820 meters (over 12,500 feet) — rises up dominantly from the foothills. To the west lies the 3000-foot Fila Brunqueña range with the Pacific Ocean beyond. Besides hiking up Mt. Chirripó (see below) and other terrestrial pursuits, there is world-class white water rafting (Classes III-V) on the General and Chirripó Rivers.

This area is reached directly via the Inter-American Highway (IAH) from San José. You'll arrive in San Isidro de El General, which sits right at the base of the Talamanca mountains, after a dizzying and often bone-chilling trip over the Cerro de La Muerte (Mountain of Death). The two major bus companies that make several daily trips down to San Isidro are MUSOC and TRACOPA, the first departing from its own terminal on the south side of San José, and the latter from the Alfaro terminal in downtown San José (see Heading Down South). The Blanco Lobo buses — who have their own station here — also pass through on their way to Pto. Jiménez, as do almost all other bus routes to the south (the only exception at this time being the Jaco Beach/Uvita-bound buses). By car, just hit the IAH and you'll get to San Isidro in about three hours — barring road crew delays, accidents or landslides. (Can you tell I like the coastal route better myself? I just can't seem to get that surfer/beach bum perspective out of my system [the coast is always better]. . . . I also have a certain fondness for remaining alive, the drivers and road conditions over these mountains being what they are. Just be careful, eh?). At least they finally patched up the road again. Anyway, this area, currently the primary gateway to the southern zone, is fairly quick and easy to get to.

SAN ISIDRO DE EL GENERAL

This city (or the closest thing to a real city that this region contains) is the largest, most commercially active and most politically important in the southern Pacific zone. It has stores for just about everything, and caters primarily to traveling salespeople, politicians, students, and a relatively substantial local population. It is a major commercial and social hub, and the people are exceptionally friendly. Unfortunately (depending on your viewpoint), the only interesting places for most tourists within the city are the perennially active central park and the regional tourist information center at **CIPROTUR**, located in the offices of the *Cámara de Comercio* or Chamber of Commerce (on Calle 4, Ave. 1/3; ciprotur@racsa.co.cr; www.ecotourism.co.cr, www.costaricasur.co.cr; #770-9393). CIPROTUR is a nonprofit organization dedicated to the promotion of tourism in the southern Pacific zone, or the Brunca Region in their terminology. Here you can get lots of information — in English — on all the various areas in the region, brochures of dozens of hotels and resorts, and even see a professionally filmed video on the area if you'd like. They offer internet service as well. They are open regular business hours Monday through Friday. There is really nothing else of overwhelming interest within the city for the traveler here, with the possible exception of a few good inexpensive restaurants and some decent shopping, though just outside of town and in the mountains nearby you'll find absolutely superb areas for hiking, picnicking and daytripping (see below). The city itself is laid down on a grid, with the lines radiating out in three directions from the central park and plaza just west of the towering Catholic church. One block to the east of the park is the highway. There are several bus stations: TRACOPA, MUSOC, Transportes Blanco (or the Quepos/Puerto Jiménez terminal as the locals know it), and others. The local buses up to San Gerardo de Rivas leave here from the plaza area and the El Mercado bus station.

LODGINGS

The accommodations in San Isidro consist primarily of small

and mid-sized low-budget hotels, a couple of which get sophisticated enough to offer hot water showers (important in this area -- the water is freezing!). Several of these are listed at the end of this section (be aware that some rent rooms on an 'hourly' basis). Fortunately, there are now several exceptions to this generalization, most of which are described below, only two within the city itself.

Finca Buena Nota – Up in the mountainous watershed above San Isidro, high in the cool, virtually bugless air 1,000 feet about the city and over 3,600 feet above sea level, lies five hectares of manicured park-like hillside perfect for getting away from it all. If experiencing Costa Rica like the old *campesinos* lived it – with substantially more comfort and style, to be sure – then this is a place to seriously consider. Only around ten minutes from downtown San Isidro by car, or equally distant from the Quebradas Biological Reserve with its butterfly farm and waterfalls, this verdant retreat has magnificent views from its high perch in Miravalles in a very tranquil and private setting. Wide green lawns dotted with dozens of types of fruit trees, stands of pine and eucalyptus, flowering bushes, and tall decorative shrubs and tall hedges, all serve as the backdrop for three modern houses spread widely apart on the spacious *finca*. Besides the two nicely finished gazebos – both lighted and fully furnished – and a grass volleyball court for the more active guests, there is a deep spring-fed pool established in what archaeologists believe was an ancient indigenous reservoir. The three rental houses are accessed via a private concrete and grass driveway, and then by stone walkways through the surrounding greenery. Casa Miguel is a large one-bedroom cottage with huge closets, a big double bed, night stands, a fully tiled bath, tiled floors, a full kitchen with lots of cupboard space, a spacious dining area, and a tiled porch with fantastic views of the city. The house is furnished with top quality bamboo furniture with floral cushions. Hot water is on tap throughout the house. Casa Isabel is a two-bedroom-plus-studio house complex specially set up for two couples, families or small groups. The main house is a large two-level room with a huge kitchen space stepping down into a spacious dining and lounging area whose three walls are floor to ceiling walls, all furnished with bamboo and glass furniture. All the floors are tiled as are the two bathrooms, both of which have bath tubs. The two bedrooms are set away from the house and attached studio via a covered walkway. They are furnished similarly to Casa Miguel, but a bit more cozy and warm. Totally private, you can hear one of the three streams on the property cascading down the mountain nearby. Casa Ricardo is a large, three-bedroom house with two full baths. The living area is more like a large terrace, and it is equally well furnished. The houses are all furnished with double and single beds, with nice firm mattresses. ***Rates:*** $35-$45 per night double depending on the house. Weekly and monthly rates available. Children under 16 free. All tours can be arranged, including a coffee tour, river rafting, Chirripó tours and trout fishing. Laundry facilities are available on site. Reservations recommended. Call direct 770-1920 or 820-8002, or e-mail buenanota@pocketmail.com. Web site: www.dominical.net/buenanota

Hotel del Sur— Centrally located for travels into the southern zone, this modern, Best Western-like complex is quite extensive with a square, two-story building complete with a richly landscaped court-yard housing the guest rooms, a nice restaurant, a separate bar, two conference rooms, two classrooms, a recently renovated swimming pool area with nice tile and stone work and two large swimming pools, an associated palapa snack bar which doubles as a dance hall on Wednesday nights, a huge outdoor Jacuzzi tub, two tennis courts, a soccer field, a large private and secure parking area off the highway, and even a modern casino. Whew! Outside of the language difference, foreign guests will feel right at home as they view the buildings and layout of the complex. Adding to the ambience is a lush garden in the courtyard formed by the standard and superior rooms, which are built in a square two stories high. There are 48 rooms total, all built with thick concrete walls, tiled floors and baths, nicely decorated, and all details up to modern standards (including large mirrors). All the rooms feature private baths, hot water, air conditioning, telephones, full closets, cable TV, glass windows with heavy curtains, and *room service*. All have both double and single beds with firm mattresses. The 20 Superior rooms have mini-bars, safes, small desks, and are generally a bit nicer. Also available are 10 fully furnished villas with small refrigerators for up to 5 people each. The large open-air restaurant, cooled by large ceiling fans, offers international cuisine ranging from $5 breakfasts to $10 lunches and dinners, all in a relaxed yet classy setting with linen nap-kins and tablecloths, padded wooden chairs, and light Latin music to set the tone. They offer both a 'fast food' menu with $2 sandwiches, hot dogs, burgers, fries and more. The main menu is highlighted by main courses such as Grilled Chicken Juliana, Trout Meuniere, and Filet Mignon. There are also many of the standard rice and pasta dishes. There are several great desserts, and a wide selection of soups and entrees. The prices are very reasonable, with dinner courses going for from $4-9 each. Their casino is the *only one* in the southern zone; it has slot machines, black jack, roulette, and more. It's open much of the day and well into the night for guests and visitors alike. Other services include laundry, transportation, and a tour desk. **Rates:** $40 for a Standard room and $60 for a Superior room. The villas rent for $55/night (no A/C). Call 771-3033, fax 771-0527, or e-mail htlsur@racsa.co.cr. Web site: www.hoteldelsur.co.cr

Hotel Los Crestones – On the southern end of central San Isidro, on the road to Dominical and the coastal highway, this modern motel offers mid-level comfort at reasonable prices. The gated entrance to the three-story, 21-room motel is located across from the SW corner of the public stadium, a few long blocks from the center of town. You pass through a tall sliding iron gate with multi-colored ornamental plants on either side, shielding the parking lot and complex from the road. The reception area, a small restaurant, and a private conference room with tinted glass windows are immediately on the left, with the paved parking lot a little farther ahead. The reception area is very tidy and professional, situated next to the restaurant with its own lounge area with wicker furniture. The parking lot actually has lined parking spaces and decorative palms covering the end wall, and the owners' house sits at the far end of the area. The main building with the rooms on the right has covered, tiled corridors that run along each floor, with very attractive planters and hanging potted plants adding lots of greenery and color. The rooms are very, very clean and sharp. They have nice beds (one double and one single) with headboards, great linen, a night stand with a lamp, a wall lamp over the beds, a small table with its own wall lamp, a flat screen TV with cable, a pitcher with glasses, a closet with extra blankets, a ceiling fan with light, and a floor fan. The bathrooms are great with sliding glass doors to the hot water showers, and fully tiled with an attractive pattern. A nice touch is the oyster-shaped sink. The bathroom even has a hair drier, and a floor towel by the shower, plus a wash cloth. Guests also get their 'own' brand of soap, shampoo, and a piece of candy. Decorations include a huge dressing mirror and paintings on the nicely painted walls. Some of the rooms have air conditioning, though they are all very cool and well insulated. Added in 2004 was a nice in-ground pool for guests only, just in case you need to chill out even more. The restaurant, with fans, tiled floors and a TV, serves a wide range of typical dishes from 6:00am till around 9:30pm. They have salads, soups, rice plates, beef tenderloin, chicken breast, fajitas, pork, fish filet, and spaghetti, all at an average of about $4 a plate. Orders are prepared fresh. If you don't want to eat in public and are staying at the hotel, they will bring the meals to your room – in other words, there is room service here! There is 24-hour security for both the parking lot and the rooms. **Rates:** $30 single, $40 double standard; $40 single, $45 double with air conditioning. Call 770-1200 or 770-1500, fax 771-6012. E-mail hcrestones@racsa.co.cr. Web site: www.hotelloscrestones.com.

Hotel Diamante Real -- For those wanting a touch of class in your accommodations, this is the hotel for you. This is the newest hotel in San Isidro (at the time of my review), taking up most of a brand new 3-story building on a prominent corner in the northwest section of the downtown area, just a block from the Interamerican Highway. The hotel also caters to conferences and meetings. The first floor reception area is very spacious and austere, with white tiled floors and a long curving black reception desk. The colors are soft, and there are large paintings on the walls, and lots of attractive potted plants. You climb a short set of stairs that passes through to the other side of the building, where you find the fully enclosed parking lot and the tiled outside corridors leading to the 22 rooms. All the rooms have very heavy, nicely finished doors with fancy handles. The rooms themselves are definitely a cut above, with matching wood and material furnishings. The beds are exceptionally high, with super thick orthopedic spring mattresses. All the rooms have the following: night stands with drawers, a late-model TV with cable, air conditioning, <u>phones</u>, a big dresser with mirror, a closet with sliding mirrored doors, sliding glass doors to a small balcony, and a *triple* set of curtains. The fully tiled bathroom has a huge shower with sliding glass doors, a large beveled mirror over a spacious counter, and guests are provided with soaps, shampoo, and other personal care products. The standard room has one queen bed, with a separate room for the closet and sink. The Junior suite has both a double and single bed, a table and chairs, and is bigger than the standard room. The Master suite replaces the single bed with another double, and adds a hair drier and a bath tub. The Suite has a king bed with a Jacuzzi jet tub, and more space to move around. There are also two rooms near the reception area for handicapped persons. The upscale restaurant is located on the third floor with nice views of the area. They sport linen tablecloths, napkins in the wine glasses, and chandeliers on the ceiling. The food is an eclectic mix of international standards. They offer Caesar salads, shrimp cocktails, various soups, and many main courses. 'Honey-Lime' Chicken, Dijon Mustard-Sesame Pork Roast, and Fettuccini Alfredo are some of the choices. They are big on wine sauces here. Desserts include cheesecake, pie and flan. The average price of main courses is around $8. The restaurant is open from 7am till 10pm every day, and non-guests are welcome. Naturally room service is available – how about dinner in your Jacuzzi? The hotel can arrange many local tours, and they have an internet café off the reception area. There is 24-hour security and reception every day.

Rates: Prices range from $35 to $60 per room (single, double or triple), depending on your choice. Group rates are available. Call 770-6230, fax 770-6250. E-mail diamantereal@mypz.com.

* * * * * * * * * * *

Rancho La Botija Mountain Lodge — A cool swim in a clean pool, a good meal, a close look at a coffee plantation, an archaeological and historical tour, a quiet place to spend the night — all these and more are Rancho La Botija, situated just 6 kilometers east of San Isidro and about 2 km. before the small town of Rivas, across the street from the "Indian Rock" on the road to Chirripó. The *finca,* which forms part of the Rivas Archaeological Zone, boasts about 21 acres, and is a working ranch and organic farm. The coffee plantation, which takes up about half the property, is also organic. This is a significant archaeological area with a huge petroglyph and a cut stone shaped by the indigenous before the arrival of Europeans. Tools and implements of the old sugar processing trade, including an antique *trapiche* (sugar mill), are displayed handsomely in the restaurant and outside. A blue tile pool and separate kiddie pool are fed by a small cascade and surrounded by a nice concrete deck, lounging furniture, dressing and restrooms, an outside shower and a conference/meeting room with foosball games. There is also a picnic area, a playground for children, a volleyball court, a lookout tower, and even a small private lake with a bridge to a gazebo on a small island, and a rowboat for exercise (or romance). There is also fishing available in their own tilapia ponds, and mountain bike/hiking trails. The restaurant is spacious and very classy, and serves a wide variety of typical Tico dishes as well as Mexican and fast food snacks, all priced at $2 to $10. Most of the fruits, milk, eggs, chicken and herbs come from the property. The lodgings consist of a *casita* near the pool with a separate attached room, four private cabins, and several rooms in a new building down the hill from the rest of the complex, for a total of 11 rooms. All have tiled or varnished hardwood floors, and private tiled baths with hot water showers. They are furnished with closet areas, tables, fans, and night stands. The *casita* has two bedrooms with three beds and views of the mountains. The adjoining room also has three beds, with lots of space and a view. The style and impression is definitely a cut above, as befits a bed & breakfast. English is spoken by the owner/manager who lives on the property; laundry service, tours and transportation are available, as is a phone and fax. There is even medical service available by one of the owners. There are two rooms specially modified for handicapped persons. **Rates:** $54 double, $12.50 for third adult, includes a full break-fast and a tour to the river, coffee plantation, petroglyph, etc., plus use of all the facilities. For day trippers, it's $5pp for a tour and use of the pool and other facilities. Restaurant available to non-guests only after 5pm by reservation. Call 829-5650, or 770-2146 telefax. E-mail labotija@racsa.co.cr. Web site: www.ecotourism.co.cr/LaBotija

Other Lodgings: Budget hotels within San Isidro include Ho-tel Chirripó (with hot water showers), Hotel Astoria, Hotel El Jardín, Hotel Amaneli, and Hotel Iguazu. Talari Mountain Lodge is located in Rivas and run by a Euro/Tica couple. Chucuyo Mountain Lodge is farther up the mountain towards San Gerardo.

DINING

Fortunately, there *are* a few good places to eat in this town, and after the harrowing drive over the mountains, you'll probably need a bite to eat and a little quiet time to get your wits together again. Here are several good places to do just that:

Taquería México Lindo — As a Californian, I was raised with Mexican food as a regular part of my diet. As an adult, I grew to love it even more. So when I found this quaint little Mexican restaurant — with an actual Mexican doing the cooking — I was overjoyed (Do you know how hard it is to find *real* Mexican food in Costa Rica?). I had to try it out, and I was not disappointed. Located at the back of the small commercial center next to the Chirripó hotel across the street from the park, the Mexican owner Armando Tapia and his wife Patricia cook up and serve a wonderful variety of real Mexican specialties, like burritos, tacos, nachos, flautas, and fajitas. All the meats are specially pre-pared by Armando, and he even has his own meat roaster for that authentic country flavor. The flour tortillas are thick and soft. There is always a choice of beef, pork, chicken or vegetarian fillers. He also serves up snack plates and appetizers like real nachos or mini-burritos for those of you with a lighter appetite. They make their own guacamole (by necessity) and standard non-spicy salsa, and offer three different hot sauces. The spacious new restaurant location is set up like a bar and grill, with both bar and table seating. There are lots of nice tables with cushioned chairs, widely spaced for privacy. The space is very nicely decorated with real piñatas, colorful hangings, tastefully done color washed walls in pastel colors, and even photos of old Mexico. There is always some nice traditional Latin music playing to set the appropriate mood. There are strong ceiling fans to keep the aromas circulating, the personal and polite service will not let you down, and nor will the healthy and well-presented dishes. In addition to the regular Mexican menu, a unique specialty here is the "volcano", made with pita bread and your choice of meat or veggies. And as a real treat after a satisfying meal, get this: homemade hot apple pie! The homemade coconut and vanilla flans are fantastic, too. Try the Jamaica flower drink for something different in natural taste. The prices are very reasonable, too, especially compared to California: $3-$5 for most lunch and dinner plates. They're open from 10am to 8:30pm every day except Sunday, and they can do take-out. English is spoken by Patricia, and a lot of USA expatriates living in the area eat here. Call 771-8222 to order ahead if you're in a hurry.

Marisquería Don Beto – You want seafood? You'll definitely get it here at one of the best – and definitely the least expensive – seafood restaurants I've dined at in Costa Rica. By far the best value in seafood in the southern zone, this wonderful place specializes in delicacies from the sea, but offers many other dishes as well, all made fresh to order and served by an excellent wait staff. First I'll describe the food. Their ceviches – fish, shrimp, clam and mixed – are about the best I've ever tasted, including my own! A medium serving, of healthy appetizer size, is only $1.25 (for fish), and is served with either real tortilla chips made at the restaurant or boiled bananas. A large shrimp ceviche, enough for a tasty meal, is less than $3. The large fish ceviche (usually marlin) is only round $2. The MOST expensive dish here at the time of my review is a dinner platter of jumbo shrimp or lobster cooked any way you like it – for only about $10. One of my favorites is the seafood soup which includes crab, fish, calamari, mussels, shrimp, and more. They have absolutely the best value on a fish filet platter I've ever seen anywhere, only $2.25 for a 'medium' plate of marlin or dorado cooked your way with salad, rice and boiled bananas. Their rice dishes are some of the best I've ever had (and the least expensive), with their special Rice Don Beto being well worth a try. Their "Mariscada" seafood plate serves two people, and includes whole fish, lobster, jumbo prawns, fish filet, crab, calamari, octopus, shellfish and salad. They also have spaghettis, stuffed sea bass, and grilled specialties. They offer French fries and typical breakfasts as well (with fresh squeezed OJ). New in 2004 are quick, inexpensive breakfast and lunch buffets. Their current location is just a few blocks south of the central park. They have a fountain in one corner of the restaurant, tiled floors, and lots of nice table seating. It's very cool and open. They have a stereo with great music playing at low volume. The place is _very_ popular with the locals, especially their 'express' take-out service, though more or less undiscovered by expatriates living in the area or tourists. I guarantee you the 5-minute walk to their main restaurant (leaving from the central park) is more than worth the trip. I go there myself rain or shine, even without an umbrella. For those of you stuck somewhere out of range by foot, they have a delivery service. You just call them at 771-7000, order your meal, and they'll bring it to you. Nice. I think you need to speak Spanish, though. They have another location about 2 km. south of San Isidro on the IAH, more convenient if you're staying at the Hotel del Sur or driving along the highway. In any case, *don't miss this one*.

Bazookas – With a motto like 'American As Apple Pie', any North American tourist will feel right at home with this restaurant's extensive menu. Located in a little commercial cul-de-sac next door to Banco de Costa Rica, tucked away at the back, this real U.S.-style diner owned by 'Chef Burns' Bernie and his wife Laura has a wide variety of choices for those seeking a taste of home. Many North American ex-pats come here regularly for both the food and hospitality. The chef/owner learned how to cook in various restaurants Stateside, and brought both the recipes and language back to his native Costa Rica. Well, let's get to the fantastic food. . . . Appetizers include Buffalo Wings, Mozzarella Sticks, Potato Skins, Nachos and Chicken Fingers. For breakfast, you've got to choose among several types of Belgian waffles, pancakes, French toast, and excellent omelets. Lunch is a treasure trove of burgers and sandwiches – 6 kinds of burgers and no less than *eighteen* sandwiches, including hot, cold, toasted and melted. Salad lovers will marvel over their grilled chicken, antipasto, green, vegetable, and four other types of salad. Their full dinner plates include several pasta dishes. They feature international specialties like Fajitas, barbecued pork ribs, Chicken Parmesan, Pasta Primavera, and Vodka Rigatoni. They also have their own special items on the menu (Bernie's Pasta, Bazooka's Burger, Chicken Bazookas, etc.) for something a little different. Side orders? Check out their *real* cole slaw, and American-style mashed potatoes. Their French fries are excellent. They have some Mexican specialties, too. Desserts include chocolate cake, lemon pie, banana splits and, of course, homemade apple pie. Every day they also run special lunches like fried chicken, fish filet, or grilled chicken salads for only about $2.50. They also feature rotating daily dinner specials, with one usually being a T-Bone or Prime Rib Steak. Prices for the regular menu are very reasonable, with a burger or sandwich with fries averaging around $2.50, and the dinner plates averaging $4. The portions are large, and all the ingredients are bought fresh daily from the central market across the street. You can choose any meal from the entire menu any time of day (Omelettes for dinner? No problem!), and the menu comes in both English and Spanish. They have an espresso machine for getting a needed lift, and all the other standard drinks. There is a bar next door for alcoholic drinks (opens at 6pm), which you can bring to your table. There are two rooms for dining inside, one with bar seating, and an outside patio. There have a TV and small stereo, and there are chocolate and candy for sale. The owners speak very good English, and can help you with local information, facilities, and suggestions.   Call to order ahead, or make reservations for their extra special Thanksgiving Dinners. They will deliver free around the downtown area, too, and take-out is available. Regular hours are 8am to 8pm every day except Sunday. Phone 771-4956.

Strapless Kafé / Kafé de la Casa -- These two eateries, true 'cafés' in the European and North American sense, are both located in the downtown area a few blocks from each other. They are owned and managed by the same creative Costa Rican lady, who converted an old Costa Rican house and an otherwise nondescript business into two nice meeting and dining places. Kafé de la Casa was one of the original houses of the old city, and the owner transformed it into a classic Euro-Bohemian style coffee shop decorated with hundreds of black and white photos of the old San Isidro during the first half of the 20th century. Each room has its own décor: There is the 'dining room' with a huge solid wood table and high-backed wooden chairs, lounge seating in classic cushioned naugahyde chairs at a round table, bar seating by the sidewalk, small café tables, front patio seating, and backyard garden seating in the fresh air. The mood is set by a mix of light jazz, soft Latin and romantic music, perfect for a café. The menu includes both American and European breakfasts, with real omelets and pancakes. There are both hot and cold sandwiches available for lunch or dinner. Other choices at Kafé de la Casa include homemade lasagna, nachos, fajitas, burritos, hot dogs, hamburgers, club sandwiches and various salads. Every day there are three to four lunch specials, and there are also some house specialties available any time. The best reason I found to visit, however (besides the great décor), was (1) the incredible variety of espresso drinks, and (2) the equally impressive and delectable variety of sweets. They not only have all the classic coffee and espresso drinks, but have lots a flavors to add in, including several liqueurs. They also serve a variety of hot and cold teas, and the full range of fresh fruit shakes and smoothies, including malts. The Strapless Kafé, just half a block from the central park, has a more cozy, modern décor, with all indoor seating. The focus here is on breakfast, plus a classic menu of coffee and espresso drinks. They also have lunch specials, and a wide variety of sweets and desserts. Both cafés offer fast, friendly service, and the prices are *very* low for the quality of food and drink. The cafés are really well located for travelers, one up by the MUSOC bus station and the Hotel Diamante Real, the other closer to the very center of town (and the other bus stations). Kafé de la Casa is open 10am to 9pm Mon-Sat, 9am to 6pm Sundays. Strapless Kafé is open 7am to 7pm daily except Sunday. Phone 771-5707.

Restaurante El Tenedor -- This nice modern restaurant on the second floor of a commercial building downtown, one of the most well-established in San Isidro with over 25 years of history, is one of the most popular eateries among both Ticos and ex-pats living in the area, especially for their pizza. The convenient location near the park, choice of inside or balcony dining, large tables with padded swivel chairs, fully padded booths, exotic fish tank, and lots of fans make this an attractive place to dine in comfort. Primarily visited by couples and families, the Tico and New Yorker owners learned their trade in the States. The specialty here is pizza, with several pasta dishes and international items rounding out the menu. There is also full bar service with cocktails and wines to help wash down the meals. A very nice aspect of this restaurant is that all the pizza sauces, all the mayonnaise, all the sauces for the dishes, and even the honey-mustard salad dressing, are made *from scratch* right here with fresh ingredients. They even make their own delicious cole slaw, which is served with most meals. OK, the menu: They have fast food choices like tacos, hamburgers, and gyros (wow), plus a variety of sandwiches. They offer six different types of spaghetti, all with homemade sauces. Dinner plates include both Tico standards such as chicken with rice and *casados*, plus steak plates. There is Cantonese rice, sizzling Cajun steak, filet mignon, Mexican-style fajitas, Chicken Parmesan (excellent), fish filet, and barbecued pork chops. They offer palm heart, chicken and Caesar salads, plus soups. And now for the pizzas: Hawaiian, mushroom, vegetarian, hot pepper, fruit, chicken, and even shrimp. You can mix and match the toppings, add more cheese, whatever. The crust is excellent, and the cheese they use is very good, too. It's one of the best pizzas I've ever eaten anywhere. Drinks include chocolate malts, frozen orangeade, flavored ices, and all the regular natural drinks and sodas. The prices are surprisingly low, only about $2 for sandwiches and 'fast food' choices. Most plates run from $4-$5, and their most expensive large pizza is only around $9. The menu is in both languages, and there is usually English-speaking staff on hand (including one of the owners). They are open 10am to 11pm every day. Delivery is available anywhere in town for about 50 cents. Call 771-0881 to order.

Restaurante y Bar La Reina del Valle -- This two-story business was completely rebuilt and reopened in early 2004 directly across from the northwest corner of the central park. If quick eats on a low budget in a decent, convenient place is what you're looking for, this is the place. The main restaurant is on the first floor, set right on the corner of the block off the sidewalk. The fully tiled interior has varnished teak furnishings, fresh breezes and fans, and a great view of the park and streets to check out the local scene. Upstairs is more seating with an even better view of the park, and a full bar with nice padded bar stools. All the finish work is exceptionally nice marbled tile, varnished wood, or finished bamboo. There are three flat-screen TV's upstairs, a 4-speaker stereo, videos, and ceiling fans to keep things cool. There are live plants in tiled planters both upstairs and down. Even the bathrooms are beautiful, with lots of space and huge mirrors for the ladies. The employees wear clean uniforms, and are very polite. The restaurant has a wide variety to choose from on a menu in both English and Spanish, and downstairs you can pick your combination of dishes at their cafeteria-style counter. There are breakfast foods, rice dishes, pastas, soups, inexpensive lunch plates (*casados*), fried chicken, fajitas, salads, sandwiches, steaks, burgers, fries, and desserts. The prices are among the lowest in the entire *country* here – seriously. Here the proof: sandwiches for $1.25-$2; soups for $2; salads for *under* $1; and full meals for only $2-$3.50 (the steak platter topping the list). You can choose among several types of *picadillo* for under $1! For good, fast meals on a low budget, this is a great spot. Of course all the standard drinks and sodas are available, and there are drinks and food to go. Upstairs you can take advantage of both a good snack menu and a drink menu (in English) at the bar. Snack items include buffalo wings, huevos rancheros, ceviche, fajitas, and seafood soup. Both national and international liquors are served, and there are many mixed drinks and cocktails on the drink menu. Restaurant hours are 6:30am to 9:30pm M-F, and 7am to 3pm Sundays. The bar is open from 10am till around midnight daily. To order take-out ahead, call 771-4860.

Other Dining Options: There are two Chinese restaurants near the park (not reviewed). There are dozens of small *sodas* in town, also, too many to list, a few other restaurants, and several bars that serve food.

OTHER SERVICES

BruncaNet Café – This modern internet café has everything you need for rapid and efficient internet service in downtown San Isidro. Right across the street from the central park (next to Banco Nacional, with green stairs leading up to its second floor location), Bruncanet Café offers 15 modern computers for navigating the Net and doing your e-mail via a direct line to the national server. It's very fast. International phone calls are available, too, via Net2Phone, for just pennies a minute. The office-style swivel chairs are comfortable, the air conditioning helps keep things cool, and the free coffee and filtered water are nice extras, especially if you take advantage of the cakes and other sweets they have for sale. They sell or trade used paperbacks, some guide books, and even an organic-based insect repellent and sunscreen. English is spoken pretty fluently by much of the helpful and friendly staff. Many of the locals do their e-mail here, and there is a bulletin board with local events, tours, rentals, etc. The spacious café is always kept very clean and orderly. The rates are very reasonable, around $1.25 an hour, and with a minimum of only 15 minutes. Their sister café Talamanca Net is located on the other side of the park, directly across from BruncaNet, on the right side of the Restaurant Chirripó dining terrace as you look in from the street. They offer dirt cheap Internet service on six computers via standard phone line. Talamanca Net, due to the slightly slower service and less modern computers, runs less than $1 an hour with a half-hour minimum -- the cheapest Internet service in the southern zone. BruncaNet's hours are 8am to 8pm M-Sa, 9am-5pm Sundays. Talamanca Net is open 8am-6pm M-F, 8am-1pm Sat. Telefax 771-3235 for BruncaNet, 771-0487 for TalamancaNet.

HIKING AND CAMPING

In the Rivas area, Rancho La Botija is especially convenient for a half or full day excursion, especially if a coffee plantation, foosball, or a nice swimming pool are things you enjoy. Also along the road to Rivas, La Pradera (when it's open) is nice for picnicking, walking, checking out the view, or just getting out of the city for a bit. Generally, the serious hikers head up to San Gerardo and the Mt. Chirripó area, while campers head to the coast.

FUDEBIOL (Foundation for the Development of Las Quebradas Biological Center) is a nice place for a day trip just a few kilometers outside of San Isidro in the Las Quebradas Protection Area, which forms the watershed for the area's water supply. This is a community-protected reserve located along the Quebradas River, and has magnificent scenery and interesting attractions. The Center has a butterfly farm, small pond, nature trails and picnic areas, all very nicely maintained. Both national and international volunteers staff the Center, endeavoring to participate in a successful conservation initiative in practice and experience the lushness and biodiversity of the area first hand. $5 gets you into the reserve all day, and includes entrance to the butterfly garden and access to all hiking trails. There is also a meeting hall available for lectures, and a lodge for up to 35 guests. Call or fax 771-2003 or 771-4131 or 770-9393, or drop by CIPROTUR (see beginning of this section) for more information.

SAN ISIDRO

1 Taquería Mexico Lindo
2 BruncaNet Café
3 Marisquería Don Beto
4 Hotel Diamante Real
5 CIPROTUR
6 Kafé de la Casa
7 Strapless Café
8 Rest. El Tendor
9 La Reina del Valle
10 Bazookas
11 Hotel Los Crestones
S Bus Station
B Bank
P Park
C Cathedral
G Gas Station
O Post Office

SAN GERARDO DE RIVAS

Whether you are heading to San Gerardo and/or Mt. Chirripó or not, the Rivas area just a few minutes outside of San Isidro at about 800 meters of altitude can be well worth a visit, even if just for a swim, a meal or a picnic. The Chirripó River passes through this area after plunging down from the highlands and merging with the Buena Vista River to form The General River, and both the bird life and mountain vistas are captivating. The area is locally famous for the "Indian Rock", a huge ancient stone carved with pre-Columbian glyphs. The road is paved all the way into the town of Rivas itself, located on the other side of the bridge 12 kilometers or so after leaving San Isidro, where it changes to packed gravel as it continues up into the mountains to San Gerardo de Rivas.

Although I've never been to mainland Europe the small, quaint village of San Gerardo de Rivas at ~1,400 meters (4,600 feet) on the southwestern flank of Mt. Chirripó strikes me as something plucked right out of the Pyrenees or Lower Alps and dropped into the heart of Costa Rica. The town itself, a small collection of houses, tourist accommodations and just a few small businesses, is strung out along a single curving road that passes over the White River just before it merges with the Chirripó River, a boisterous torrent bouncing and churning its way around massive boulders as it plunges through the narrow valley on its way down the mountain. The air is clear and crisp at this high altitude (sweats or sweaters are recommended, while fans are not necessary), and pine trees lend their aromatic scent to the alpine ambiance. Chirripó National Park is the primary attraction here, and the park office is located on the lower side of the town below the concrete bridge. Whether or not you are going to take on the challenge of climbing Mt. Chirripó, this is a nice place to get away from the lowland heat and go hiking, bird watching, waterfall bathing, or dipping in nearby natural hot springs. There is also mountain trout fishing available, a rarity in Costa Rica. You can actually catch your own dinner at one of several trout farms.

The local bus to the area (named "El Chirripó") can be boarded at the El Mercado station, or at the central plaza, from

5am-7:30pm. The bus leaves the plaza for San Gerardo at 5am and the station at 2pm daily, passing through the Rivas area about 10 minutes later. By car, just head south along the IAH from San Isidro. Take the first left after crossing the Río Jilguero bridge only a short ways from downtown (at a flashing overhead signal light near the top of the first hill). This road winds slowly up the valley towards the town of Rivas, passing Rancho La Botija along the way, just a few minutes from San Isidro. Cross the bridge into the main part of Rivas and follow the road up and left through the town, making a right turn where the pavement ends at the top of the town. Stay on the main gravel road till you get to San Gerardo.

LODGINGS

The various *cabinas* and lodges in San Gerardo de Rivas cater primarily to those heading up to Mt. Chirripó, these being typically frugal Europeans and backpacking Americans who do not want to spend much on food and lodging. Also, there is much competition for the tourist dollar. Therefore, rates tend to be among the lowest in Costa Rica, and the facilities clean and comfortable. All the basic lodgings here are currently run by Ticos, usually families. Also, nobody has fans since the nights get pretty chilly and there are really no biting insects to speak of. Rather, blankets are provided to keep warm. The first place you come to (reviewed below) is by far the nicest in town, actually the only one in town for those desiring more than just a cheap room to sleep in. It is the only one built and currently owned by a foreigner, and both the style and quality reflect that distinction. The 'backpacker' lodgings start just east of this one, spread out along both sides of the road towards the entrance to the park.

Hotel Río Chirripó -- This high altitude Bed & Breakfast describes itself as 'a place of peace', ideal for personal or group retreats. I don't disagree. This lodge, the only place approaching luxury accommodations in San Gerardo, is an excellent place to either cool down from the lowland beaches, or base a trek up Central America's highest mountain, or both. The ten acres of lush greenery is set right on a private stretch of river, where white water bounces around huge boulders and little eddies form secluded swimming holes. If the wild river is not your style, a stone and grass path leads down to a large concrete and tile swimming pool with a wraparound wooden deck, lounge chairs, and a really nice bath house with hot water showers and beautiful tile and wood work. Below the pool, partially hidden behind the abundant foliage, is a private cabin with bamboo trim, a vaulted ceiling, and lots of glass windows looking out at the greenery and river. The main lodge building is a very attractive tropical version of Southwestern U.S. style construction, utilizing wooden beams of tree trunks and branches, shaped and stuccoed partial walls painted in earth colors, and lots of decorative mosaic and ceramic tiles. The main structural feature is a large, open-air *rancho* with a nicely done fireplace alcove (with an extra large working fireplace) with lots of pillows and mats for comfort. The rest of the circular space has nice tiled floors, designed specifically for activities like yoga and tai chi. There are many indigenous artifacts and other interesting items on the shelves, concrete tables and inset nooks. A step up to one side is the kitchen and dining room, with long wooden tables, colorful woven table cloths, candles, hanging lanterns, and even a small fountain, all creating a creative, warm environment. The arched doorways and half-walls preserve the expansive atmosphere with views of the surrounding mountains. The tiled kitchen is fully equipped with excellent utensils and gas appliances. The rooms are set apart in a pair of concrete two-story buildings with varnished wood facing and trim. They are very spacious and attractive, with woven cane mats, full closets, tiled private baths with spacious hot-water showers, hand-painted patterned walls, and large glass windows with curtains and louvers. The amenities include colorful SW-style linen and bed covers, desk lamps on the night stands, and wide verandas with comfortable leather rocking chairs where you can soak up the mountain views. An international-style breakfast is included of eggs any style, toast, coffee or tea, and all the fresh fruit you can eat. Tours and bilingual guides can be arranged upon request. English, French and German are spoken. **Rates:** $39 single, $59 double, and $69 triple. Low season discounts. Groups can rent the entire lodge at special rates. The kitchen can be utilized by guests for preparing lunch and dinner. Call ahead at 771-7065 or 377-3557. E-mail watsufrank@yahoo.com. Web site: www.riochirripo.com.

Other Lodgings (in order of their appearance): El Pelícano looks like a European mountain lodge, and is one of the nicest among the low budget options. Cabinas y Restaurante Marín is next to the park station. El Bosque has a relatively large bar and restaurant. El Descanso is quiet and set back from the road. Roca Dura has good fast food and unusual rooms. Vista Al Cerro is friendly, clean, and has its own small restaurant, and good parking as well. Cabinas y Restaurante Urán is the closest to the park entrance.

FOOD SERVICE AND TOURS

See above, as the lodges and *cabinas* have their own restaurants, and there are no independent tour operators here.

HIKING AND CAMPING

The major attraction to this area is **Mt. Chirripó National Park**, San Gerardo being the primary gateway to this high-altitude reserve. Mt. Chirripó is the highest mountain in Central America at 3,820 meters above sea level. The park contains U-shaped glacial forms, moraines, glacial terraces, lakes, and ancient ravines 2-3 kilometers high formed by receding glaciers up to 25,000 years ago. The temperatures vary between -9 and 20 degrees Centigrade (16-68 degrees Fahrenheit), and there are some trees that grow nowhere else in Central America. The birding is good with the quetzals and other cooler climate species around, and animals include pumas, jaguars, peccaries, rabbits, coyotes, and squirrels. Mt. Chirripó was a sacred site to the pre-Columbian indigenous of the area. 'Doing' Chirripó typically takes 2 days, depending on your physical endurance. It's not easy, though no special training is necessary as the trails are clearly marked and well maintained. It's possible to make it up and back in one day, as the competitors in the annual Chirripó foot race do in February of each year. I'll skip that option, thank you. Regardless of your speed of ascent, you need to visit the park office in San Isidro or San Gerardo and buy a ticket before you enter the park. The park's lodging facilities, at a point just a few kilometers below the peak, are very basic — bring warm clothes, and some food. If you need more info or assistance, the staff at CIPROTUR can help you, especially if you don't speak good Spanish.

Also an option are shorter hikes within the park, like the one to Cerro El Jurán. As mentioned above, there are waterfall trips, horseback riding and trout fishing offered by locals on private lands in the area. Two kilometers above San Gerardo is the tiny village of Herradura, which has nearby natural hot springs (*aguas termales*), perfect for loosening up those hard, sore muscles after a rough hike. Look for the little black sign with red lettering on the east side of the road. Secure parking is available at Parqueo Las Rosas, which sits about 500 meters below the sign. It's about a 15-minute hike up to the hot spring. The spring water itself is piped down from under some boulders where it bursts to the surface from unknown depths, and a concrete pool has been formed in a rocky, forested area that holds up to about 20 people.

The water was pretty warm when I went, though some locals say that it varies in temperature from lukewarm to fairly hot. Maybe I'll catch it better next time. There is a small fee to take a dip, paid at the little soda on the way up.

A place in Herradura rents camping equipment and offers camp sites, as does El Descanso in San Gerardo. Camping is available on *Finca Mirador*, the private ranch of the owners of El Descanso, which has both primary rainforest and a working coffee plantation. There is also camping available at Vista al Cerro Mountain Lodge. The latter camp sites are right on the riverbank with their own bath house, all surrounded by trees and rich foliage. Roca Dura has campsites, too.

THE SOUTHERN PACIFIC COAST

Although San Isidro de El General is officially considered the gateway to and capital of the southern zone of Costa Rica, it's when you encounter the coastal areas from Dominical south that you will really begin to get a true taste of the magic of this pristine and visually stunning region of the country. Here the verdant mountains cascade down from thousands of feet, spilling down into miles of sandy beaches punctuated by numerous magnificent points of ancient volcanic rock. The rainforest of the area abounds with wildlife due to the sparse local human population, sheltering all four types of monkeys and even various species of wild cats. There are many refreshing waterfalls and natural pools to take advantage in this area, while the modern facilities will not leave you wishing for home as progress has brought both electricity and phone service to this once-isolated area.

There are two routes to this area from San José. The first is via the Pacific Coast Highway, by far the best in most people's opinion, including my own. This route takes you through the mountains west of San José, down the coast through Jaco Beach, Quepos/Manuel Antonio, and many other beach areas, and finally down along the coast through thousands of acres of African palm orchards and other agricultural flatlands to Dominical. The other route is via the California-style mountain road from San Isidro de El General, a trip of less than an hour by car, a little longer by bus.

The bus schedules for this area are more or less as follows (you can pick up the most recent schedule in Dominical in the little monthly community booklet called *Dominical Days*). From San Isidro: buses leave at 7am and 1:30pm to Quepos, passing through Dominical at 8:10am and 2:40pm respectively; departures at 9am and 4pm head south to Uvita, passing through Dominical at 10:10am and 5:10pm. From San José, buses depart at 3pm going all the way to Uvita, and also at 5:30am on weekends and every day during the summer. There are also other buses from San José going only as far as Jaco Beach or Quepos. From Quepos you can catch one of several daily buses south to Dominical, leaving between 5:00am and 7:00pm. From

Dominical heading further south, you can catch one of the several daily buses down to Cortés and Palmar (one leaves at 4:30am and another at 10:30am), one of which continues south as far as the border with Panama at Paso Canoas. Once you're in Palmar at the intersection of the Costanera Sur (South Coast Highway) and the Interamerican Highway (IAH), you can catch buses to anywhere along the IAH, as well as one of the several daily runs to Puerto Jiménez.

DOMINICAL AND VICINITY

Dominical, described as an "uncut gem" by one magazine, sits right on the Pacific shore surrounded by a river, high mountain peaks and sandy blond beaches. This is a magical area where the dolphins play with surfers out in the swells while the cooling offshore breezes tease spray from the wave crests. The town itself is a major destination for international surfers, though recently many non-aquatic tourists have been attracted by the area's impressive natural beauty and slightly cooler climate. The vibrant local scene is very laid back and friendly, a much higher percentage of Ticos speak English, and the local population takes pride in keeping things clean. There are unlimited options for adventure and sight-seeing, whether on your own or with tours, and both Manuel Antonio and Ballena Marino National Parks are within easy driving distance for day trips. This is a major pit stop for travelers through the area, with a full-service gas station 2 km. north of town near Hacienda Barú's nature reserve.

Hacienda Barú forms part of an extensive network of private reserves called the 'Path of the Tapir', a project which is striving to create and maintain a viable biological corridor along the Pacific coastal mountain range. This is part of an even larger international effort to connect the tropical forests of southern Mexico with those of Panama in an uninterrupted line of private and public wilderness reserves, the Meso American Biological Corridor. For more information, please contact Franklin Sequeira at 787-0254 or Jack Ewing at 787-0001 (jeewing@racsa.co.cr).

There are several natural attractions in the area for those seeking a little fun and excitement -- and I'm not talking about the minimally attired set cruising along the beach and around town. **Poza Azul**, a large cascading 30-foot waterfall feeding a fairly deep swimming hole with rope swings, is just five kilometers south of town, about 300-400 meters off the road above the hamlet of Dominicalito. The **Terciopelo Waterfalls**, a 3-tiered cascade tumbling down about 120 feet into several swimming holes, is up in the mountains a few kilometers north of the gas station. The **Barú River Falls** (also known as the Nauyaca Falls and Santo Cristo Falls) is a spectacular set of huge waterfalls in the mountains above Dominical, about 10 km. up to road to San Isidro and then a 2-3 hour hike in. It's best to go with a tour to both reduce inconvenience and maximize your enjoyment of the trip (see TOURS section below). There are also the gigantic **Diamante Falls**, some of the largest in Central America, where you can actually sleep overnight in a natural cave behind the falling water (see TOURS section). For somewhat less natural attractions, a local expat with a high-tech audiovisual system in Escaleras has been presenting 'Movies In The Jungle', miniature film festivals with offbeat, creative and artistic films from the past several decades. An even more valiant attempt at 'real' culture has been made recently with the formation of a local theater group, which presented the acclaimed production *The Fantastiks* in 2004.

There are several buses daily into Dominical. The following is the schedule in early 2004 for buses *leaving* Dominical (passing through, really) for other areas. San Isidro: 6:35 and 7:00am, 2:40 and 3:30pm; Quepos: 5:25 and 8:15am, 1:40 and 2:45pm; Uvita: 4:15, 10:00, 10:10, and 11:30am, and 5:15 and 9:00pm; Cortes: 4:15 and 10:00am; San Jose: 5:25am and 1:40pm.

LODGINGS

The Dominical area has quite a wide variety of lodgings to choose from, from fairly inexpensive budget accommodations to luxury villas to secluded *fincas*. The following descriptions speak for themselves. For the sake of efficiency and convenience, I will list the lodgings roughly in the order they appear coming over the Tinamaste mountains from San Isidro, over to the north of town, then into Dominical, and finally south along the highway a bit. There then follows a short section called **Dominical – Uvita**, which covers a small but growing area south of Dominical along the highway towards Uvita and **Bahía**. I highly recommend reading through both these sections (and really all the way through **Ojochal** and **Playa Tortuga**) before deciding where to stay, as these areas are all just a few minutes away from each other by car or bus. The Uvita / Bahía area (the next major section) is less than 15 minutes from Dominical by car, and the Ojochal / Playa Tortuga area just another 10-15 minutes from there. Again, there is lots to choose from, and it's all good. I don't envy your decision making here.

Mirador Los Chorros – Set right off the main road between San Isidro and Dominical, around one kilometer before descending into the small town of Tinamastes, this small but attractive set of accommodations and restaurant has three rustic private cabins available. This is a nice, photogenic place to stop on your way over the mountains, especially if you're tired and the sun is leaving for the day. It's also very cool up here (no fans needed). The somewhat hidden cabins are situated on the side of a steep ridge below the restaurant, with a private entrance coming off the main road. Built all of wood cut in rustic style, then sanded and varnished, these little hideaways are set well apart from each other for maximum privacy. They have double beds, curtains over glass windows with louvers, small porches, tables, and tiled showers with hot water. They are surrounded with flowers and ornamental plants, with stone-lined gravel paths to get you there. The views are absolutely fantastic of the deep verdant valleys below Tinamastes and the blue Pacific beyond, as you can almost feel the 3,000-ft. elevation. The clean and spacious restaurant offers typical Costa Rican food in a friendly, hospitable setting. Francisco Vargas F. built his restaurant in 2001 right on the edge of a high ridge, completing the cabins a couple of years later. Sunsets are simply overwhelming from here, and the food isn't bad either. Gallo pinto, casados, rice dishes, and fish filets are offered alongside fried chicken, chop suey, ceviche and French fries (very good here). The portions are healthy and the service is friendly by both the owner and his staff. Cocktails like piña coladas and bloody marys can accompany your meal as the restaurant offers full bar service. Snacks such as nachos, tacos, pork rinds, chicken wings and fajitas are available as well. The prices are very low, from $2-$4 for most regular plates. The menu is in English and Spanish. Take-out is available. The décor a cut above the norm, with linen tablecloths on the large tables and a long tiled bar looking out over the edge of the ridge to the view. It's very cool and breezy here, and the TV and good stereo provide background entertainment. Open 8am-9pm daily. *Rates*: The cabins rent for $20/night double. Call 770-8032 for reservations.

Finca Ipe – This working organic farm, recently certified bio-dynamic by DEMETER, exemplifies what can be accomplished by a small group of dedicated people striving to demonstrate grand possibilities. As well as cultivating the land for modest commercial gain, they have created and maintained an idyllic working and living environment for themselves and their guests. They boast a diverse collection of exotic fruit and spice trees; cultivated wood trees; systems for recycling and reduction of wastes; 100% organic pest management; two ponds for watershed management and aquaculture; bio-gas digesters fed by human and animal waste which generate gas for their stove; a solar cooker; a condenser for essential oils; greenhouses, a drying house, and a nursery; and much more. Finca Ipe members believe that sharing what they have learned with others is paramount to the health of this beautiful planet we all share. A stay at the farm is the best way to accomplish this goal, and with that in mind the owners have recently renovated and expanded their accommodations. The farm runs a WOOFA volunteer program, and they have their own housing in Casa Ylang Ylang. This recently renovated house has a massive common room for reading, lounging, etc., and an oversized kitchen for preparing the common meals. One can dine inside, or out on the 'bistro' porch. Tiled floors and colorful murals add comfort, while the arched doorways and windows create character. There are 4 bedrooms, plus a loft space for sleeping. The new (2003) 22-bed Bamboo House is the primary accommodations for overnight guests. It is ideal for yoga retreats and alternative living educational workshops. The long, dorm-style house has 5 private bedrooms lined up next to each other behind a wide hard-wood covered porch with furniture for relaxing and socializing. The separate bath area is really well done, with ceramic tile on the main floor, and mosaic tile in the compost toilet areas and showers. The main house is built almost completely of bamboo and local woods harvested from the property. The beds are primarily single and bunks, with some double beds. The Bamboo House has its own kitchen facilities. Nearby there is a new rancho with lots of hammocks for chilling out, and catching the sunset. In addition, there are three private houses for rent on the property, all very nice. *Rates*: For volunteers the cost is $10 per day (in addition to the work), which includes basic food staples. For rates for the Bamboo House, e-mail ahead of time, and/or see their Web site. Finca Ipe also offers comprehensive guided tours around the farm to daytime visitors between 7am – 11am most weekdays. They'll show you the organic farming techniques they employ, help you identify the many plants and trees, show you around the nurseries, explain the bio-gas system, and complete the tour with natural refreshments. E-mail Finca_Ipe@hotmail.com. Web site: www.fincaipe.com

Paraiso Tropical — About 2 km below the town of Platanillo on the road from San Isidro and around 11 km up the same road from Dominical (very near the office for Don Lulo's Nauyaca Waterfalls), you'll find four acres of the classy, fully self-contained retreat of 'Tropical Paradise'. Several luxurious private cabins and three rooms are spread out among several types of fruit trees and lush tropical flora, along with a nice restaurant, full bar and large recreation area with a modern pool with slide, the latter surrounded by lounge chairs, tables, patio, lawns and shade trees. There are actually two pools, one smaller and shallow for just relaxing or for smaller children. The accommodations consist of four bungalows and three private rooms total. Each immaculate bungalow and room is meticulously appointed with the highest quality materials. The 2 bedrooms and large bath of the bungalows have tiled floors, closets, lots of screened and curtained windows, vaulted hardwood ceilings, air conditioning and ceiling fans. Each bungalow is also equipped with a refrigerator/freezer, a coffee maker, a TV, and a hammock or swing on the private patio. The bungalows each have one double and two single beds to sleep up to four. The decor of the restaurant is pure class with tablecloths and linen napkins, and very nice ceramic tiled floors. The restaurant is open on three sides to take advantage of the breezes and nice views of the grounds. You look past columns supporting high arched walls, a classical touch not often found in the area. The food is mix of North American, Mexican, and Tico dishes, all prepared fresh to order. All liquors are available at the modern bar, and they can mix up many cocktails. They usually have English-speaking staff during the high season. Hours for both guests and the public are 8am-10pm, with take-out available. Laundry is available to guests staying several days or more. *Rates:* $50 double or triple for a bungalow. Rooms are less. Prices include breakfast. Discounts for stays of 1 week +, for groups, and during green season. Most credit cards accepted. Call 787-8016 telefax, 771-8182, or 787-0153. Web site: www.villasparaisotropical.com, e-mail info@villasparaisotropical.com.

Hacienda Barú — This privately owned national wildlife refuge just 2 km. north of Dominical contains over 800 acres of natural wonder representing the full spectrum of coastal tropical terrain. The mission of its expatriate North American owners, fully dedicated to the concept of sustainable development, includes both preservation and education, and the tours, lodging and restaurant service they offer help support this and other eco-friendly projects. Towering jungle canopies, captivating rainforest, primeval mangroves, pristine beaches — it's all here, along with the cabins, restaurant and visitors' center nestled in among the flora. The property includes both coastal lowlands and highland habitats, and is left more or less untouched except for the small area set aside for the buildings, which is nicely maintained and landscaped. You can drive right up to your private 2 or 3 bedroom cabin, which is more like a small house, complete with a full kitchen and living room. Each cabin has both double and single beds with fans, closets, shelving and even a safe in the bedrooms; a private tiled bath with hot water shower; a couch, bamboo table, chairs and a ceiling fan in the lounge area; a patio with bench; shuttered and screened windows; and all 110 electric. They each have a tiled patio, too. They are very private, and due to the solid concrete block construction, insulated very well for sound (though the noisiest neighbors by far are the birds – bird watchers love it here). There is a small ranchito with a thatched palm roof and hammocks nearby to just 'hang out', and 3 outside showers for people coming back from the beach only 350 meters away. The open-air restaurant is housed in a traditional rancho, its style enhanced a bit by linen tablecloths and soft music. Meals are $6-7 each and include a full main course of freshly prepared Costa Rican fare, refreshment and dessert. Full bar service is also available, and the restaurant is open to the public. ***Rates:*** $60/night double. $10 each additional person. Discounts for groups, families, and children (under 10 free). Significantly lower rates during green season. Credit cards accepted. The best part of Hacienda Barú is the tours. From self-hike trails to beach combing to wild animal observation 112 feet above the primary rainforest floor, you can really do it all here! They have added a fantastic new aerial rainforest tour to their repertoire of adventures, the 'Flight of the Toucan'. This is an exciting, primarily airborne ride through several layers of rainforest canopy via an extensive cable and platform system. They have recently added a native butterfly garden to the property, too. The tours are open to everybody, and the prices are very reasonable. See the TOURS section for more information. Call ahead for both accommodations and activities at 787-0003. E-mail: hacbaru@racsa.co.cr; Web site: www.haciendabaru.com

Pequeño Oasis — This quiet, secluded, friendly B&B across the road from the Hacienda Barú property offers North American and European hospitality and a touch of the country life to boot. The lodgings, gardens, orchards, and barn/workshed are all part of a 65-acre *finca* of mostly secondary rainforest with some primary forest mixed in, climbing from the lowlands by the road up a verdant mountainside. A lofty perch up on the ridge commands a magnificent panoramic view over the fields, forests and mangroves out to the Pacific, accented by cool breezes and a backdrop of lively old growth rainforest. Hiking trails through the property are maintained for guests while a sandy, isolated beach is only 5 minutes away, and over 1800 acres of private nature reserves surround the property. The five guest rooms are housed in the same Spanish-style house as the owner's quarters. The covered front patio has the office on one side and the owner's room on the other. After you enter the house a wide, long hallway/lounge area separates the guest rooms on either side. In this space there is a bamboo couch and chairs, coffee table, books to browse through, a all map, display case with some indigenous artifacts, and mounted insect board (very interesting). The rooms themselves are very nicely detailed, with ceiling or floor fans, hardwood queen beds with nice shelved headboards, louvered glass windows with curtains, night lamps, large mirrors, etc. A very rare treat: the mattresses are baffled waterbeds (though two regular double beds are available, too). The excellent shower has real hot water on tap in the shared bath. At the back of the building is an attached second story, which contains the kitchen and dining room. It's basically a large open deck with tables and hammocks looking out to the bulk of the property out back and into the mountains, where the bird and wildlife watching is excellent in the mornings and evenings. Sloths, monkeys and lots of exotic bird life can be spotted while relaxing with a cup of coffee or cold drink. By the way, all the wood used for construction on the property is milled right there on the *finca* from fallen trees. Conservation works here. A full breakfast is served to guests as part of their stay, with coffee, juice, and fruit plate, followed by either *gallo pinto*, bacon and eggs, French toast, pancakes, or other international standard. Your preferences are always considered. Dinner is served only upon request, and by reservation. **Rates:** $55 double including breakfast. Phone, laundry, transportation and tours are all available. Low season and group rates available. English, French, German, Dutch and Spanish are all spoken here, so communication is never a problem. Randy will gladly give you a hiking tour of the property during your stay. The owners make wood products and watercolor paintings, which are available for direct puchase. Call 787-0035 direct, or e-mail rab51us@yahoo.com. Web site: www.pequeno-oasis.com.

Hotel Villas Río Mar — This official 3-star resort is definitely the class act of the area. The hotel consists of 10 bungalows housing 40 private suites, the office and reception building, a huge restaurant, a very large pool and jacuzzi with a swim-up bar and snack *ranchito*, a fully equipped conference center, tennis courts and service buildings. It's all spread out among several acres of lush and colorful landscaping bordered by the Barú River on one side and verdant mountainside on the other. Almost a kilometer from the town on the river, the hotel has the double advantage of excellent seclusion and close proximity to both the highway and town facilities. The suites, four to a building, are exceptionally large and well-equipped. Inside is one king or two twin beds, a large closet with full-length mirror, two night stands with lamps, a dressing table with accompanying hair drier, louvered windows with curtains, and a spacious fully-equipped bath with steaming hot water showers. The large ceiling fan provides ample air circulation. Outside the French doors is a commodious and elegant verandah, fully furnished with sink, refrigerator, dining table with stools, floor lamps, its own ceiling fan and gauze curtains for bug protection. Very complete. The daily maid service makes it that much sweeter. The *rancho*-style steak house is the place to go for a classy dinner worthy of its 3-star classification. The service by the English-speaking staff is impeccable, and the food will not disappoint you either, whether you are staying here or not (Many locals dine here on weekends and brings their business clients). With bamboo and hardwood furniture, and plenty of room to stretch out, their international-style breakfast and lunch offerings will go down smoothly. For dinner, they offer international, steak house and seafood specialties that will satisfy the gourmet in you, served in proper multi-course style. There is, of course, complete bar service with many tropical mixed drinks. Despite the level of quality and service, the prices are kept reasonable, from around $4 for a typical breakfast to about $22 for the most expensive dinners (the steak platters). There is ample secure parking at the office. For hotel guests, there are both laundry and concierge services available, as well as a full service tour desk, with the whole panorama of local and regional tours. Also offered are car rentals, bike rentals, surfboard rentals and lessons, transportation, reservations at other hotels, and a computer with Internet. **Rates:** Regular rates are $70 double high season, $55 double low season. *However*, you will get <u>10% OFF</u> if you call direct for reservations and mention this book. This makes it one of the best deals in Costa Rica for this level of accommodations. Fax and international phone services are also available, and all major credit cards are accepted. Call 787-0052, fax 787-0054. E-mail info@villasriomar.com. Their Web site is www.villasriomar.com.

Río Lindo Resort – Located right at the edge of Dominical, where the road into town comes off the highway, this small Florida-style hotel complex is one of the more complete in the area. The hotel was taken over by new owners in early 2002 and completely renovated. The centerpiece of the complex is the circular pool with its central fountain and swim-up palapa bar – unique in the area. Paths lead up to the attrative two-story concrete and wood building housing the 10 rooms. There is a tiled patio in front of the downstairs rooms, and a tiled balcony up top which looks out over the pool area to the Barú River and the Pacific beyond. Across the river is a lush biological reserve. The area around the pool and hotel is very nicely landscaped with flowers, shrubs, trees and well-tended lawn. There is plenty of lounge furniture around the pool for soaking up the sun and ambience, and the expanded Sunset Pool Bar has lots of seating as well. There are even underwater stools at the bar for those desiring a cold drink and conversation without having to leave the coolness of the pool. There is also an outside shower. The rooms are very well finished with tiled floors and baths, large mirrors, bamboo furniture, ceiling fans, colorful curtains over big glass windows, and lock boxes. They each have one queen and one single bed. The downstairs rooms have beautiful wall murals and air conditioning. Each downstairs room has its own furnished patio area with ceiling fans that looks out over the pool area to the river. The upstairs rooms have vaulted ceilings and better views. Most of the rooms have hot water showers. A new addition is a combination lobby, lounge and breakfast area, built by the new owners in 2004, where guests can not only get their complimentary breakfast in the mornings but chat with the owners and other guests in a relaxed, open-air environment. There is a covered walkway from the private parking area, vibrant landscaping (one of the owner's hobbies), and a greatly expanded and improved poolside bar area. The rest of the small complex is made up of their own bar and restaurant (see DINING section), a tour operator, a real estate office, and the office and managers' quarters of the hotel. English is spoken by the owners and staff, laundry service is available, there is secure private parking off the road, and they can reserve most of the local tours. Continental breakfast is provided free with lodging, and lunch and dinner are available in their adjacent restaurant. They offer their own self-guided tours with kayaks or inner tubes up the adjacent river and to Dominicalito a few km. down the highway. *Rates:* $45 per room without A/C (upstairs), or $55 with A/C (downstairs), both for up to three people. Significant low season discounts. Phone 787-0028 or 787-0078, e-mail riolindo@baslink.com. Web site: www.riolindo.com.

Sundancer Cabinas – Probably the quietest and most removed from the action of the town of those lodgings within Dominical itself, these motel-style rooms are tucked away off the road right near the center of the community. To get there, you enter a concrete drive bordered by tall flowering bushes and mature palm and forest trees. The lot is large compared to others in town, and there is lots of mature foliage and shade trees, including fruit and deciduous species, and has plenty of room to park your car. All is housed in one single-story building, next to which there is a really nice pool. The murals on the hotel and pool's pump house are spectacular. The deep concrete pool itself was specially designed to host water volleyball tournaments, with special bench sections on either side having their own cold water jets, and plenty of room to swim around. It's nicely finished with attractive tile trim. The owner plans to add a palapa bar and grill next to the pool in the near future. A winding concrete path leads from the parking area to the rooms, which are 4 on either side of the office. The entrance to the building is a large living room, and then locked doors lead to either side of the building, each of which has its own furnished lounging area with wraparound couches and large tables, and even a refrigerator if you want to keep something cool. A short hallway leads to the rooms, with each four sharing two full baths. The rooms are well set up, each with a full closet, shelf, both desk and powerful ceiling fans, curtains over louvered glass windows, electrical outlets, and vaulted ceilings. Very comfortable. Each room has either a double or two single beds. A couple of nice amenities are quality bedding on soft mattresses and real, thick bath towels. The ample tiled baths all have hot water showers. The best feature in my opinion is that the most noise you typically hear are the birds in the morning. Everything else sounds far away. If you want to be close to everything in town (and on the beach) by foot, yet also want your quiet and privacy, this place will work for you. Breakfast is also offered by the bilingual manager. **Rates:** $20/room, for up to 3 people. Negotiable in low season. Half the building, made up of 4 rooms and two baths and their associated living room, can be rented out as a package at a substantial discount – perfect for groups. Telefax 787-0189. E-mail wildcard@wildcardethnographics.com. The owner spends most of his time in the States, where he runs a Art of the Americas and antique circus poster business off the Web. The site is www.wildcardethnographics.com. It could be interesting.

Complejo Turístico Diuwak –This is a quiet place where one can choose to either relax or have fun 24 hours a day. The entrance to this "complete tourist center" has a furnished terrace with a nice fountain for relaxing or having a cocktail. There are two restaurants, a small general store, and a communications center associated with the hotel on the property. The construction of the guest rooms is all concrete and hardwood. This 16-room resort has two types of accommodations to choose from. The standard rooms have tiled floors, built-in closets, bamboo chairs and tables, and both double and single beds, all ventilated by strong ceiling fans. The nice private porches are tiled and enclosed with funky vinewood. The private baths have tiled floors and heated water showers. The four suites in their separate building across the driveway are nicely furnished, with a fully equipped kitchen, dining area and small living room. The separate bedroom has two beds and some furniture, as well as air conditioning. All the rooms have phones with international access. In 2003 a new area in back of over an acre was finished with wide green lawns, colorful landscaping and a huge, magnificent pool fed by a cascade. The pool is surrounded by an extensive lounging deck, and has an attached bar and restaurant. It is very private and quiet, surrounded by trees, tall palms and chattering birds. This area is ideal for group activities such as parties, weddings, group karaoke or just socializing. There is a separate open-air restaurant on the property with a large color TV and a comfortable lounge area. It is a very spacious affair covered by an open beam rancho and decorated with beautiful wall murals and relief carvings of indigenous icons. The menu is varied, featuring both Tico and American breakfasts, including breakfast omelets. There are ceviches, salads, soups and full bar service with a wide variety of cocktails. There are most of your standard meat, seafood, and pasta dishes, as well as sandwiches and burgers. Prices range from $2 - $12. There is a ping-pong table and lounge area across from the restaurant. Next door is a small convenience store where you can find most of the things you may run out of. Next to this is an 'international communications center' with faxes, phones and several modern computers for Internet services. Almost everything a tourist would need is available right on the property, which is why they call it a 'Tourist Complex'. **Rates:** $60 double standard room, $70 double with A\C, and $10 more for an extra person; the suites are $80 a day, with steep discounts for weekly or monthly rentals. You will also get a 10% discount if you present or mention this book when making your reservation. All credit cards accepted. English is spoken. Laundry, transportation, and tours are all available. For reservations call 787-0087, fax 787-0089, or e-mail diuwak@racsa.co.cr. Their Web site is www.diuwak.com

El Coco Suizo Cabinas, Restaurant & Bar — These are decent budget accommodations in Dominical, and one of only two formal camping areas, located right in front of the beach at the south end of town. This small complex has little traffic, quiet mornings, and lots of shade and breezes. The 2 acre plus property has wide green lawns under huge mango, almond and coconut trees, which is lit at night so campers can find their way around. The main group of rooms are contiguous with the restaurant and bar, though positioned away from any noise. The restaurant is housed in a large rancho open on two sides, one of them facing the beach and surf. There is a snack bar on the street side around the corner from the bar. A private cabin is available closer to the beach across the yard, and there is a 4-plex of two stories at the edge of the lawn looking right over the road to the beach and waves. The restaurant is open for all three meals from 7am-9pm, with the bar closing at around 1am. The snack bar sells chips, crackers, sodas, milk, juices, and other items to munch on or take to the beach. The restaurant has lots of tables and space to stretch out, Latin and American music, and excellent air flow. Many locals eat and drink here regularly, which speaks well for the prices (very reasonable) and portions. There is a typical variety of dishes available, from fish filet and shrimp to soup and sandwiches and French fries, all highlighted by friendly table service. The rooms by the restaurant are small but clean, with one large screened window. They have concrete floors with varnished hardwood walls, shelving for clothes and such and a small table. They have 2 or 3 beds, double and single. The 5 rooms on the road side are screened from the light traffic by a natural wall of thick foliage, and a covered walkway leads around the building past the communal baths and other 5 rooms and back to the restaurant. The newly renovated private *casita* has 3 beds in two rooms and a private bath. It has a full kitchen, a telephone and air conditioning. The rooms in the two story 4-plex are spacious with double and single beds, private baths, hammocks and sofas on the deck and porch, and great views. For those who want to cook for themselves there is an area set up with a sink, barbecue and other facilities. There is a phone available for calls and messages. Camping is available, either in your own tent or in theirs, on a soft lawn under the trees. Campers share four showers and one restroom. Parking is inside the property right next to the rooms. *Rates:* $12 double, $18 triple for rooms with shared baths, $30 for rooms with private bath. The private little house is $100 per night for up to 5 people. Camping is around $2.50pp in your own tent, $12 per tent in theirs. Call ahead at 787-0235 or 787-0076 for weekend stays.

Tortilla Flats Cabinas & Restaurant — This comfortable and modern hotel-on-the-sand has a classic setup right on the main beach of Dominical. It's just the spot to meet tourists and surfers from all over the world checking out the waves and the local beach scene, and have a great meal as well. One 2-story and two 1-story concrete and varnished hardwood buildings sit on either side of a nicely furnished open-air restaurant right across from the long sandy expanse of Dominical Beach. There is a popular new bar with DirecTV and great stereo built in 2001. On the sand out front is a volleyball court and several concrete umbrella tables and benches for lounging, drinking or even dining. The hotel buildings and restaurant are clean and modern with tiled floors, surrounded by tropical foliage and rock gardens. There are 18 rooms available, and the international restaurant is open to the public for all three meals. The large rooms of the hotel have double and single beds with carved wooden headboards, tables, mirrors, ceiling fans, large screened windows with glass louvers and curtains, electrical outlets, ample private baths with tiled hot-water showers, and a bench and sometimes a hammock on the porch outside. Some rooms have air conditioning, too. The construction is of concrete and hardwood, so they're very cool and quiet. There is also one suite available that sleeps up to 8 people, with a private bath and nice view of the beach from the 2nd story. The restaurant menu — in English — lists all types of international dishes from real French toast and banana pancakes for breakfast to hot chicken wings and chicken nachos for appetizers. Their low-cost sandwiches on toast (grilled cheese, tuna salad, etc.) are a rare treat. Many standard seafood dishes are available, of course, as well as real submarine sandwiches, which is a specialty here — Hawaiian, chicken parmesan, and mahi-mahi are just a few of the exotic options. You will taste the fruits of a real chef with 9 years' of restaurant experience in Colorado and Alaska under the direction of top gourmet chefs, who can whip up anything from shark-sized standard lunch plates (*casado*) to perfectly grilled tuna filet with wasabi and grilled pineapple. There are several nightly dinner specials emphasizing the abundant seafood of the area (seared ahi tuna, curry jumbo shrimp), a full range of tropical drinks from the bar, and both ladies' night (Thursdays, with free shots for the women) and daily happy hours from 4-6pm with 2-for-1 beers. They even have karaoke on occasion. ***Rates:*** $25 - $30 per room high season. Low season rates are $15-$20 per room. Long-term and group discounts available. VISA accepted. Owners Jennifer and Gino and their staff will arrange tours (Green Iguana Surf Camp is based here), and there are personal care products available at their office. Call or fax ahead at 787-0033. E-mail tortflat@racsa.co.cr or information@tortillaflats.com. Web site www.tortillaflats.com.

Roca Verde — Tucked away in its own secluded cove about half a mile (1 km.) south of Dominical, Roca Verde is a 12-room boutique hotel designed in casual elegance for the discerning traveler. The open construction style of the restaurant and bar area, the complete yet unobtrusive style of the rooms, and lots of artistic touches in the decor impart a tasteful yet informal atmosphere for beachside relaxation. The enormous building housing the restaurant, bar and offices boasts a soaring vaulted roof held aloft by natural round wood beams, with plenty of natural breezes to keep the air moving. The bar is a half moon shape with lots of stools, a satellite TV with programs in English, and tropical style full bar service. The high concrete walls behind the bar are finished in blue and green color washing, with cool designs worked in. The view is directly out to the beach and surf a stone's throw away, and the good tunes will help you enjoy the brisk sea breezes wafting through the restaurant. If you need some distraction, a nicely finished shuffle board table is available. The food is a mix of international (American, Italian, Mexican) and Tico fare with an emphasis on seafood, prepared by U.S.-trained chefs fresh to order. This is THE place to dance on Saturday nights in the Dominical area, with a mix of rock, reggae, salsa and merengue to get you moving. The substantial pool next to the rooms has an encircling concrete patio with lounge furniture, outside speakers for constant background music, and nice landscaping. The rooms are all in a long 2-story building behind and above the restaurant and bar. They are very commodious and amply furnished with full dresser drawers and large mirror (very rare and thoughtful), night stands, a closet with hangars, double and single beds with real box springs and orthopedic mattresses, and both thin gauze and thicker curtains for maximum flexibility of lighting and privacy. Air conditioning will keep things cool. The impeccable tiled baths have a nice glass block wall for the shower, which has plenty of hot water on tap. **Rates:** $75 double regular, $55 double low season. Group rates and tour packages available. Phone, fax and laundry services are available. All credit cards and American Express are welcomed. Call 787-0036, fax 787-0013, or go to their Web site at www.hotelrocaverde.net. Their e-mail is info@hotelrocaverde.net.

Posada del Sol – Set around 30 feet off the main road through Dominical with a grassy parking area surrounded by shade trees and ornamental plants, this small inn has nice modern rooms at reasonable rates. The two women owners run the small inn themselves, and they speak English in case you need help with booking tours, making phone calls, or general area information. The one long building starts with the small office and reception area, with an attractively tiled corridor running the length of the building from there to their small backyard with a round umbrella table. There is a high wall between the inn and the neighboring property which is lined with lots of ornamental plants to add color, with a green belt serving as a buffer as well. You pass through a tall wrought iron security gate to get to the five rooms, which guarantees excellent security. The corridor has several hammocks ready for guests, as well as several small tables and chairs for lounging which are routinely utilized for reading and socializing. Both candles and outside lamps illuminate the corridor at night. The standard rooms are very spacious with full closets, luggage tables, night stands, reading lamps, wall fans, and nice hardwood bed frames with real orthopedic mattresses. The floors are tiled, and the decorations are attractive. The tiled baths have bamboo shelving and mirrors, and hot water showers. All the standard rooms have two large, curtained windows on either side of the space for good cross-ventilation, with wooden shutters as well if privacy is what you want. The concrete construction provides excellent sound proofing from the other guests. There is one single room available, somewhat smaller than the standard rooms, at the end of the building. There is also a fully furnished 2-bedroom apartment available upstairs above the office. The apartment has a big kitchen table, a living room, and a fully equipped kitchen. As it is on the second floor, there is even more privacy and quiet. The water for the inn comes from their own deep-water well, and has been thoroughly tested for purity. *Rates:* $35-40 high season for the standard double rooms, $25 for the single room with one single bed. Low season discounts. Ask for the apartment rates. Tours can be arranged by the owners. Call 787-0085 telefax.

Other Lodgings: Thrusters Cabinas, which is also a popular local watering hole; and Antorchas (not reviewed), primarily for backbackers and campers.

FOOD SERVICE

Café Río Lindo and Rum Bar -- This Italian restaurant with its attached rum bar is conveniently located right at the entrance to Dominical, adjacent to the Hotel Río Lindo. The same North American owners of the hotel have renovated and remodeled both the restaurant and the bar, and both are better than ever. The restaurant specializes in homemade pastas and pizza, with lots of seating at glass-topped tables in an airy dining space with nice murals, lighting and music. The ceiling fans will keep you cool as you munch on appetizers such as buffalo wings and Cajun cheese fries. Soups (both hot and cold – ask the waiter) and salads are available to prepare you for more of the quality menu. Sandwiches include real meatball with melted provolone, chicken parmesan, and steak and cheese. They make their own stromboli, both classic (ham, pepperoni, and mozzarella) and veggie, either in small or large servings. Homemade ravioli is also available, and they have a rotating menu of Italian and international specialties for lunch and dinner, including lots of seafood. The delicious pizzas come in three sizes, with your choice of over 11 toppings, including roasted garlic and pineapple. The prices are reasonable, with the biggest cheese pizza running about $9 (toppings are around 80 cents each). Sandwiches run about $5 each. English, Spanish and Italian are spoken. Hours are 11am till late, and you can order from the bar next door. Speaking of the bar, the owners completely rebuilt it in 2004, and hired a famous local artist (see my book cover) to do up the entire place in style. It's definitely one of the biggest bars in the southern zone, and has lots of seating choices. There are massive concrete circular booths in the main lounge, a corner area with bar seating, a semi-separate room by the road with small counters and seating, and the long bar itself. They also added a pool table in its own room across from the bar – check out the artwork! They boast a large TV with satellite feed (all the major sports events), a good stereo, and a cool local cadre of English-speaking bartenders. Naturally they can set you up with a huge variety of cocktails and mixed drinks, with both national and imported liquors. Get it all in one place. Call 787-0072 for restaurant take-out orders.

Fish Lips Restaurant -- Owned by a long-time sport fisherman, this restaurant on the main street through town was created primarily to serve the abundant seafood brought in by the owner/boat captain from his regular trips out into the deep blue. Located in a modern building that the owner fixed up a couple of years ago when he took over, one has the choice of dining in the popular open-air patio on one side with a partial view towards the Barú River, or in the fully enclosed air-conditioned dining room. The patio has strong ceiling fans, subdued lighting, polished resin-topped wooden tables and chairs, and colorful murals. Next to the patio is an uncovered space with concrete furniture for yet another option. The enclosed dining room, behind the front terrace, has long polished bamboo tables and cushioned bamboo chairs, perfect for spinning those long, tall fishing tales with friends. The best reason to come here, however, is for the food. It's absolutely fantastic. The Tico chef was originally trained in San José, then taught further by the owner himself in what foreign tourists (and residents) really love. Every day's options are different depending on the catch, and the daily specials are posted up on a big board. A partial list of what you can find here: lobster, clams, grouper, snapper, mahi-mahi, snook, and marlin. They also offer meat platters, featuring aged beef of the best quality they can find. Filet mignon with Béarnaise sauce and Beef Wellington are often available. Many locals come here just for their incredibly delicious desserts (they have quite a selection). When I was there for dinner, here is what they had on the board: Lobster (blackened, garlic, teriyaki, or fried); grouper almandine; fish cayla; fish or chicken Vera Cruz; kabob of jumbo shrimp, chicken and fish; four different types of fish cooked any way you want; and fish, chicken or beef fajitas. It was *really* hard to choose. My soup of blackened grouper in cream sauce was beyond delicious, and the garlic bread was some of the best I've ever tasted. The appetizers are amazing, too – I had fresh oysters *flown in from Texas*. Of course, there is full bar service with cocktails and mixed drinks to wash it all down, plus the standard assortment of sodas and fruit drinks. The prices are very reasonable when compared to an equivalent restaurant in the States. Appetizers, soups and salads run $3-6. The main courses run from about $7 to a max of $18 (large lobster with all the trimmings), with the average falling at only about $8. Actually, you probably couldn't get meals of this size or quality in the States at these prices, especially in a tourist area like San Francisco (I know). Feel lucky to be in Costa Rica. If you love seafood, and you feel like 'splurging', this is a good place to do it. Hours are 11:00am to 9:30pm daily except Wednesdays. English is spoken by the wait staff, and take-out is available. Phone 787-0091.

Restaurante Su Raza – For typical Tico fare done the *right* way, this place is hard to beat. The vegetables are crisp, the rice well cooked, the fish sautéed, and the salads are first rate. They are just across from the telephone booths by the soccer field in the 'central district', with a *mini-super* general store attached. There have not only your typical variety of Costa Rica dishes, but several additions like French fries (which are pretty much standard in this country now anyway) and hamburgers. They specialize in ceviches and seafood (my favorite), but all their dishes are extremely well prepared and politely served. Their *casados* are the best I've ever had, with bounteous portions, a real mixed vegetable and greens salad, the standard rice and beans (though you can substitute in their world-class French fries, which I highly recommend), and a more than generous helping of fish filet, beef, pork or chicken (the chicken in salsa is fantastic). They have soups, full salads, rice dishes, and more, all prepared fresh to order by a trained cook. They even have items like chicken fingers and onion rings, very hard to find around here. Check out their "Su Raza Salad" and "Su Raza Rice Dish", or fried chicken. They offer "starving surfer" breakfast specials at around $3, as well as various pasta dishes. All this is served to you either next to the small store near the road or out on a covered hardwood deck in the back with a good view of the Barú

River rivermouth and peeling waves beyond. The music is a soft mix of Spanish and English hits. They have DirecTV for entertainment as well. There are 6 tables out on the deck, and 3 large booths on the road side. The prices are at the low end of the spectrum, with cheap *gallo pinto* breakfasts and the excellent *casados* going for around $4, with fresh lobster being the only 'expensive' plate at about $10. The menu is in both Spanish and English, and the owner speaks English. I would rate this restaurant the best value for typical Tico meals in the area. You be the judge. An additional service offered at Su Raza is the availability of coastline sportfishing. There is a small motorboat (*panga*) offered at $35/hour to anglers looking for snook, snapper, roosterfish, jack and other inshore game fish. Just ask one of the male staff. Taxi and laundry services are also available here. Phone 787-0105.

Jazzy's River House — "At Jazzy's River House you can play us your homemade tune, dance to a fiddle, read a novel or make a basket from tropical plant pittle — with Jazzy et al — on the banks of the Río Barú . . . ." This café/tea house/gathering spot is a musician's home away from home, a two-story open air modern tropical house with a hint of Bohemian flavor whose soft colors and warm hosts will soothe your nerves and loosen up your creative spirit. The cool tiled floors, high varnished ceiling and rivermouth views from the public area of Steve and Kim's home, situated right on Barú River in central Dominical, are conducive to relaxing your spirit and giving you pause from your busy adventures and travels. With the only lending and swapping library in the area and a wide selection of herbal teas, coffees, espressos and natural fruit drinks, Jazzy's is an ideal place to say good-bye to your tension and hello to your creative energies. For the musicians who visit, they have guitars, drums, flutes, a fiddle, a mandolin, an electric piano, and more. Wednesday night jam sessions are a tradition here now, and all are welcome to participate as it often gets pretty energetic with both locals and travelers blending and synthesizing their musical talents, the owners' "folk-Baroque" style complementing their visitors'. For those with a literary bent, they'll help you put your prose into poetry and your poetry into music. They even have a real live chat room for those more social beings among you — unplugged! If hunger pangs hit, their natural pastries, snacks and good vibes will fill the pit. They also host a very popular Wednesday night dinner event (reservations mandatory), with exceptional dishes and a casual, friendly ambience unparalleled in the area. Although easy to get to – just follow the short road down to their house opposite the soccer field – and the house is very secluded and surrounded by lush foliage and tall shade trees. Check out the natural basketry workshops given by Kim (check with her for days and times), and yoga classes hosted personally by Steve. You'll be welcomed any day, however, for a taste of both their culinary and spiritual treats. They also have unique handmade artworks for sale. Call 787-0310 for dinner reservations, classes or more information. E-mail: jazzysriverhouse@hotmail.com. Check out their Web site at www.dominical.biz/Jazzys. Ask for Jazzy!

San Clemente Bar & Grill, and Visitor Center – This unique North American-owned complex in central Dominical offers not only an American-style eatery but several additional services as well, all tailored to foreign visitors. The Bar and Grill welcomes travelers with 6 large color TVs featuring CNN, sports events and other English-language programs. There is a unique 'Cool Bus' with non-stop surf videos, a fan, and a long couch along one side of the former school bus for major chilling. Both Elvis and Duke Kuhanamoku will supervise your meals from their respective shrines (with eternal flames, no less) to help you digest your American, Tex-Mex and seafood specialties from 7am to 10pm daily, with a full selection of cocktails and international liquors to wash it all down. Featured is an 'oxcart grill' on weekends (dinner only), serving fresh international cuisine focused on seafood, all prepared by an experienced chef. There is also 'Taco Tuesday' when from 6-10pm you can get $1 tacos (fish, chicken, beef or veggie) and $2 Margaritas. The regular menu has 'starving surfer' specials all the time, and you can lay on all the Spicy Mike's Hot Sauce you can handle. The tropical décor of the bar and recreation area is augmented by pool tables, a foosball table, a ping pong table, and lots of surfboards (including a table made of one). They even have their own T-shirt display – for their own T-shirts, of course. In addition to the restaurant and bar services, there are Friday night discos with a live DJ (no cover charge). The center was expanded in 2004, and now has a surf, gift, and souvenir shop with a full selection of beachwear, surfwear, arts and crafts, etc. They rent beach bikes, too. The Internet café is upstairs, with modern computers, a rare super-fast ISDN connection, laptop hookups, multilingual staff, and even bagels and espresso drinks. New is an adventure tour office and info center for the more adventurous among you. The San Clemente center also offers laundry service, postal service and money exchange services for both US dollars and travelers checks. For those in need of lodgings, they have rooms right on the beach, right in front of the most popular surf breaks. There is a choice of nice *cabinas* at Cabinas San Clemente, featuring 16 standard rooms and 6 deluxe rooms in two buildings of two stories each. The rooms are large and nicely finished, with earth tone color washed walls, tiled floors downstairs and varnished purple heart wood floors upstairs, bamboo and hardwood furniture, tropical lampshades, shelving, and varnished cane ceilings. Both hot water and air conditioning are available. Just across the street is the Dominical Backpackers' Hostel. At some of the lowest rates in the area you can enjoy full kitchen facilities, hot water showers and satellite TV, all shared with fellow backpackers. Surfboards and boogie boards are available for rent for guests at either place. For more info on any of the above, or reservations, phone 787-0055 or 787-0026.

Coconut Spice -- If an exotic Asian dinner in a modern, comfortable environment is what you're looking for, this restaurant in the Plaza Pacifica is the place to go in Dominical. Thai, Indonesian, Malaysian and Indian dishes are featured at this second floor space above the store, where you can choose between indoor or outdoor dining. The earth tone walls of the restaurant are accented by dark hardwoods, and there are attractive wall paintings over cool tiled floors. Strong ceiling fans keep the air moving while modern Asian music sets the atmosphere. The comfortable furniture is enhanced with woven natural fiber placemats and linen napkins. Outside on the wraparound balcony one can dine *al fresco* under the stars. Paul, one of the two owners, personally takes care of the diners while his partner Eugene directs the kitchen staff. Eugene was formally trained as a chef in England, and has worked in various upscale restaurants in both Great Britain and Costa Rica. The extensive standard menu, with over 35 individual items, has everything from starters to main courses, and varies a bit over time as the owners discover what their guests prefer and, of course, depending on what is available (lamb, prawns, lobster, etc.). There is also an Indian menu of 12 main dishes and 8 side dishes, making a total of over 50 dishes to choose from! Here are some samples: Appetizers such as chicken or pork satay, spring rolls, spicy prawns, and Thai meat balls; soups like Tom Yam Goong (prawns and lemon grass in hot and sour soup) and Chiang Mai (fish and noodles in coconut soup); and salads like Thai-style chicken and Chinese cabbage. They have three different curry sauces (yellow, red and green) that they use on chicken, pork, beef, lamb, and seafood in a variety of ways. Main courses include whole fish in ginger sauce, sweet Thai pork, chicken in lime sauce with cashew nuts – the list goes on. All main courses are served with jasmine rice. Both lamb and fresh lobster are often available. On top of all these wonderful plates, there are rice, noodle and vegetarian options, including tofu. The Indian menu includes Tandoori Chicken, Rogan Josh, and Paneer A Chaari. Fortunately you don't need a translator to order here as all the dishes have a brief description of their main ingredients and style – in English, thank the Universe.

Only the best spices and ingredients are used, many of them imported (by necessity). All of this exotic richness can be washed down with mixed drinks, cocktails, beer or Chilean wine from their own bar. Prices: Starters run from $3-5, soups and salads from $7-9, and main courses from $8-15. Hours are Tuesday thru Sunday from 4:30pm to closing. Call 829-8397 for take-out or reservations.

Hammerheads -- With a motto like 'Cold Beer – Great Food – Good Times', how can you go wrong? This popular bar and grill on the north side of Plaza Pacifica has 'meals you can recognize' for those looking for a taste of home. The owner/managers Dan and Diana are originally from California (like me), and have strived to create a restaurant with the same food and feeling as a classic California bar and grille – something I can definitely relate to. This is a casual, clean, friendly place to hang out and get a good Stateside-style meal, and maybe meet some of the wild and wooly local ex-pats. There are eight wooden tables, some with high stools and others with low padded chairs, plus bar seating up a couple of stairs at the upper level. There is even a hammock for ultra casual dining. Tall planters and ornamental palms screen the restaurant from the parking lot, while the breezes, shade and ceiling fans keep things cool. They have a set main menu, plus daily chalkboard specials. Appetizers include hot & spicy chicken wings, both 'real' and 'unreal' nachos, and ceviche. Hamburgers have names like 'No Ham About It', 'Makin' Bacon', and 'Wild Thing'. Sandwich names are equally crazy with 'Club Me Tender', 'Snapper Head', and 'North Beach' among the choices. They even have 'Chic Food', made up of salads and vegetarian choices. Real onion rings? You got 'em! They also have their own assortment of scrumptious homemade desserts (brownie sundaes, mango cobblers – yum!), and lots of side orders. Chalkboard specials include things like Caesar Salad, Garlic-Mushroom Cheese steak with Potato Salad, and Grilled Dorado with Baby Greens. Full bar service is available, and they'll mix up almost any drink you can think of. The music here is great, too, as the owners have one of the largest collection of classic rock, blues, and jazz CD's around. And the prices? Really low for this type of food, especially compared to what they'd cost in the States. Burgers are only $2.00 - $3.25, sandwiches $2.75 - $4.00 (the Steak Sandwich). The specials are inexpensive as well. Hours are daily from 11am till around 8pm for meals, with the bar staying open till the last patron leaves, or 2am, whichever comes first. Phone 787-0125.

Guido's South – Just a few kilometers north of Dominical, in the secluded beachside area of Playa Guapil, is this funky little eatery-cum-surf camp where one can get New York style pizza on a Costa Rican beach. Run by a North American named Rick, who used to make pizzas himself on the Jersey boardwalk, the big open-air rancho about 100 meters from the shore serves up hand-tossed pizzas with a flair. The paint work on the wooden tables, walls and tree-trunk posts will dazzle you, and the log seats at the L-shaped bar add character to the place. Rick serves all different kinds of hand-tossed pizza, and of course will whip up custom pizzas throwing on whatever you want that he has, all made fresh to order. Cheese, mushroom, pepperoni, ham, pineapple, beef, and many other toppings are available. A large 14-inch pizza runs $7-10 depending on the toppings. There is full bar service with most liquors in stock, and a full range of cocktails to cool you down. Both English and Spanish are spoken fluently. The place is getting popular not only for the pizza, but for special occasions as well. Another thing you can do here is learn to surf, with **Las Olas Surf Camp**. Rick is an ex-pro snowboarder, and he's bringing down his professional surfer buddy to help teach surfing, along with some local Tico experts. Instruction is available all the way from your very first wave up to the finer points of aerials and 360's. He even has plans for a skateboard park next to the restaurant for practice and fun. If you'd like to learn more about the surf camp, e-mail gr8pza@aol.com, or check out the web site at www.lasolassurfcamp.com.

TOURS AND OTHER SERVICES

Dominical Visitor Information Center -- Get all your questions about the Dominical area answered here! Located right at the entrance to the town of Dominical next to Century 21 in the Pueblo Del Río commercial center, this community supported information center is run by North Americans fluent in Dominicalese English. They not only share free information with visitors, but can make reservations with various lodgings and tour operators as well. The office is nicely laid out, with huge varnished purple heart wood tables and desks specially brought in for this office, one of which is full of dozens of brochures, with a wall of fliers and other information behind it. They have guide books for sale of the whole southern zone, and can provide personal knowledge of the immediate area. What do you want to do? This is the most important question, because there is a lot to choose from. Need hotel arrangements? Car rental? Arrange a tour? Curious if you can count on that taxi you just hired to pick you up at 5:30 AM to get you to your fishing tour on time? Need laundry service? Need a friend? ... I think that you get the idea. Based on the personality and style of the manager, Mark, they wanted to call it "Radar O'Reilly's", but that wouldn't fly. Despite the fact that they couldn't name the business Radar O'Reilly's, you can still call Mark by that handle. The webmaster of Dominical.Biz (who hosts their site) has received a number of 'really interesting requests' about the area. When all else fails, he goes to Mark. Mark and his energetic, amiable assistant Amanda know everybody, and so can therefore get almost anything done or acquired that you can think of. Not just a visitor's information resource, Mark offers invaluable help to residents as well, or those looking to relocate to this area. For more information on lodgings, tours, rental cars -- or whatever -- call 787-0096, or fax 787-0149. E-mail infocenter@dominical.biz. Web site: www.dominical.biz/info.

Don Lulo's Nauyaca Waterfalls — A trip to the Barú River Falls is a definite MUST DO, according to all the locals and tourists who have been there! The Nauyaca / Barú River Falls are by far one of the most visually impressive and picturesque waterfalls in all of Costa Rica, if not in all of Central America. They are the highest and largest falls in the country, cascading down from over 150 feet into a huge natural pool that is 20 feet deep and boasts around 3000 feet of surface area to wade, swim, tube or dive into. The area surrounding the falls is lush rainforest, and many birds and animals abound. Señor Braulio Jiménez (known simply as Don Lulo) and his family have been guiding trips to the waterfall since 1992, and have the 6-8 hour tour down to a science. You start from their office on the main road with a bilingual guide, riding horseback on very tame, reliable horses, and wind down to Don Lulo's personal home where you are treated to a sumptuous breakfast of typical Tico fare and copious fruits right from his property. A small zoo is maintained at the house, where you can get up close and personal with toucans, pacas, scarlet macaws, parrots and a pair of beautiful young deer, plus other native species. Due to their familiarity with the area, your guides will be able to point out all types of flora and fauna as you make your way to the falls themselves. Once there, their changing room and inner tubes take away any excuses you may still have for staying on shore. After your time at the falls, Don Lulo will have a tantalizing meal awaiting you back at his house, of excellent quality, cooked the traditional way over an open flame, and with plenty for all, including refreshments. From there it's back to the office at a leisurely pace. This entire package costs only $40pp. Custom tours are available for groups, too, with alternate paths and itineraries. The office is located right on the road to the coast ~26 km. from San Isidro, or ~10 km. up the mountain from the Dominical side. Look for the sign.

Reservations are needed at least one day in advance. You can call 787-8013 or 787-0198. E-mail ciprotur@racsa.co.cr. Their Web site is www.ecotourism.co.cr/NauyacaWaterfalls

Bella Vista Horseback Tours – This exhilarating horseback riding tour takes you from the lofty heights of upper Escaleras area above Punta Dominical down to the pristine beach of Playa Dominicalito, and then up to a secluded waterfall. Your personalized horseback riding tour begins with a healthy breakfast on the balcony of Bella Vista Lodge, with views of the Pacific Ocean and coastline all the way from Manuel Antonio to the Osa Peninsula. There is the option to go later in the morning or in the afternoon as well, when you will enjoy snacks and beverage of your choice after the tour. Either way, you get to sit and take in all the views of the deep blue Pacific, and bird watch while you eat. An experienced guide is provided to point out the different trees, animals, and birds along the trail. You leave from high up in Escaleras, passing down through winding mountain trails with streams and forest, with the opportunity to spot lots of wildlife like monkeys and exotic bird species. When you arrive at the beach, you can walk or run your horse on the beach to your satisfaction, or dismount and use your own legs. The calm waters of Dominicalito Beach are fine for swimming. Afterwards, you can stop and relax with a cold drink provded by your guide. Next you continue to a beautiful waterfall where you can enjoy a stimulating fresh-water swim. Towels will be provided, and nobody will be checking a watch to hurry you back. When you're ready to leave, it is a short ride back up the mountain to Bella Vista Lodge. The unstructured nature of this tour allows everyone to enjoy the lush countryside at his or her own pace. If you're like taking pictures, don't worry — the guide stops for photo sessions along the way if necessary. The tour takes 4-6 hours, and costs $40pp. Contact Bella Vista Lodge at 787-8069 or 388-0155. E-mail info@bellavistalodge.com or bvlodge@mailstation.com. Web site: www.bellavistalodge.com.

Hacienda Barú Tours – Probably the most popular and diverse destination for day tours in the Dominical area, Hacienda Barú provides a wide selection of beach and jungle adventures for those looking for a little excitement. All the tours are available to the general public, and are run very professionally with some of the best guides in the region. All tours are led by an experienced local guide, fully bilingual and trained as a naturalist. All the equipment used is impeccably maintained to assure comfort and safety for all. The following tours can be experienced right on the Hacienda Barú's extensive grounds and associated wildlife refuge. The Canopy Platform Tour lets you experience the rainforest canopy from a wooden platform located at 110 feet above the forest floor. You and your naturalist guide are hoisted up with a special winch and harness where you can observe a fascinating tree-top ecosystem that you would simply miss from the ground. For a more physically demanding treetop excursion, you can also go on a tree climbing tour where you ascend through different layers of the canopy to a height of 112 feet from the ground. The Flight of the Toucan is an exciting zip line trip back and forth across a lush gully of heavy rainforest. You fly through the treetops from 14 different platforms, as well as zipping to one canopy platform for bird's eye observation. This is definitely one experience that will leave you breathless. A more sedate Rainforest Experience hike is also available, where you walk through primary, secondary and selectively logged rainforest environments, your guide carefully pointing out flora and fauna that you may otherwise miss on your own, and explaining their significance in the rainforest ecosystem. For the birders among you, there is a Mangrove Hike which includes a visit to a bird blind near a rookery for cattle egrets and boat billed herons. The hike visits forest, mangrove and beach environments with a specially trained guide for spotting those elusive rare species. Two adventures which immerse you even deeper into the tropical experience are the Night In The Jungle and Night On The Beach. These both include 2-hour hikes to secluded spots where you can really get in touch with nature for a longer period. Roomy tent lodging, dinner and breakfast are included. Hacienda Barú also has seven kilometers of all weather self-hike trails in both the coastal lowland and the highland primary forest. The $6 fee for the trails includes entry to a butterfly garden, an orchid garden, and a birding tower. An excellent trail guide called *Paths of Discovery*, which contains loads of information about the trails and the flora and fauna found at the wildlife refuge, is available for $3. The guided day tours run from $20 - $45pp, with the overnight excursions costing $60pp. For inquiries and reservations call 787-0003. E-mail: hacbaru@racsa.co.cr; Web site: www.haciendabaru.com

Southern Expeditions — David Mora is a friendly bilingual guide with several years of experience doing all types of excursions all over the southern zone. From his modern office right at the entrance to the town of Dominical he offers a wide variety of custom-tailored tours to just about any destination in the region, for groups as well as individuals. For exploring this rich and vibrant zone, a good guide is a great asset for optimizing your safety, enjoyment and education on your journey. A partial list of available trips are: white water rafting on one of several big local rivers, scuba diving out at the world-class Caño Island outside of Drake Bay, sport fishing either inshore or far offshore for the big sails and marlin, horseback riding in the mountains or at the beach, mangrove exploring by boat or kayak, and exciting waterfall treks. He'll take you to both Corcovado and Ballena Marino National Parks, get you out to Drake Bay, and show you around Wilson Botanical Gardens and La Amistad International Park. He has his own kayaks for mangrove or coastal tours, and access to the Guaymí Indian reservation for special cultural tours. He even rents cars for those who want to manage their own trek. One of his special tours is the 'Caves and Waves' kayak adventure out near the south end of Ballena Marino National Park. You want a real adventure, something both cool and exciting, fun and interesting? This is it! You can paddle right through high rock arches and naturally formed sea caves while discovering for yourself the stunning beauty of this sparsely populated stretch of Pacific coastline. Many customers have raved about the tours, and some have claimed it to be their best experience in Costa Rica. Most of the tours are done out of Playa Piñuelas, about half an hour south of Dominical. Transportation is provided, and a light lunch is served as part of your tour. No kayaking experience is necessary, as he can teach you the basics before your trip if necessary. Guided kayak fishing? No problem either. These shores host many species of large snapper, roosterfish, snook and other challenging sport fish. David's large office — with a spacious furnished terrace, hundreds of brochures, and fully modern telecommunications – is in the first building you come to on the right upon descending off the highway into Dominical. You can't miss it. Call 787-0100 or fax 787-0203, or drop by the office on your way in to Dominical. E-mail expedicionessur@racsa.co.cr. Web site: www.costarica-southern-expeditions.com

Tree of Life Tours -- These amazing waterfall adventure tours have been one of Costa Rica's best kept secrets over the past several years. Not any more. This is more than just another tour company with run-of-the-mill sightseeing tours. The owner is a non-profit organization, assisting individual spiritual renewal through tour adventures and experiences. The tours are designed not only for the eyes, but for the mind, the body, and the soul. The Tree of Life property is situated in 200 acres of pristine cloud/rain forest with pasture lands, mountain ranges and river valleys. The property encompasses 2 mountain ranges, 12 waterfalls, 4 swimming holes, over 15 miles of hiking and horseback riding trails, and unique accommodation in a fully-equipped *natural cave* behind a 90 foot waterfall. They have half-day to full 3-day (or longer) tour packages, all fully inclusive with accommodation, meals, equipment and any necessary training for rappelling or horseback riding.

These tours are suitable for young and old alike. Some of the activities include rappelling, canyoneering, swimming, horseback riding, hiking, and group activities. Tour Package One is set atop beautiful Barú Falls, which has 2 different picturesque waterfalls ranging from 60 to 120ft. You can reach this location either by a 30-minute hike or by a one-hour horseback ride (recommended) along a panoramic ridge top into the valley below. Once at the falls, you are first trained on how to properly and safely rappel on a small training hill. After completion of this training, you begin your exciting 120 ft rappel down the face side of Barú Falls. Once you complete the rappel, there is a short hike to a spectacular viewpoint at the bottom of both waterfalls where there is a large natural 20ft-deep swimming hole. You then have the option to engage in a variety of activities. Tour Package Two is set atop one of Costa Rica's most beautiful natural terrains. Home to the howler monkey, exotic birds and wildlife, here you will discover some of the most spectacular rainforests and extreme river gorges in the country. It is approximately a challenging 2 to 2 1/2 hour hike to get into the pristine cloud/rain forest. Your accommodations will be inside a very large, magical cave behind two 90ft waterfalls with a kitchen and sleeping facilities, with all equipment and provisions provided. On the mountain there are 10 spectacular falls, including Costa Rica's tallest at 600ft. While at the top you are able to hike to other waterfalls with diving and swimming areas, plus a range of other activities listed below. Tour Package Three combines Tours One and Two in a multi-day, all-inclusive experience. Phone 787-0183 or 392-4307. E-mail infocenter@dominical.biz. Web site: www.treeoflifetours.com.

Green Iguana Surf Camp – Playa Dominical has several excellent surf spots, and is the ideal place to learn to surf. They have some of the most consistent surf in Costa Rica, with a variety of nearby beaches and reefs to choose from. Area waves range from small, easy beginner surf, to larger more challenging waves. Green Iguana's surf school can teach you everything you need to know to get started in this wonderful sport. They offer a unique combination of fun, learning, adventure and total relaxation. The camps are designed for everyone - from surfers of all abilities, to the tourist looking for a great vacation package. This well-established surf school, based out of Tortilla Flats hotel right on the beach in Dominical, offers a wide variety of surfing options. All of Green Iguana's instructors are highly experienced surfers and strong swimmers, and all have previous surf instruction experience. Both male and female instructors are available for those with a preference, and even 'all girl' surf camps are available. Classes are available for children, older people, beginners, and even experienced surfers. They have lots of boards to choose from, including both short and long boards, and even soft-top boards for those just starting out. Beginner surf lessons last two hours. They start with a safety chat, with a description of how the ocean moves (especially the currents and tides). It's not nearly as easy or simple as it looks, my friends (I'm a surfer). After the talk, you learn how to paddle out, how to punch through the whitewater, and how to stand up and ride to the beach. Green Iguana guarantees that each and every student will get up on his or her feet on the first lesson. If more than one lesson is desired, Green Iguana offers multi-day arrangements either independently or with a hotel package. They can set up your entire itinerary, which would include airport pick-up, a room at Tortilla Flats right on the beach, transportation to various surf breaks along the coast for your lessons, local adventure tours, and even meals while you are here. 5 to 10-day packages are available for any level of instruction. Individual classes start at $50 for one person, $40pp for two or more. The price includes 2 full hours of instruction, plus surfboard rental for 24 hours (you'll need to practice afterwards, too!). Walk-on students are welcome. Call 787-0157 in Costa Rica, or e-mail admin@greeniguanasurfcamp.com. Check out their web site at www.greeniguanasurfcamp.com.

Costa Rica Language School -- The philosophy at the Costa Rica Language School is learning doesn't happen in a vacuum, but within rich layers. This Spanish language school, headquartered in San Isidro with classes in both that town and Dominical, has programs for individuals, families, children, business professionals and high school and college students. In addition, they have a growing Medical Spanish program for physicians, medical students and others in health-related professions. All the teachers are graduated from the best universities of the country. The CRLS has been teaching Spanish for more than three years to people from all over the world. Their approach to teaching Spanish is to blend classroom learning with real-life experiences in our culture. You study the language and then we put what you have learned to work — the quickest and most effective way to learn and retain a new language. They hold intensive, small-group language courses during the week, using solid academic curriculum. They then combine classroom training with afternoon and weekend activities that are chosen by the student group along with the instructors. The classes are normally held in open places outdoors, or in open classrooms close to the river and the ocean depending on the preferences of the students. After lessons, the class may go hiking in the rain forest, swimming at the beach, shopping, or sit down and chat with locals over a cup of coffee. They also set up volunteer activities for students, giving you the opportunity to have authentic and meaningful interactions with the local people. Students learn Spanish while becoming immersed in the cultural heritage of the country. In the Medical Spanish program, they combine classroom lessons with visits to local clinics and hospitals. Classes start at 8:00 am every day. Lunch is at 12 noon. Then there is a two hour break. The cultural activities are done in the afternoon or nighttime depending on the type of activity, which can include cooking, surfing, and even dancing. Rates for group classes start at $12 per hour per person, with a two-hour minimum. For 10 hours or more of instruction, the rate is $10 per hour. Private lessons are $15 per hour. They offer fully inclusive packages as well starting at $280 per week, which includes three hours daily of lessons, a weekly tour, lodgings with a family or in a hotel, laundry service, cooking lessons, dancing lessons, and surf lessons (one a week). Also included are a welcome drink, class materials and a graduation certificate. Multi-week discounts are available. E-mail costaricaspanishschool@yahoo.com or gafastio@hotmail.com, or go by the Dominical Visitor Information Center. They have an extensive web site at www.costaricalanguageschool.com.

CAMPING AND HIKING

Camping is fine right at Dominical Beach. I recommend the rivermouth area on the north end of the beach, or the long sandy coconut groves south of El Coco Suizo for privacy. For facilities, you can pay a small camping fee at either Antorchas or El Coco Suizo, both of which specialize in hosting campers, and can even provide tents on their properties. Dominicalito would work, too, though there are fewer facilities. If you speak good Spanish, however, this may work out better for you, as several families and fishermen live right on and near the beach here, and there are at least three eateries within walking distance. Poza Azul is a short walk up from Dominicalito Beach, too, and you can hike for miles into the forest-clad mountains of Escaleras high above the coast from here.

In addition to the waterfalls mentioned earlier, a great area for hiking is Hacienda Barú, which is an official wildlife refuge. They offer a wide variety of tours in an equally wide variety of spectacular wildlife habitats, from birding in beachside mangrove swamps to a exciting cable and platform tour zipping through the canopy high above the floor of a virgin rainforest. Overnight camping trips are also available. See above for a more thorough description of both their lodgings and tours (in their appropriate sections).

DOMINICAL

1 Hotel Villas Rio Mar
2 Southern Expeditions
3 Hotel Rio Lindo / Rest. & Bar
4 Dom. Visitor Info Center
5 Jazzy's River House
6 Fish Lips
7 Restaurante Su Raza
8 San Clemente B&G / Center
9 Posada Del Sol
10 Sundancer Cabinas
11 Centro Turístico Diuwak
12 El Coco Suizo
13 Tortilla Flats / Iguana Surf
14 Restaurant Coconut Spice
15 Hammerheads
P Police Station
B Bus Stops

TO QUEPOS

TO HACIENDA BARU & PEQUENO OASIS

TO SAN ISIDRO

BARU RIVER

1

—N—

PACIFIC OCEAN

SOCCER FIELD

3 2
4
5 6
7
9 B 8
13 11 10

15
14
PLAZA PACIFICA

P
12
B

To Roca Verde, Dominicalito & Escaleras

← PCH →

To Uvita & Bahia

65

DOMINICAL – UVITA

The following businesses are located along the beautiful, pristine coastline starting just south of Dominical. Only minutes from Dominical itself, I placed them in their own section due to the very different environment they inhabit. Either right on the shore or up on the steep ridges above the coast, these destinations are set like jewels in the green crown of a magnificent Pacific dreamland. The area reminds me of a tropical Malibu – though with only about 5% of the population, and about 1000% of its beauty. The tiny communities of **Dominicalito**, **Escaleras**, and **Puertocito** are represented here. Enjoy.

Costa Paraíso Lodge— Just 2 km. south of Dominical, before you get to Playa Dominicalito, you'll find this lush seaside vacation spot ideal for those looking for a more homey and private retreat. Set below the highway and right above the roaring surf on a rocky shore, the lush landscaping flows down gently from the owner's home and guest rooms to a picturesque beach of part sand, part volcanic reef that makes the perfect setting for romantic sunsets. Just down the road a few steps is a beautiful, fully sheltered beach that is ideal for safe swimming, the outer reef keeping both the waves and rip tides away. Just another kilometer or so south is Punta Dominical, a surfer's Mecca, and the Poza Azul waterfall. There are several sitting areas for gazing at the Pacific, one with table and hammocks under a thatched-palm *ranchito*. The guest houses above the owner's quarters feature complete living spaces with bedrooms that accommodate up to four persons. They all have tiled porches with ocean views, fully tiled private baths with hot water showers, nice modern kitchen facilities, living rooms with vaulted ceilings, and both floor and ceiling fans. The houses are architecturally designed for maximum ventilation from the cooling breezes, and the materials and decor are top quality. The "Pelican Roost" and "Dolphin Lodge" apartments feature bedrooms for 3 or 4, respectively, and fully equipped kitchens. The separate "Coconut Cove" bungalow features two rooms, one with a double bed and the other with bunk beds, which can be rented together or separately. It also has a full kitchen. The "Toucan Nest" bungalow has even more privacy, a fabulous ocean view, large patio, and a small fridge and coffee maker. The "Monkey Loft" is a two story cabin with a full kitchen and two sleeping areas (one is a loft). For those returning from the beach or wishing to wash their own clothes there is a covered outdoor shower and sink. The Monkey Loft also boasts air conditioning for warm summer days. English, German and Spanish are spoken by the European owner Desi, who also sells her own handmade pottery and paintings and a few other little items you may need. *Rates:* $75-90 plus tax for the cabins, depending on which one you choose, based on double occupancy; $12 more for each additional person. Children under 10 are free. Weekly and monthly rates available, as well as low season discounts. Best to call or fax direct at 787-0025. E-mail is costapar@racsa.co.cr, Web sites: www.worldheadquarters.com/costarica/hotels/costa_paraiso, and a page on www.dominical.biz.

Coconut Grove – As you cruise down the Pacific Coast Highway just a couple of kilometers south of Dominical (and about 100 mts. past the entrance to Costa Paraíso), you will see a colorful painted boulder at the entrance to this tranquil seaside complex where the North American owners promote a friendly, familial atmosphere to enhance your relaxation and comfort. Cruise down a hibiscus-lined lane and to the right you will find the owners' residence, while to the left are two guest houses and three cottages available to guests. There are lots of shade trees and rich landscaping on the large lot bordering the shore. A large pool sits above the path leading to the shore, complete with poolside furnishings, inflatable mattresses and tubes, and a furnished *ranchito* with a bar and barbeque. A short path, Coconut Grove's own private entrance to the beach, leads to the protected sandy cove where fantastic swimming and boogie boarding can be enjoyed in safety. Looking back towards land you see only a high forested ridge, as the highway just disappears from view. The large private guest houses, recently renovated with stucco exteriors painted in nice earth tones, and with interior upgrades as well, are set closest to the beach. They are fully tiled and furnished, with a large, fully-equipped kitchen with tiled counters and a nice breakfast nook. The vaulted ceiling of varnished wood adds space to the rooms while the ceiling fans keep the air-conditioned air moving, and the tiled and furnished patio with a big hammock gives you the chance to get outside in comfort and soak in the view of the sea. The bedrooms have either queen or full-sized beds with nice sheets and covers, while the spacious and nicely finished bathrooms have plenty of hot water. One really outstanding feature is the French glass windows, which are screened and have folding and locking wooden shutters. The concrete walls and distance from other buildings keep things quiet and private. The three cottages are somewhat smaller, yet also fully furnished with their own kitchenettes. They have tiled floors, a large closet, vaulted hardwood ceilings, and a covered porch with chairs and hammocks. The glass windows slide open, though they too have air conditioning. They also have private tiled baths with sliding glass doors on the nice showers with hot water on tap. The cottages are set higher on the ridge, so they still have a view of the sea over the guest houses lower down. All the lodgings are immaculately maintained, and the atmosphere is relaxed and 'homey'.

Rates: $65 double for the cottages, $100 double for the guest houses, all taxes included. Lower rates apply during green season, and also for stays of 7 days or longer. English is the primary language, as the owners are North Americans. Phone, fax and e-mail is available here on their own phone line. Call or fax 787-0130, or e-mail info@coconutgrovecr.com. Web sites: www.coconutgrovecostarica.com, and www.coconutgrovecr.com.

Punta Dominical — For those who enjoy both seclusion and lofty vistas in tranquil abodes above the sea, this place is for you. Located approximately 5 kilometers south of the town of Dominical near the small community of Dominicalito, these lovely private cabins and restaurant are perched high above the Pacific at the end of Dominical Point. Nestled among large shady mango and palm trees, with well-planned terraced landscaping and inlaid stone walkways, the cabins climb back from the restaurant situated right near the tip of the small peninsula, above a convenient parking area below. The views are stunning to both the north and south, with the picturesque harbor and beach of Dominicalito on one side and rugged volcanic reefs on the other. The La Parcela restaurant gives you a choice of either view while you dine, and a menu in English for those who need it. There is lots of shade and an abundance of cooling breezes. Frommers travel guide rated the restaurant here as having "the best food in Dominical" — maybe that's why travelers staying elsewhere come here to sample their fresh seafood specialties. Chef Román invites you to sample both his traditional dishes and the Italian specialties he has introduced to his menu, like antipasto and fresh pasta. Of course there is a full range of typical dishes available, with rice plates, meats and chicken all available, as well as complete bar service – including imported wines — and appropriate dining music. All is served on nice linen tablecloths on large tables. The individual cabins, built of local tropical hardwoods, are positioned on the edge of a bluff looking south over the rolling surf on the reefs below to the coastline beyond. The full-width front porch with hammock and chairs makes enjoying your private view more comfortable. Each cabin has two double beds and bunk beds, a bamboo night stand, a large closet, and a full private bath with tiled shower, hot water, cabinets, mirror, towel racks and a separate changing room. The main room has floor to ceiling wooden louvers on three sides to precisely control the air flow, and a ceiling fan just in case the fresh ocean breezes aren't enough. *Rates:* $50 double includes tax and a continental breakfast, $5 each additional person. All major credit cards accepted. All local tours can be arranged. To get there, watch for the big 'La Parcela' sign on the ocean side of the highway at the southern edge of Dominicalito about 1/2 kilometer past the bridge. Turn right there, follow the gravel road towards the left at the fork, and you'll run right into the restaurant and parking area after a few hundred yards. English is spoken. Call 787-0016, or fax 787-0241. Web site: www.laparcela.net. E-mails info@laparcela.net, ehrcr@racsa.co.cr.

Pacific Edge – Built on a finger ridge 600 feet above the coastline just minutes from Dominical, one can spot humpback whales from your cabin's private deck while toucans and howler monkeys cry plaintively in the background. Over 135 bird species have been seen from the property. Although just 1 kilometer above the coastal highway, this small getaway perched on the edge of the mountain feels a million miles from civilization. The views are absolutely spectacular, boasting year-round sunsets over the deep blue Pacific, and white-water vistas north to Manuel Antonio that blow the mind. You don't need to go to the beach to cool off, however. They have their own free form concrete pool, partially covered by a lofty lookout rancho —even the rain won't get you while you swim — and you can enjoy the poolside garden with indigenous artifacts and sculptures. Behind the pool and deck is the dining terrace and common lounge area, open on two sides. The tiled floors and vaulted ceiling keep the heat at bay, while the bamboo and cane walls and cushioned bamboo seating add genuine, classic tropical décor. Several indoor games are available to pass the time, and these can be taken up to the other lookout tower as well past the colorful landscaping, or to the patio furniture next to the lawn. Lighted concrete paths lead down to the three cabins and private bungalow. There is one standard cabin with two single beds (can be combined to make one king) that sleeps 2, and two deluxe cabins that sleep up to four (2 doubles or 1 double and 2 twin beds). All the cabins have nice varnished hardwood finishing, spacious private decks, and lots of room to move around inside. They all have a hammock, table with chair, an oil lamp, a kitchenette with fridge and coffee maker, upgraded fixtures, fans and paintings. All the private baths have hot water showers. Very cozy and comfortable. The bungalow is like a small house, with two separate bedrooms and a spacious kitchen area. The large deck is totally private, and has a dining table with chairs facing the view. In the living room is a couch and coffee table for lounging inside. The windows are all sliding glass, with screening as well. Some features of all the accommodations are really nice curtains, patterned fabrics, and quality linen. Breakfast and dinner are available to guests upon prior request. The excellent international dinner menu, with 15 main courses to choose from, emphasizes seafood, poultry and pasta, with vegetarian options available. Wine, beer and some mixed drinks are available. All the area tours can be arranged by the owner/hosts. *Rates*: The standard cabin rents for $50 plus tax per night. The deluxe cabins start at $60 double. The bungalow starts at $75 double. Discounts for groups and stays of 4 days or more. 15% discount during low season. Phone 787-8010, e-mail pacificedge@pocketmail.com. Web site: www.pacificedge.info.

Bella Vista Ranch & Guest Lodge – Woody Dyer, a long-term resident originally from the southern U.S., carefully shaped his sprawling tropical ranch high above the Pacific coast over the past two decades into an idyllic mountain lodge that anyone can appreciate and enjoy. The lodge and nearby corral sit on top of a hill looking out over the ocean. One of the most attractive features of the lodge is its view: an unparalleled vista stretching from Manuel Antonio to the north down to the Osa Peninsula to the south, and countless miles out into the Pacific. The view of the forested mountain range thrusting skyward behind the lodge is also remarkable. Open fields mix with secondary forest as the property slopes steeply up the mountainside to a high ridge beyond, a fertile land with abundant bird life. The wooden lodge – built primarily with wood from the *finca* – has ceramic tile floors in the common areas and hardwood floors in the several guest rooms. The view from the long wooden deck and lounging area is spectacular, and you can even see the Nicoya Peninsula and Caño Island on clear days. Hammocks and comfortable chairs line the deck alongside carved stone indigenous tables. There is also a display case full of Indian artifacts and such next to a large table in a more sheltered common area. The bird watching is exceptional right from the lodge, some birders even rating it better than Monteverde. The rooms are constructed of varnished hardwoods, and have ceiling fans with lights, full closets, large screened windows with wooden shutters (country style), and private tiled baths with hot water showers. A 2-story cabin sits about 40 yards below the lodge, surrounded by banana and other fruit trees and foliage. This private cabin has two bedrooms, a living room, full bath and full kitchen, and a long deck having the same excellent view. Secluded and serene on top of a high ridge, this lodge lends itself to deep relaxation. *Rates:* $45 double for rooms in the lodge, $75 for the cabin (up to 4 people). Breakfast included May through November. Discounts for groups. Lunch, dinner and snacks are available upon request, with Italian, Mexican, or local Costa Rican dishes prepared with fresh fish, vegetables and fruit salsas. Laundry, transportation, and tours are available. Particularly special is their own horseback adventure tour down to the beach (it is available to non-guests, too). See their tour in the Dominical section for more details. Also available at or near the lodge are bird watching and hiking, with the manager Barbara able to hook you up with all the other area tours upon request. Call direct 787-8069, or 388-0155. E-mail info@bellavistalodge.com or bvlodge@mailstation.com. Web site: www.bellavistalodge.com.

Villa Escaleras Inn -- This secluded, private inn set high above the Pacific in the Escaleras area boasts wide panoramic views of the ocean spanning all the way from the Osa Peninsula far to the south up to the Dominicalito area and Punta Dominical. Available in 2, 3 or 4-bedroom options, the inn has modern, comfortable accommodations for up to 10 people, spread out over 4,500 square feet of living space on multiple levels. The main part of the inn is a three-story structure surrounded by lush vegetation. It is built of concrete and local hardwoods varnished to a shine, with Spanish tile or polished purple heart wood floors throughout. Tastefully furnished in traditional Central American style, the owners incorporated natural fabrics and Latin American art to create a warm, attractive environment. There is also a full compliment of entertainment equipment: DirecTV, VHS and DVD players, and a stereo with CD and tape players. There is a large multi-depth pool to one side of the main building, with a furnished stone terrace for lounging and a smoker/barbecue for outside feasts. The landscaping is very thick and colorful, with most of the four acres given over to Nature. The top floor has a wide deck running the length of the building, fully furnished with tables, bamboo seating, four hammocks, and even a leather rocking chair. The main living area is very spacious, with a big kitchen, commodious dining area, and a separate bar behind the cozy entertainment alcove. Your eyes rise up along the gigantic mural on the wall to the varnished vaulted ceiling, though you can't miss the tapestries and artwork hung throughout the inn. One bedroom is on the upper floor, with two more on the second level. The best room is the master suite on the lower level, big enough for a party. The room is fully tiled with a private stone floor patio and massive bath with stone floors, shelving, a stone bench, and shower, all open to the breezes and view. Inside is a big couch that makes a futon bed, a full closet, several bamboo chairs and a table, nightstands, a dressing mirror and more. The other bedrooms are also fully furnished, and all have private baths with nicely tiled showers and floors. There is hot water on tap in all the bathrooms, as well as in the showers. The glass windows have louvers and screens so the fresh mountain air can blow through. There is a large laundry room with both a washer and drier, too. The kitchen even has both a microwave and a dishwasher. **Rates**: The inn is only available exclusively – one set of guests at a time – and there is a 3-night minimum. Rates start at $240 per night for up to 4 people. Weekly discounts. Catered meals are available, and tours can be arranged upon request. Low season discounts. Reservations are mandatory. Call (773) 279-0516 in the U.S. E-mail villaescaleras@yahoo.com. Web site: www.villa-escaleras.com.

Casi El Cielo -- This classy luxury inn perched high in the hills of Escaleras is the perfect place to spoil yourself. Your enjoyment of the spectacular panoramic white water views of the Pacific Ocean, verdant coastlines to both the north and south, and the not-too-distant Osa Peninsula are dramatically enhanced by the sophisticated yet warmhearted southern hospitality of the owner, Barbara Kocak, and her staff. Any written description I could give you would fall far short of the reality, so I will just try to highlight a few salient features. There are four air-conditioned bedroom suites, each with a theme: Bird, Shell, Jungle and Fish. Each has a thick queen sized mattress and box springs with a custom-made frame. The bathrooms are equally unique, with thematic customized tile work. Each room has nightstands, lamps, large closets with safes, clock radios, and even robes. The spacious baths have detachable shower heads, bench seating in the shower, hair driers, a make-up mirror with lights, and more. Naturally there is hot water on tap. The huge tinted windows of the bedrooms have sliders and retractable blinds. Wide sliding glass doors – and sliding screens – lead out to private terraces, all with ocean views. The main living area upstairs consists of five commodious spaces: The fully equipped kitchen with wraparound bar and library/game room on the upper level; the dining and entertainment rooms on a second level; and the wide furnished outside terrace. There is a TV with DVD and VHS players in the living room, along with a karaoke-capable stereo system. The décor and furnishings are simply too much to describe, many pieces crafted especially for the inn by well-known artisans. Some examples are an absolutely magnificent glass coffee table with a very accurate scaled-down dolphin leaping *through* it; a 12-foot seascape mural that swings up to double as a buffet table; and a hand-made floor lamp made of intertwined driftwood. The tropical décor is accented by curving archways, colorful murals, potted plants, beautiful fabrics, and polished hardwoods. The villa is surrounded by expertly manicured tropical gardens, with a gorgeous infinity swimming pool at its base. The pool has its own waterfall, a swim-up bar, and a furnished stone deck. Breakfasts are your choice of Costa Rican and International, with lots of fresh fruit always available. Room service in the morning anyone? No problem. Lunches are light but tasty, featuring pastas, grilled meats and seafood, sandwiches, and such. Dinner is by request only. Full bar service with Italian wines is available. The inn has its own English-speaking guide, and even a van, for custom local tours, plus can arrange any other area adventures. On-site massages, manicures and pedicures available. *Rates*: A room is $175 double, which includes breakfast and lunch. Both group and weekly rates are available, and low season discounts apply. Phone (843) 873-6991 in the U.S., 813-5614 in Costa Rica. E-mail info@casielcielo.com. Web site: www.casielcielo.com.

Las Casitas de Puertocito — Midway between Dominical and Uvita (about 9 km. from either) you'll find this enchanting little resort in the seaside development of Puertocito on a high ridge above the Pacific. The neat and well-kept landscaping and lawns add color to this quaint and intimate corner of paradise, with many flowering shrubs to create a garden atmosphere. There is lots of rainforest nearby, so monkeys and other animals are constantly cruising by. Just a few minutes' walk away is the development's 'private' beach. Your friendly Italian hostess has refurbished the two 4-plexes that house everything including the 5 rooms, large apartment, and a small private restaurant. There is a very nice pool of varying depth with a table and bench seat actually built in, and an outside shower and lounge chairs to stay refreshed and relaxed. The split-level rooms have a queen-sized bed, two night stands with lamps, a ceiling fan, cathedral hardwood ceilings and a view window looking out towards the ocean or mountains in the upstairs loft. The downstairs living area has a built-in closet, tiled floor, large bamboo table and chair, an extra single bed, and a nice tiled bath with large mirror. The shower has full-time hot water on tap, and the glass windows have screening and dark curtains. Double glass doors open onto a spacious private furnished terrace with an attractive white cane ceiling. One room has 4 beds, sleeping up to 6 people. You can also get a room with a kitchenette if desired. Also available now is the former owner's apartment, with two sleeping rooms, one with a queen bed and the other with two single beds. The apartment has a larger bath with a great shower (glass blocks), a large kitchen, and a huge veranda with bamboo furniture. There are two wooden cabins available for rent as well. Lots of options. The cozy guest restaurant is situated on a large terrace and wide wooden deck extending out over a lawn with a view towards the sea. The food is primarily Italian, but with the options of 'fast food' or Mexican on request. There is lots of fresh fish, shrimp and lobster served. Mexican entrees and snacks like nachos, guacamole and tacos are available. Homemade breads and pizzas are featured. There is full bar service and Italian wines. The prices are very reasonable. Continental breakfast here is included with your stay. Several local tours are offered, like horseback riding, fishing and water-fall treks. *Rates:* $49 + tax double, with $8 + tax more for a third person. For groups or families up to 6, it's $75 for the room. A room with a kitchenette is $5 extra. Ask for prices on the apartment and wood cabins. Low season discounts. Call 200-0139 or 393-4327. E-mail ahead at lascasitas@pocketmail.com; Web site: www.lascasitashotel.com. They are located on the west side of the highway at the top of a rise almost exactly halfway between Dominical and Uvita. There is a sign next to the concrete entry gate.

Sun Storm Mountain – On the southern side of the Escaleras area, 1.7 kilometers up the official Escaleras road that leaves the high-way a few kilometers south of Dominicalito, this North American-owned and managed lodge is a self-contained hideaway. The several build-ings are spaced out on the side of a ridge on a 5-acre property overlook-ing the Pacific. Secondary forest covers much of the property while yellow-flowered manicillo and rocky soil surround the main lodge struc-ture and guest rooms. The view from the lodge is a sweeping vista out to the ocean and south along the coast to the Osa Peninsula. A large pool below the rooms provides welcome relief from the tropical heat. The main building is a large rancho with a huge open deck facing the sea. There are 2 duplexes for visitors having large rooms with fully tiled baths. Extremely hot water is provided by a solar system in both the sinks and showers (on tap). Furnishings include double and/or single beds, full closets, night stands, and shelves, all on either ceramic tile or hardwood floors. Vaulted ceilings with ceiling fans keep the rooms cool. Covered porches with hammocks run the length of the duplexes. The main building functions as Jolly Roger Restaurant and Bar, with the owner Roger Watson doing most of the cooking and serving. Fast food, steaks, real stews – basically standard Canadian fare is offered, with full bar service. The restaurant and bar are open to the public. Also available at Sun Storm Mountain is a two bedroom cottage. The cottage is fully equipped with a full kitchen, and features new oversized spring mattresses on new bed frames. It is set apart above the lodge, near the road with its own entry and carport. It has it's own electric hot water heater and a gas stove. Amenities include a fully tiled bath, a vanity, pinewood doors, louvered glass windows, tiled floors and full closets. Rates: $30 double for the rooms, and $60 for the cottage for up to 4 people. Laundry and transportation available. Open from Nov. 1st – April 31st. In the U.S. call (716) 542-4863, in Canada (705) 753-0262 where Roger has another, larger lodge. Phone 305-2414 in Costa Rica. You can get to the lodge two ways: by following the main Escaleras road from the upper ridge down to the south back towards the coastal highway. It will be on your right hand side. If you come up from the south, there is an entrance to the Escaleras area across from the Puertocito area. The lodge is less than 2 kilometers from the highway via that road. 4wd is recommended in the winter months.

Other Lodgings: Finca Brian & Emilia, which is a large *finca* owned and run by a North American ex-pat and his daughter.

UVITA AND BAHÍA

These small coastal villages on the Pacific Coast Highway (PCH) are set just north of the border of Marino Ballena National Park, a coastal and underwater paradise of protected marine life, with submerged reefs and jutting offshore islets whose beauty defy description. The park extends south from Bahía 15 km. to Punta Piñuela and 15 km. out to sea, protecting not only several fantastic beaches (Playas Ballena, Ventanas, Piñuelas, etc.) but also about 4,500 hectares of marine sanctuary, including the largest coral reef on the Pacific coast of Central America. The town of Uvita starts just south of a gas station about 18 km. from Dominical. Bahía – according to the locals – starts on the south side of the large concrete bridge over the river, and lies on the ocean side of the highway. Smaller and more idyllic than Dominical, there are fewer locals and a lot less tourists in this area. Activities for the rugged set include waterfall treks, jungle hikes, horseback riding, kayaking, boat tours of the park and out to Drake Bay and Caño Island, snorkeling, beachcombing, etc. There is a nice waterfall (*catarata*) just a couple of kilometers from the highway, easily reached by car or foot (follow the signs up the road across from the Uvita bus stop, east of El Viajero Restaurant). Rainforest cloaks the Fila Tinamaste mountains behind the town where spider and howler monkeys abound, and crocodiles reside in the lagoons and mangroves around Bahía, which forms the park's northern border. There is also a well-developed private butterfly farm (they call it a 'colony') where you can see hundreds of butterflies close-up, and all their develpmental stages from egg to adult. Guided tours are available.

This area is now being rapidly developed for tourism as the *Costanera Sur* (PCH) is completely paved and capped through this area. The wide and scenic highway is now considered by many to be the best in the country, Costa Rica's own version of California's Highway 1 (once they get the lines painted, that is). If you're up north in Jaco Beach or Quepos / Manuel Antonio and thinking of coming down, have no fear – the way is clear.

The national park here is sparsely visited — for now,

that is. There are now formal entrances in Bahía and on the south side of town where you must pay a fee to enter. Like I said, this area is now getting developed for tourism.

Buses run to and from Uvita several times a day both up and down the coast, and to and from San José. See departure times from the north earlier in this section. Buses leave Uvita at 10am and 3pm for Cortés to the south (there may also be an early morning bus to the south). For Dominical, departure times are 4:30am (to San José via Quepos and Jaco Beach), 6am and 2pm (to San Isidro). Buses to Uvita from the south leave from Palmar and Cortés at least twice a day. Palmar's local bus station is right in the center of town.

LODGINGS

Cabinas & Restaurante Cocotico — This tranquil locale, run by a friendly local Tico and his wife, is located about 400 meters east of the main Uvita bus stop on the highway, towards the mountains in a very quiet area surrounded by forest and open pastures. The property of over 60 hectares has three main buildings near the road, the rest consisting of forest and pastures with meandering streams and over 100 species of birds counted so far. Two of the buildings sit right off the road, housing the restaurant, several guest rooms, and the family's living quarters. The third is set ~100 meters back into the property with 6 more private guest rooms. There is also a private rustic cabin ensconced in the surrounding forest. A gravel road leads back to the far building over a small stream and through a wide lawn surrounded by tall stands of laurel trees and other indigenous flora, all teeming with bird life. It's very peaceful and secluded. There is also a grill and barbecue area for guests. The main building itself is motel-style, all concrete construction with artistic murals and wide tiled porches in front of the rooms. The 12 rooms next to the restaurant and family kitchen are housed in a 2-story concrete and hardwood structure, have two beds each and tiled private baths. The rooms in the back building have a double and single bed, shelving, huge screened windows with curtains for privacy, paneled wood ceilings and lots of space to move around. The private bath has a large tiled shower and an electrical outlet, and a hot water shower. One of the rooms has its own full kitchen. There is also a separate wash room in this building with a large sink, table and stool for guests to do their own laundry. The private cabin is set back from the rooms, surrounded by secondary forest. It has its own full kitchen and private bath. The restaurant is very spacious and attractive, serving freshly prepared Tico meals (lunch and dinner only, 11am - 9pm) along with some delicious international dinner specials prepared most nights by a North American chef. Full bar service is available, and many locals come here to relax and socialize. Prices are very reasonable. A new attraction is a **surf school** here at Cocotico. The owner and other local surfers will teach you basic wave riding skills with brand new boards made just for the school. Some of the income from the surf school will go to a local reforestation program (hence the 'eco' aspect). Other tours available here are sport fishing, birdwatching, and horseback riding. ***Rates:*** $17 for rooms by the restaurant, $22 per room in back building, both for up to 4 people. The private cabin is $30, as is the corner room with the kitchen. Discounts for long stays (3+ days) and groups. Laundry service is available. Call 743-8032 or 743-8174 direct. E-mail info@ecosurfing.com; Web site www.ecosurfing.com.

Balcón de Uvita – The Dutch and Indonesian owners of this popular restaurant high above Uvita also have three very comfortable guest bungalows for rent. All are of concrete construction with varnished hardwood trim, and have a big balcony of 60 square feet which overlooks the Pacific, complete with a nice sitting area with a table and hammock as well as an outside sink and counters. The fully tiled, oversized bathrooms all have a shower and bath with hot water from a solar system, and more comfort is added by the orthopedic mattresses. Air-conditioning is not necessary due to the cool ocean breezes, and there are 3-speed portable fans to keep the air circulating under the high vaulted ceilings of rich varnished hardwood. You can always open up the large windows with screens to keep the bugs out, or close the thick wooden shutters for privacy and quiet. You can also cool off in their very nice pool located just a few steps away from the bungalows and surrounded by colorful foliage. For one week or longer rentals, there are cooking utensils and a gas stove, while all the bungalows have refrigerators. For those who want to get out a bit, there is a short path on the property that leads through secondary forest to a 10-foot private waterfall with a small wading hole underneath for a natural deep tissue massage. The restaurant, getting more famous year by year, is run by the owners themselves. You will not only be able to dine on fine food, but be able to partake of the breathtaking panoramic vista laid out at your feet from their lofty perch above the coast. The emphasis is on Indonesian cuisine, which is similar to Thai food with some influence from Chinese styles, yet a bit more tropical and exotic with a unique blending of ingredients like coconut, ginger, hot chilies and peanut sauce. With names like Loempia, Nasi Goreng, and Lawar to choose from, this dining adventure is equivalent in the hiking world to coming face to face with a wild panther — and having it purr for you. Prices vary from $2-3 appetizers to the $6-10 main dishes. Beer, wine and some liquors are served. The menu is in both English and Spanish, both of which are spoken fluently here, as well as Dutch and German. Although group reservations (and reservations from their bungalow guests) will be taken for any day, they are generally only open from Thursday through Sunday, 11am - 9pm, so plan your trip accordingly. It'll be worth it. **Rates**: $59 per bungalow high season (Dec. 15 – Apr. 30), $49 low season, including taxes. $10pp extra over 3. Weekly rates available. Guests of the bungalows can reserve the restaurant for any meal, any day. Many tours are offered, including horseback riding and scuba diving. A 4wd is recommended to get up to the property, though the owners can pick you up if necessary from town. Phone direct at 743-8034, or e-mail info@balcondeuvita.com. Web site: www.balcondeuvita.com.

Rancho Pacifico -- This brand new lodge up in the mountains above Uvita bills itself as 'Your luxury base camp in Costa Rica's last best place'. The lodge was opened in mid-2004, just as this book went to print. Co-owner Silvia Jimenez, a former Miss Costa Rica, is a retired ENT surgeon. Her husband Garrison is a former PBS personality with a passion for the outdoors in general and fly fishing in particular. The 28-acre complex almost 2000 feet above the Pacific is teeming with wildlife, backed by primary rainforest and boasting some of the best panoramic views on the coast, including the famous Whale's Tail of Marino Ballena National Park seemingly right at your feet, *and* both Caño Island and the Osa Peninsula to the south. Accommodations are a choice of four one bedroom suites, one 1-bedroom villa, and two 2-bedroom villas, all of which are very spacious. The 2-bedroom, 2-bath villas have a 1400 sq. ft. upstairs master suite, 400 square ft. downstairs porch and 300 sq. ft. private upstairs balcony. Plenty of room to move around, yes? A large open-air clubhouse serves as the gathering place with its guest-only restaurant and bar. The architecture is unique and airy featuring big round beam construction, vaulted ceilings, private decks, naturally landscaped gardens and local art and artifacts as part of the furnishings and décor. The white stucco walls and red tile roofs remind me of Mediterranean villas. There are spring-fed plunge pools to escape the heat. Amenities include air conditioning, turbo ceiling fans, oversized showers, deluxe bath products, high quality European bedding, and complimentary room service. One of the nice features of Rancho Pacifico is not only the personal management and participation of the owners, but the fact that there are normally more staff than guests, so your personal needs will get immediate attention. Of course there is 24-hour security at the lodge. Garrison also runs Rancho Pacifico Outfitters, a fly and light tackle fishing operation that heads out into the sport fishing mecca of the surrounding Pacific hunting for snook, pompano, milkfish, dorado, sailfish, and more. **Rates**: Daily rates are as follows: The 1-bedroom suite is $120-140 per night; the 1-bedroom villa is $160-190; the 2-bedroom villa goes for $200-250 per night. Adjoining suites can be shared. All rates include both breakfast and cocktail hour. Special weekly and monthly rates are available, as well as adventure, fishing and spa packages (massage and other personal care services are available). Call toll-free (800) 621-1975 in the U.S., 383-3966 in Costa Rica. E-mail flyfishing@ranchopacifico.com. Web site: www.ranchopacifico.com.

Cabinas Los Laureles – Several hundred meters off the highway, and before you get to the Cocotico complex, Los Laureles offers two different types of simple but comfortable accommodations. The small 4-plex near the road is a concrete and wood structure with a long porch out front of four large rooms. There is a big almond tree out front for shade, and you can park right there next to the rooms. The grounds on the front part of the property are attractive, with lots of green lawn and ornamental plants. There are lots of trees on the large property of around 10 acres, much of which is forest on the back side of the complex. There is a nice trail that runs through secondary forest, and the bird watching is excellent. The rooms near the road have tiled floors, wooden frames with headboards for the double and single beds, and a picnic bench on the porch for relaxing. Two of the rooms here have private tiled baths, and one has a refrigerator. An open-air rancho sits nearby next to the managers' house with tiled floors, a long dining table, and rocking chairs. The rest of the rooms, located in the back of the property, are much nicer. They are actually very private cabins, ensconced in forest and gardens. They are around 200 meters back from the main road across a stream. A gravel road leads you there, and you can also park here right by your room. There are two independent cabins, both of concrete and tile, and one two-story duplex. One has a refrigerator. They have nice double and single beds, one with separate bedrooms and a living room with its own bed. The bird life is fantastic. *Rates:* $15-30 per room depending on which you choose. Meals are available to guests, prepared by the family and served in the tiled rancho next to their house. Call 743-8008 (Spanish only).

* * * * * * *

The following accommodations are located in the hamlet of

Bahía, which officially starts on the south side of the large concrete bridge and sits between the highway and the beach, where it butts up against the national park. There are several inexpensive places to stay in Bahía. The beach here is still primarily a Tico tourist destination, though it is becoming more popular among foreign tourists due to the paving of the PCH and its total lack of crowds -- for the moment, that is. Modernization and expansion has hit even here now, however, and many foreigners have purchased land near the beach. This area will grow dramatically over the next few years.

Cabinas Gato – Conveniently located on the corner of the coastal highway and the main entrance to Bahía and the local beaches, this set of brand new rooms (2004) are a nice place to overnight, or set up a base for exploring the area. Owned by Jose 'Gato' and his wife Marlene, there is plenty of parking right in front of the five rooms in the large gravel parking lot next to the owners' house. The rooms are set back from the highway about 100 feet, with a long covered and tiled corridor running the length of the building. A nice white wooden fence surrounds the property, lined with ornamental palms and colorful shrubs. From the back of the rooms you can actually see the ocean, and hear the waves crashing on the beach not too far off. On the lower portion of the property, down a small path, there is an open-air *rancho* with kitchen facilites for guests. It is a very private area, with its own well and surrounded by many fruit trees, grass and pineapple. The building with the rooms has a furnished patio running its length for outside lounging. All the rooms have tiled floors with fully tiled private baths, all of better than average quality and design. The big glass windows have screened louvers. The heavy cedar doors – great for keeping out any traffic noise – are polished to a shine. All the rooms have full closets next to the bathrooms, and the showers, with nice sliding glass doors, are very spacious and tiled all the way to the top with a nice design. The ceiling fans have decorative lights, and each room has a stylish night lamp outside by the door. Four of the rooms are virtually identical in size and design, while a fifth is larger with special features for handicapped persons. All of the beds are new, with thick mattresses and varnished headboards, and one even has drawers on the sides. The other rooms have nightstands between two of the beds. Each room has either one double bed, a double and single bed, or one double and two single beds. They are all extremely clean, and very cool inside (good temperature and noise insulation). The owners' house is only steps from the rooms, so there is 24-hour security every day and night. Guests can cook for themselves in the *rancho*. **Rates**: $16 double, $23 triple. Low season, group and multi-day discounts available. Good English is spoken by Gato, who is a biologist and author. Besides arranging many local tours, Gato has his own 22-foot launch with a 55hp Johnson that fits 10 people for aquatic tours. Sport fishing, snorkeling, whale watching, and trips to Caño Island are possible. Phone 818-2484.

Cabinas Las Gemelas – Another small set of rooms, these are located a little ways off the main road in town, closer to the beach towards central Bahía. The owners live in a house at the entrance to the property, with the five rooms lined up past the house next to each other on a wide greenbelt. There is about an acre of green lawns, ornamental plants, and some mature fruit trees. You can actually drive right up to your cabin on the grass if you like, or park by the small concrete rancho opposite the rooms. The rancho serves as a common kitchen for guests, with gas burners, a barbecue, and lots of bar and table seating. All the landscaping is very neat and well-maintained, and the property is well hidden from neighbors and far from the center of town. The owner Giovani is the local bus driver, so you'll never be late for the bus if you stay here. It's also easy to find if you're riding the bus to the area – just tell the driver you want to go home with him (you know what I mean). The rooms are only a couple of years old, concrete construction with nice glass windows, glass louvers, open beam vaulted ceilings and nice curtains. They have strong ceiling fans with various speeds, wood frame beds with headboards and spring mattresses, and really nice tiled floors. The private baths are all fully tiled. All the rooms have televisions, shelves or full closets, and thick wooden doors wth heavy locks. They are nicely painted outside with either murals or natural scenes. Each has its own covered front porch on the greenbelt. One room is actually a separate cabin, and is outfitted for handicapped persons. Two of the rooms have air conditioning. Once again, 24-hours security is provided by the family. *Rates*: Standard rooms are $12 single, $20 double. Rooms with A/C are $25 single or double, $5 each additional person up to four total. Phone 743-8009.

Cabinas Maria Jesus — These Tico-owned *cabinas* with six rooms and a tranquil, homey atmosphere are located just 400 meters from the beach in central Bahia, right at the intersection of the two roads leading in to Bahia from Uvita and the highway, across from the *pulperia* where one of the buses stops. The working *finca* covers about 7 hectares of fruit trees and pasture, with several milk cows and a couple of pet sheep. There are animals (probably anteaters) that sleep in the trees and steal honey from the insects, and lots of avian activity. There is a wide greenbelt at the front of the property, and you cone first to the owners' home on the left. Far behind the house is the corral, and behind that another 15 meters or so are the rest of the rooms in two recently renovated buildings of concrete and wood. There is lots of shade and some nice ornamental landscaping. Five of the rooms are housed in the front building, with a large furnished and tiled patio out front facing the front part of the property. The rooms are clean, basic and fairly spacious, and have night stands, shelving, a chair and ceiling fans, all with private baths as well. They also have shelving for clothes, and some have open closets. The separate cabin behind this building has a fully tiled bath and a table fan, and offers more privacy and solitude. All the rooms have air conditioning except one now (a rarity in the area, especially at these low rates), and most of the rooms have hot water showers. Televisions and refrigerators are planned for some of the rooms. In addition to the rooms, campers are welcome to pitch their tents on the shady lawn, and they are planning to segregate specific sites for this purpose. Meals can be arranged in advance with the family if desired. Spanish is necessary. *Rates:* $10pp without A/C, $12pp with A/C. Ask about camping rates. A nice option here is to help milk the cows in the morning. You can also rent horses for beach or mountain excursions, or take a free walking tour of the property. Call 743-8121for reservations, or 771-9814 as a backup. They are located right across from the *parque,* at the intersection of the two roads into Bahía.

Cabinas Rana Roja – Located right on the main road to the beaches of Bahía, just west of where two roads into town converge at the little park (across from the preceding business), these four rooms in one square building are inexpensive and convenient. The fifth room in the 5-plex is occupied by the owner, so there is good security all the time. There is a yard on one side with a hammock and picnic table, and a small grassy area for parking. There is a public phone right out front if you have a phone card. There is a covered outside corridor that wraps around the entire building, which serves as access to the rooms. The concrete and wood construction is better than basic, and the rooms are very spacious. The glass windows have double curtains of lace and dark material to control the light getting through. The ceilings are high and vaulted, with a varnished hardwood finish. They all have tables with shelves for your luggage, and ceiling fans to keep the air circulating. They all have televisions, too. The fully tiled bathrooms are very commodious. I liked the nice touch of the towels folded like t-shirts on the bed, something unique in my experience. Each room has at least one double bed, and up to three single beds. The 'honeymooners suite', the largest, has a sofa, a small refrigerator, bamboo shelves in addition to the regular table with shelves, and is more secluded. *Rates*: $14 single or double, $7pp extra for each additional person up to 5 total. $20 for the big 'honeymooners suite', which only has one big double bed. Laundry is available for an extra charge. Phone 743-8047. Ask for Freddy.

Villas Hegalva – These rooms are spread out amidst a nice verdant property near the airstrip and only a few minutes' walk from the beach. There is a large restaurant, a few private cabins, and rooms adjacent to the owner's house and restaurant. The property has lots of rich lawn area with many fruit trees and flowering bushes. Most of the rooms are pretty basic, with a couple of beds and a fan. One cabin to one side of the restaurant in its own building has its own private bath, and was recently renovated and upgraded a bit. It is spacious and comfortable, with its own porch out front. It sits next to the airstrip, which is used by regular airplanes about as often as pigs fly (though the local ultralight pilot uses it often -- I've never seen a standard airplane on it). The other two private cabins are located between the driveway and the wide grassy field with the camp sites. They are small, but have high roofs. They are fine for low budget travelers, a cut above camping for sure. The rooms around the corner from the restaurant, facing the field, are typical for budget accommodations. They have concrete floors, curtains, and fans. The place isn't bad at all -- I have stayed here myself several times. The food in the restaurant is typical Tico, plus fast food and sandwiches. Spaghetti and seafood is featured, with very low prices. There is some bar service for diners. Restaurant hours are 7am-8pm daily. **Rates:** $10 single and $15 double for a room with private bath, $5pp with shared bath. Discounts in low season. The camping is excellent here, with lights and facilities on site, for around $2.50pp. They offer their own popular horseback tour to the local rainforest for $25pp, plus island or fishing boat tours. Call 743-8016.

Cabinas Dagmar – These nine rooms were being completely refurbished, and some built brand new, when I reviewed the place in early 2004. They are located next to Cabinas Hegalva (the two used to be one business), a little farther north along the same road with a separate private entrance. The large lot is fully planted with large ornamental shrubs, mature fruit trees, and a wide lawn. There are lots of birds all over due to the abundant foliage both on the lot with the *cabinas* and on the lot next door, which is owned by the same person. You can actually hear the surf from here, a short walk to the beach, though it is very quiet and secluded in this area. The two buildings are set far back from the road at the end of a driveway. The original building houses the owner's quarters downstairs, plus a small private eatery which was scheduled to be open soon to guests serving typical Costa Rica meals. The upstairs is set up like a big apartment, with four furnished bedrooms and a spacious common porch. One room has two double beds and an attached kitchen, while the others are just simple rooms with beds, drawers or closets, a fan, and a mirror. The rooms have now all been remodeled and fixed up. The new 4-plex is a two-story concrete, wood and fiberboard building. The downstairs rooms are solid concrete block with concrete ceilings, tiled floors, and extra large tiled baths. One of the lower rooms has a full kitchen with a unique rock sink, a refrigerator, coffeemaker, rice cooker, toaster and breakfast island. This one has one double bed, while the other three rooms have a double plus a single bed. The upstairs rooms, with wood and fiberboard walls, have tiled kitchens as well. All the rooms in the fourplex have a porch in front. The back side of the building faces the air strip. **Rates**: $10 - $25 per person, depending on the room, number of people, etc. Laundry service is available. Group and multi-day discounts available. Tours can be arranged, and discounted tickets to the marine park (the beach) are available here for foreigners. Phone 743-8181.

Villas Maria Luisa Lodge – These spacious two-story *ranchos* near the beach and national park are an excellent private getaway for couples and groups. Four fully equipped lodgings are set on several acres of verdant property only about 3 minutes from the shore by foot. The lodge qualifies as an ecological development due to its use of natural fertilizer, well water, and other environmental considerations. The relatively large complex boasts a large swimming pool with special night lighting, barbecues, wide manicured lawns with lush landscaping, plenty of healthy fruit trees, and lots of privacy. It even has two soccer fields, one miniature and the other almost full sized – with lights for nighttime play! They even have a gym and a volleyball court. It is ideal for active, sports types. Nice concrete paths wind through the property. They have their own artesian well of aerated and filtered water -- certified pure -- with a 25,000-liter tank to supply the complex. Next to the well is a covered hot tub and deck for guests. The grounds come alive with over 150 fruit trees, whose organic produce helps supply food for the staff and guests. They also have chickens, turkeys and pigs, all raised with wholesome feed (like fallen fruit and coconuts) and no added hormones. Organic turkey eggs for breakfast! Pig roasts are common here -- pick your own pork. Next to the manager's house is a screened pool room with both a standard pool table and a small child-sized version, and its own bathroom. The whole place is very clean, green and private. These are the best lodgings by the beach in this area. The two-story accommodations are set up with the open-air living area, kitchen and bathroom facilities downstairs, and the huge sleeping area upstairs. The living area is fully furnished, and has nice ceramic tiled floors. The fully screened kitchen has all the cooking and eating utensils, a refrigerator, and a tiled sink. The upstairs sleeping area is made of all wood with three very large screened windows for lots of airflow under a high roof. The six single beds in each room can be pushed together, and there is a wide covered deck for more private lounging. There is a newly constructed suite towards the back of the property, fully equipped for up to 6 people. It has everything including a toaster, rice cooker, refrigerator/freezer and even a bottle of wine. **Rates:** $80 per rancho for up to 6 people, and $100 for the new suite. Low season discounts. Call 743-8094 or 743-8095 (Spanish only), or 391-9780 (English spoken).

Other Lodgings: Toucan Hotel, Cabinas Punta Uvita, Cabinas Betti, Cabinas El Tucan, Cabinas El Bambu, Villas El Bejuco, Cascada Verde.

FOOD SERVICE

Restaurante El Viajero — Right on the highway, on the main intersection of Uvita on the northeast corner across from the bus stop, this Tico-run eatery serves up excellent typical fare with a strong emphasis on seafood. Their ceviche is purported to be the best in the area according to locals, and after trying it I can't disagree. The clean, modern dining area is open to the breezes on three sides, with a nice high ceiling and ceiling fans to keep the heat off. There is plenty of space and six big hardwood tables, all spread out on an immaculate tiled floor. The menu runs the gamut from typical *casados*, fish filet, pork chops and chicken to hamburgers, tacos, French fries and nachos to satisfy those demanding foreigners. Of course, they have the natural fruit drinks and shakes, as well as sodas and complete bar service. The prices are relatively low, with a sautéed fish filet with fries and salad going for about four bucks, and an equally complete plate of shrimp in garlic sauce for less than seven. The ceviches (several types) are excellent, as are the fruit shakes. For those speaking Spanish, lots of free local information is there for the asking, including bus schedules, directions, inside tips and the like. Very friendly people. This is an ideal place to wait for the buses that pass through Uvita on their way north and south on the coastal highway. This is also a popular meeting place for both Tico and expat locals. They're open from 6am - 8pm daily. Take-out is available. Phone 743-8060. There is a public phone out front, the kind you need a calling card for.

Restaurante Marino Ballena – Located around 50 feet off the highway in the commercial center south of the big bridge in Uvita, this spacious open-air restaurant has friendly, efficient service for travelers. The posts and beams of the soaring *rancho* are made primarily of whole trees and branches, while the roof is all rough-cut boards, all of which is treated and varnished. There are 15 wooden tables, some of them like long dining room tables, over nice tiled floors. The chairs around the two big glass-topped tables are made entirely of solid *cristobal*, one of the most beautiful and rare hardwoods in the tropics. There are nice breezes, lots of ornamental plants around the perimeter, and both a TV and stereo for entertainment. The restaurant has its own full bar on one side, complete with bar stools and mirrored liquor shelves. The head cook here spent 10 years working in the U.S. in various restaurants, and both the menu and quality reflect that experience. The menu runs the gamut of typical Costa Rican dishes, plus many international standards. There is a choice of Tico, American or continental breakfasts, plus small fruit plates, yogurt, granola, etc. Omelets and hot oatmeal are served, and eggs any style. Appetizers include several soups, ceviches, and heart of palm cocktails. There are chef, shrimp, and mixed green salads. For main courses, there are rice plates, the typical *casados*, and spaghetti. Seafood choices include snapper, dorado, shrimp and lobster. They serve sautéed chicken breast, fajitas, and chicken in wine and pineapple sauce. In beef they have both tenderloin and Filet Mignon. They have several sandwiches, including clubs and beef tenderloin, as well as hamburgers. If you still have an appetite after lunch or dinner, they offer several desserts like ice cream and fresh fruit. They naturally have all the regular sodas and juice drinks, plus milk shakes, and have full bar service with both national and international liquors. The menu is in both English and Spanish to avoid confusion. Prices run basic breakfast items for around $1.50 to $2 sandwiches to $8 Filet Mignon in wine and mushroom sauce. Fresh lobster will run you about $20 when it's available. The average main course is around $6. Two nice features of this restaurant are (1) they have a children's menu, and (2) they accept credit cards. English is understood by the administrator, and spoken by the head cook. Hours are generally 6:30am to 9:00pm daily. There is take-out.

Other Dining Options: Cabinas y Restaurante Hegalva, Rest. Cocotico, and a few other small *sodas* in the area.

TOURS AND OTHER SERVICES

Takbeha - This no-cost stop (especially for those with this book in their possession) offers free help for those who have urgent problems, including emergency translation services. At-cost services include EMERGENCY ONLY direct dial to anywhere telephone services, as well as emergency fax and e-mail service. Some people have trouble with the cultural differences between their home country and Latin America. Things are done just a little bit differently here, although most of the time there is no problem. When there is, however, you can go to Takbeha, and Mark will straighten it out for free. Mark can give directions, find a horseback riding tour geared to what you want, get that air-conditioned hotel room for a little less or show you where to camp with a toilet at rock-bottom prices. In other words, if it is in the Uvita/Bahia, Parque Marino Ballena area and you can't find it, just go find Mark, and your challenge will be resolved. TAKBEHA is located at the juncture of the Uvita and Cortezal rivers about 500 meters past the cemetery on the main road in Uvita (yes, they moved since the last edition of this book came out). Both the business and owner live in a small river rock house, the last one on the right before you cross the Rio Cortezal river. If you have any trouble locating the house, just ask almost anybody in Uvita or Bahia and they can tell you where to go – to find Mark, that is. Also, if a more permanent stay is on your mind and you just love the Uvita area and are SERIOUS and not looking just to look, Mark can also help you find a property at local prices, guide you through the legal and logistical challenges, and/or refer you the right professional, all at no cost. You can contact him before your arrival via e-mail at markmkahle@yahoo.com, or call or fax country code 506 then 743-8142. He answers all serious inquiries. He speaks both fluent German and English, so there will be no language barriers. Be warned that these services are FREE, and because of this Mark can get surly with those who waste his time or think they know his home town better than he does. The information he gives is extremely accurate and up-to-date and is indeed free. Take advantage of it.

Dolphin Tour – This independent tour operator specializes in aquatic tours of the Marino Ballena National Park, Caño Island, Corcovado National Park, and the surrounding areas. They have three of their own covered launches for tours, always clean and well-maintained. They are currently located right in 'downtown' Bahia, very close to the entrance to the park and beaches. The office has tiled floors and air conditioning, and is very spacious and comfortable. The Costa Rican owners manage the business themselves, with Sindy taking care of the office and Victor running the tours. They have several souvenirs for sale, which you can peruse while you're deciding on which tour to sign up for. The dolphin and whale tour lasts around three hours, and includes water, fruit, and snorkeling equipment. They cruise around the area offshore looking for whales (in season) and dolphins and, if they are encountered, one can jump in and attempt to interact with them. The snorkeling tour takes you out to the Ballena Islands where you can observe birds, corals and many types of fish. This tour lasts around two hours. They offer their own inshore sport fishing tour, with four fishing poles, lures, fresh water and fruit for the fishermen, and ice for the fish. The tour to Caño Island leaves at 7:00am and lasts around 7 hours. Snorkeling at the island is fantastic, typically with great visibility. You can also walk along paths on the island itself. Underwater you can see a bewildering variety of sea life, including sharks and turtles. On the way out and back you can spot dolphins and whales if your luck is good. There is also a 7-hour tour to Corcovado National Park, where you can hike around and try to spot the abundance of wild animals that live there. The longer tours include lunch. You can also combine different tours, like dolphin watching and snorkeling, or sport fishing and whale watching. Prices range from $30pp to $380 per boatload, depending on the type of tour and number of people. Some English is spoken by the owner/operators, leaning primarily towards the lexicon of the sea. Phone 743-8169, 743-8013 or 825-4031. E-mail delfintour1@yahoo.com.

Skyline Nature Ultralight Flying Tours – How would you like to see the Whale's Tail from the air? Or get an aerial view of hundreds of miles of pristine tropical coastline? The wind caressing your face, feeling as free as a bird... Imagine that the moment to live your dream has arrived.... Skyline Nature Flying Tours is committed to helping you experience the pleasure of this tri-dimensional experience in a unique and unforgettable way. You can live new and intense emotions as you discover a bird's-eye view of the enchanting scenery in the Southern Pacific region of Costa Rica and, armed with a camera, bring back a scaled-down sense of the adventure to share with those unfortunate enough not to be with you. This company specializes in airborne recreational sports in an area of extraordinary natural beauty, owned and operated by a master pilot who originally learned his trade in the Amazon jungles as a bush pilot. He flew ultralights in Brazil, Bolivia, and Peru as well, improving his skills with experience. He has a degree in design and construction of vehicles from notable German schools, so he takes care of his own machines with an expert's hand. Under his guidance you can explore and enjoy this sport with total ease, as you fly in the legendary *Challenger II* (a two-seater), known for its excellent flight performance, operational safety and extraordinary gliding capacity. Comfortably seated in an open cabin, you travel accompanied by one of the experienced sports pilots on staff, or the owner himself. Because every trip is private – just you and the pilot —you are in permanent contact with your 'driver' and can converse with him through the entire trip via helmet radios. He will guide you into what is probably one of the most exciting adventures you have ever lived, an extraordinary experience in communion with nature. With Skyline, you have the unique opportunity to experience marine and tropical forest biodiversity from above, instead of just on the ground. **Skyline Ultralight Flight School** provides the opportunity to continue flying while you become an authentic Ultralight Fixed-Wing Airplane Sports Pilot. The school offers instruction from your first ever flight to advanced tactical and emergency maneuvers for experienced pilots wanting to hone their skills. For more info or flight bookings, call 743-8036 or 743-8037. E-mail skyline@racsa.co.cr, or redbaronul@yahoo.com.ar. Web site: www.flyultralight.com.

CAMPING AND HIKING

The *Refugio Nacional Mixta de Vida Silvestre Rancho Merced*, located just two kilometers or so north of Uvita, is a private reserve of over 2,500 acres between the highway and the sea. They offer hiking (I do not know if there is a charge), as well as horseback riding and a boat tour (definitely a charge). Oro Verde, on the east side of the highway across from Rancho Merced, offers hikes to a waterfall, horseback riding, and camping.

The mountains above Uvita are very accessible for hiking trips, and the beaches in this area are fantastic for beachcombing. There are several waterfalls not far from the highway, like the one just a few hundred meters past Cabinas Cocotico right off the road (ask at the restaurant for specifics, or just follow the *catarata* signs). Cocotico also has several loop trails through forest, streams, and pastures on their private *finca*, where the bird watching is exceptional. Camping is offered by Cocotico, Toucan Hotel, Cabinas Hegalva, Cabinas Punta Uvita, and Cabinas Maria Jesús. The camping area at Cabinas Hegalva is particularly attractive. The area's sparsely populated beaches are also a good bet, though most of the beach area in Bahía is now controlled by the park authorities, and there is a charge for using the facilities. The long sandy beach is lined with swaying coconut palms, the surf is abundant and almost never ridden, and you can walk right into the seemingly endless shoreline which forms part of Ballena Marino National Park.

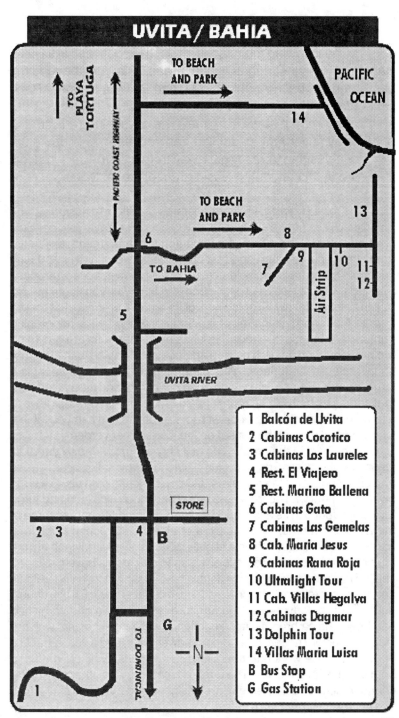

UVITA / BAHIA

PACIFIC OCEAN

TO PLAYA TORTUGA

PACIFIC COAST HIGHWAY

TO BEACH AND PARK

14

TO BEACH AND PARK

13

6 8

7 9 10 11 12

TO BAHIA

Air Strip

5

UVITA RIVER

STORE

2 3 4 B

G

TO DOMINICAL

—N—

1

1 Balcón de Uvita
2 Cabinas Cocotico
3 Cabinas Los Laureles
4 Rest. El Viajero
5 Rest. Marino Ballena
6 Cabinas Gato
7 Cabinas Las Gemelas
8 Cab. Maria Jesus
9 Cabinas Rana Roja
10 Ultralight Tour
11 Cab. Villas Hegalva
12 Cabinas Dagmar
13 Dolphin Tour
14 Villas Maria Luisa
B Bus Stop
G Gas Station

UVITA - OJOCHAL / PLAYA TORTUGA

The following four places are located between the Uvita/ Bahía and Playa Tortuga/Ojochal areas. **Playa Ballena** is the southernmost beach within the Marino Ballena National Park, while **Playa Piñuelas** and **Playa Ventanas** are just a bit further south, just north of **Playa Tortuga**. The coast along this stretch of highway is verdant, unspoiled and very sparsely populated. For those desiring to *really* get away from the crowds (what few there are in this region), this is a great place to do it.

Finca Bavaria – Fifteen hectares of hilltop seclusion can be found just 5 kilometers south of the Uvita bridge in Playa Ballena. Just finished in 2001, this German owned and operated resort is situated among secondary forest and fruit orchards between a river and high ridge with hiking trails a full kilometer from the highway above the coast. Although you are less than a mile from the highway, you might as well be ten times as far away for the negligible amount of sound that makes it up to the resort, almost all of it being absorbed by the intervening rainforest. Mangos, oranges, bananas and other fruits are grown on the property, with an herb garden adding organic spice to the international restaurant offerings. The centerpiece of the development is a large, open-air space with a high open beam roof and nicely tiled floor that serves as both dining room and common area. You step down to a terrace on the edge of a slope with lounge chairs and bamboo tables, with a perfect view of the sunset on the Pacific over verdant rainforest (one of the best in the area). The building is surrounded by carefully planned lush landscaping, including well-tended lawns, flowering bushes and ornamental plants and palms. Down a concrete pathway is a large swimming pool with ocean views, a bar and much nice lounging furniture being found in its associated gazebo. Behind the pool sit three of the available rooms. The triplex is of all concrete construction with hardwood detailing, each on a slightly different level, and each having their own private covered patio. The spacious rooms have tile floors, vaulted hardwood ceilings, nice double beds, ceiling fans, halogen lights and thick concrete walls for privacy. Gauze curtains cover French double doors of glass louvres. All the furniture is of finished and varnished bamboo. The bathrooms are exceptional, with large showers with detachable shower heads, glass block shower walls, and a very attractive ensemble of tile work and trimming. Hot water is available on tap in both the sink and shower. The duplex, located on the other side of the central *rancho* and kitchen/bar, are designed and furnished similarly to the lower rooms by the pool, but are larger and have an extra bed. They also have a wider patio from which you can catch the sunsets. All the construction is a cut above the standard, with lots of special attention to details. The guest-only restaurant prepares "good" meals by prior reservation for guests. The menu is a mix of Tico and international fare, with many liquors available. **Rates:** $52 double for a room in the triplex, $59 double in the duplex. Discounts in low season and for long stays. A walking tour of the property is available, and transportation and other local tours can be arranged. The owner can pick you up from Uvita by prior arrangement. Both English and German are spoken fluently from November to May when the owner Rudi is here. E-mail info@Finca-Bavaria.de for reservations. Web site: www.Finca-Bavaria.de

Centro do Creación de La Costa – This attractive complex just off the highway just south of the park border in the Playa Ballena area has all you need for a relaxing getaway. Formerly known as the Flamingo complex and Cabinasana, the owners have created a 'meeting point for different cultures to share the fruits of their creation.' The complex is owned by a non-profit organization dedicated to long-term integrated sustainable development where alternative modes of thought lead to both healthier living and biosphere conservation (see their web site at www.syntonia.net). With four rooms in 2 duplexes close to the highway, plus three rustic cabins hidden near the shore, a full-service bar and restaurant on the property, and the beach only a few steps away, there is nothing lacking that a weary traveler would need. The combined properties encompasses over five hectares of bright, thick grass and scattered trees and shrubs on the former Flamingo side, and even has a crocodile pond. There is a stand of tall forest near the edge of the beach, and a path leads through to the other side where the sand goes on seemingly forever. The restaurant and bar are situated next to a gravel parking area just below the highway, while the duplexes are set farther in. They are very well built and nicely finished, with ceramic tiled floors, fully tiled private baths, a high ceiling under a vaulted roof, and a hardwood loft. French windows adorn the white concrete walls, while two regular beds and a bunk bed furnish the downstairs. A fourth bed is found up in the loft. One of the rooms here has a kitchenette. The second duplex is set at the far end of another verdant field, and sits under tall shade trees. The very spacious restaurant is housed in a huge rancho with partial thatched-palm roof, tiled floors, and a stone wall and polished hardwood bar. There are many unique tables of stone and rare hardwood. For entertainment there is a large color TV and a ping pong table, plus the cosmopolitan staff. The food runs the full gamut of standard Tico fare, plus sandwiches. Prices here are also at the low end of the scale. In keeping with their theme, some special meals and events are hosted by the owners, including International meals (Thai, Indian, etc.) on Thursdays, Reggae Night with DJ on Fridays, live music on Saturdays, and barbecues on the beach on Sunday afternoons with music. On the other side of the property, the three rustic cabins are open and spacious. There is a large bathroom with a huge bathtub of molded concrete. Unique murals add lots of color, while basic kitchen facilities allow you to cook for yourself. They also have a platform, where the calls of the birds and howler monkeys can be heard best. *Rates:* $20 single, $10pp additional up to 5. Group and low season discounts. Laundry, transportation and local tours are available. English, French, German, Spanish and Italian spoken. Call 835-7222, or fax 743-8145. E-mail info@syntonia.net. Web site www.ecoarc.org

Cristal de Ballena – How would you like to stay in a beautiful private park overlooking rainforest, mountains, and the wide Pacific? Full of lush vegetation and high energy, this stunning mountain-top retreat and conference center only two minutes off the coastal highway above Marino Ballena National Park is a special place to visit. The 30 acres of impeccably maintained grounds is made up of a verdant mix of forest, open fields, wide lawns, thick hedges, and radiant landscaping. Hundreds of fruit trees of all types dot the property, while all the water is from their own pure springs and wells. You can hear howler monkeys in the primary forest across the valley, and one man spotted 32 species of birds in only two hours sitting in *one place* on the property. Even the outdoor construction is unique, with features like white stuccoed retaining walls, large white planters, real stone walls and large concrete sculptures. They have the largest swimming pool I have ever seen in Costa Rica, all finished with mosaic tiles, including the dolphins. There is a waterfall flowing into it, and a giant covered Jacuzzi tub nearby. If the pool isn't enough for you, there is a 400-FOOT TOBAGAN that slides you down to another pool with a swim-up bar! Next to the upper pool is the second story conference center with the open-air restaurant and bar underneath, with a huge tiled terrace and very classy and tasteful furniture and décor, like the fluted columns and balustrades. The air-conditioned conference center, ringed by sliding plate-glass windows, can hold up to 60 people, and has its own bar and sliding glass doors that go to a small terrace overlooking the pool area. On the other side of the pool is a raised gazebo surrounded by a wide lawn lined by tall traveler's palms. Try meditating there at sunset. Up higher on the hill, above the large parking lot, is a brand new hotel going up as this book went to print. Opening in 2005, it will have 19 top shelf rooms, all with spectacular ocean views from large private terraces. There will be an office, a gift shop, and more. There will also be 4 deluxe rooms with Jacuzzi hot tubs, and two rooms for handicapped persons. When I was there the two private cabins were available, tucked away off the main road up to the restaurant and new hotel. They are very spacious, with a canopy queen sized bed, night stands, an extra single bed, tables and chairs. They have full vanities with dressing mirror and chairs and full closets, and the tiled baths have oversized step-down showers. All the furniture is varnished wood and bamboo – very nice. The food at the private restaurant is international gourmet, all dinners by prior reservation. English, Spanish and German spoken. *Rates:* The cabins are $55 double, including breakfast. Call or e-mail for hotel rates. The restaurant and cabins re-open on Sept. 15th of 2004, and the hotel is scheduled to open in February of 2005. Phone 365-6258. E-mail info@cristal-online.com. Web site www.cristal-online.com.

Villas Leonor – These secluded private cabins are set right near the beach at the end of a short private road off the coast highway. The entrance is just south of the Flamingo complex (Creación de La Costa), and ends at a small group of buildings surrounded by wide lawns, tall coconut palms, fruit trees, flowering bushes, and a meandering stream in a beachside forest. Monkeys, coatis, toucans and parrots can be readily spotted right on and around the 2-acre property. There are lots of melodious birds and hooting howler monkeys to add the authentic jungle background atmosphere. The semi-private sandy beach (no public access) — which is great for swimming and sunbathing, and part of the national park — is only a minute away via a wide coconut-lined grassy path. The property has a small river that opens up right near the beach to form a small lagoon, where one can bathe in calm waters. There are excellent tide pools at the point just a few minutes down the beach. One can walk to a secluded 30-foot waterfall, too, up the river the runs through the property. Two of the cabins are about 30 meters from the guest-only restaurant and bar, and the other is hidden between the restaurant and the stream. They have big screened windows on three sides, curtained for privacy. The floors inside the cabin and out on their private porches are tiled, and they have nice bamboo double beds with extra single beds as well. Each cabin has a private bath. The restaurant and bar is an open air *rancho* with a high thatched palm roof. It is spacious, has several large tables plus barstools with a view of the verdant grounds, and breezes pass freely through the dining area. They were remodeling in 2004, just in time for the public electricity that arrived (at last!). Food service is by guest request only, with the full range of typical fare available, and full bar service as well. They have their own water supply from an excellent mountain spring. *Rates:* $20 per night depending on the cabin, for up to 5 people. Group rates available. Low season discounts. Transportation, horseback riding, waterfall tours, and a motorboat are all available. Call or fax 225-8151, or call 837-6333.

Other Lodgings: Pensión Roca Paraíso, La Cosinga

OJOCHAL / PLAYA TORTUGA

This special little area of beach and mountains has become an increasingly popular destination, a cosmopolitan enclave of European and North American expatriates with more fine dining and atmosphere per square kilometer than most other areas. It has a very wide sandy beach which is easy to get to, and you can still see turtles finishing their annual egg-laying odyssey on the shore. The mountains above the highway to the west are steep, high and cloaked with rainforest. There is a nice river that winds its way through Ojochal on its way to the sea at Playa Tortuga. As more tourists are just beginning to travel this stretch of coastline and discover this area, there are fewer crowds, and lots of space and privacy. The locals have formed a real community, and cooperate in many projects. Since this is above all a residential settlement of expatriate foreigners there is very little of that 'touristy' atmosphere, and the impression of down-to-earth living and community-wide friendliness can be felt and hopefully appreciated by all visitors. The area is progressing rapidly, with a shopping center just 2 kilometers up the road in the Playa Ventanas area. Tours in the area include sea and river kayaking, boat tours, snorkeling, birding, fishing, waterfalls and horseback riding. It's similar to Uvita in many respects, but with much more modern construction styles and somewhat closer proximity to the mountains and beach (the highway was cut narrowly between the two). The community is located about 24 kilometers north of the town of Palmar, and about 19 kilometers south of Uvita.

LODGINGS

The lodgings in this friendly enclave range from very good to excellent, with the foreign expatriates bringing their construction talents, styles and tastes into an area that was not much more than jungle and cattle ranches before. It might be a tough decision, but it's one you should make, for this area is definitely worth a visit. Stay at more than one place if you have the time.

Hotel Villas Gaia — This 12-room hotel is a contemporary style collection of private bungalows between the highway and the coast.

Rated as "the nicest hotel south of Dominical" on this stretch of coast by *Costa Rica Handbook* a few years ago, it's located just 100 meters or so north of the concrete bridge on the highway as you're coming down from Dominical, set on the top of a little rise in the road. The restaurant is right next to the parking area above the highway, and the bungalows are spread out amidst tall rainforest trees and bushy, colorful foliage, with lighted concrete paths winding through the attractive complex. The friendly, multilingual Dutch owners Luuc Van Wezel and his wife Anna left as much natural forest as they could while building, then filled in the spaces with fruit trees, large ornamental plants, and flowers. The property dips down into a shallow ravine full of rainforest where monkeys pass through almost every morning, then back up to the expansive pool area with impressive views of a rivermouth, mangrove forest, Playa Tortuga, Isla Garza and the Pacific Ocean. A small artificial cascade adds soothing accompaniment as it spills into the multilevel tiled pool, there is a separate wading pool, and you can lounge on the copious patio furniture or in the covered bar area. There is also a private path to the beach for guests if you're in the mood for salt water. The wooden bungalows with finished concrete floors are all done up in earth-color pastel decor and minimalist furnishings. The double and single beds have orthopedic mattresses and several huge pillows. There is a built-in closet, vaulted ceilings, and a set of large sliding doors leading to a private, fully furnished patio. The spacious tiled bath has hot water showers. One of the cabins has been extended to two bedrooms and equipped with a TV, refrigerator, and A/C – it is now called 'La Casa'. Other bungalows now have A/C as well. The very mod restaurant has funky tree-root chandeliers under a high vaulted roof and is open to the breezes while surrounded by colorful landscaping on two sides. There are novels and non-fiction to browse through, as well as post cards, insect repellent and guide books for sale. The food is a mixture of Costa Rican, European and tropical styles. They have nice touches such as fresh squeezed orange juice, homemade breads, and antipasto, in addition to several European sauces for dishes like macadamia fish filet. There is full bar service also. Box lunches and take-out is available. *Rates:* $85 bungalow with A/C, $75 without A/C; $10 for an extra bed, all including taxes. There is an optional meal plan available. La Casa is available for a minimum 3-day stay at $95 per night for up to 8 persons. Over 30 tours are offered here, and can be customized to fit your needs. Phone 244-0316 or 382-8240, e-mail info@villasgaia.com, or visit their Web site: www.villasgaia.com

Villas El Bosque – Across a deep gully on a paved driveway off the main highway and up into a stand of old growth forest, one comes into the heart of an attractive 1-hectare property known as The Forest Villas. Surrounded by towering primary rainforest with lianas and "monkey ladder" vines where monkeys, sloths and exotic canopy birds roam, this secluded and tranquil locale is another small jewel where one can really get away. There is a pool with colorful landscaping and lounge furniture, and lighted paths with low stone walls lead to the two bungalows and three rooms. There is a nice private path which takes you directly to the long sandy beach in around 10 minutes. The independent bungalows are very spacious and modern, with bright tiled floors and baths, open beam vaulted ceilings, and a roomy kitchen. The kitchen is fully equipped for self-cooked meals, and has nice tiled counters and lots of cupboard space. Each bungalow comes exceptionally well furnished with a queen-sized bed with built-in headboard and night stands, a full closet, a futon in the living area, two ceiling fans with lights, fully tiled baths with hot water showers, a tiled sink with a lighted dressing mirror outside of the bathroom, a spacious deck with its own ceiling fan and light, and large screened and louvered windows. They are very clean and spacious. The terraces look right into the middle of forest, high above the ground, and have lounging furniture to relax and enjoy the scenery and wildlife. The rooms are similarly finished less the kitchen facilities. They have nice tiled porches, too, with hammocks. All the lodgings are set on the edge of a low bluff amidst the forest, so the animal and bird watching is excellent right from your deck. You can also hear the ocean on occasion rumbling not too far away near Garza Island. **Rates:** Cabins are $50 double and $35 single (lodging only). The rooms are $35 per night double including breakfast. Long-term rates available. Dinners available upon request. English, French and Spanish spoken. Phone 398-2112, fax 786-6358 'Villas El Bosque', e-mail villaselbosque@yahoo.com. Web site: www.villaselbosque.com

Hotel Posada Playa Tortuga – Cooling breezes, the ambience of an old Spanish mission, and a relaxing home-like atmosphere with modern comforts makes this B&B a special place. This hotel, owned by gracious hosts "Gringo" Mike and Karen Terzano, is set high on a bluff looking out across Playa Tortuga to Isla Garza and the wide Pacific. The main hotel building is a long two-story concrete and heavy wood beam structure stretched out along the ridge. A tiled corridor runs the length of the building in front of the downstairs guest rooms to the common areas on the north side of the building, where a huge solid wood table under two wrought iron chandeliers makes a fine centerpiece for the spacious dining and lounging terrace. The furniture is specially selected custom made Spanish colonial style, of hand-carved, antique-style wood. Upstairs is another set of five rooms lined up along a wooden balcony facing the ocean. Just a few steps from the main building is a covered, furnished patio with a spectacular view of sunsets over the Pacific. Down another set of steps and you're at the very large pool and tiled Jacuzzi tub. The pool area has a wide concrete patio and lots of lounge furniture surrounded by coconut palms and ornamental plants. From here a path leads directly to the beach only 5 minutes away. The spacious rooms have large ceiling fans, air conditioning, indirect lighting over the two double beds with box-springs and orthopedic mattresses, commodious tiled baths with powerful hot water showers (and sinks), and something that really does it for me: thick terrycloth towels and real wash cloths. Extra amenities include wrought iron lamps, huge mirrors over nice dressing tables, spacious night stands with drawers, and large, beautifully framed oil paintings from the Cuzco school in Peru. The new two-story building (2004) houses seven new upscale rooms, including a 'romantic nook' with a jacuzzi tub on a private balcony overlooking the Pacific. All these rooms have king-sized beds, both A/C and fans, bathtubs, top-shelf tile for the floors and baths, spectacular ocean views, and TV's with DVD players. The first floor houses a multi-purpose conference and communications center. The hotel restaurant is open to the public most days for dinners, featuring family-style dining during the week, and the original Gringo Mike's special all-u-can-eat pizza nights on Saturdays. English, Spanish, Dutch, French and German are all spoken. *Rates:* $65 + tax single or double in the standard rooms, and $10pp for additional guests in the same room. The new rooms run $75-95 double with breakfast. children 12 and under are free. VISA and MasterCard accepted. Rates includes a fantastic buffet breakfast featuring homemade baked goods. They can arrange all the local tours, including their own Flying Dutchman Tours and an overnight jungle trek (see TOURS section). Call 384-5489 direct, or e-mail ptortuga@racsa.co.cr. Web site: www.hotel-posada.com

Rancho Soluna — Located down on the river in Ojochal just east of the highway, this small, attractive establishment is owned and run by trilingual French Canadians. The quaint complex sits among wide lawns, fruit trees (bananas, plantains, pineapple, and papaya), and a strip of tall forest along their private river frontage. There is both lodging and food available here, as well as camping. The grounds are very well kept, it's very peaceful here, and there is always lots of melodious birdsong in the background to add ambience to the setting. They boast a large in-ground pool, 9 x 4.5 meters, complete with floating mattresses, inner tubes, and lounging furniture. For accommodations, there are two large rooms and two small *casitas* for guests. The rooms are near the open-air restaurant, boasting huge screened windows, louvered shutters, tiled floors and private baths with hot water showers, ample shelving, vaulted ceilings, ceiling fans and a covered patio. The *casitas* have half-walls with screening all around, lights and ceiling fans, shelving, hammocks, night stands and kitchenettes. They also have a full bath with a hot-water shower. The restaurant is a breezy thatched-palm *rancho* with a long bar along the open kitchen and lots of table seating, surrounded on three sides by tall flowering shrubs and green lawns. The music is great. To one side of the restaurant they have a nice gift shop area. Meals run from about $2.00 - $6.50, and consist basically of fast food plus some interesting Italian and American twists like "French fry - cheese melts". The owners Michelle and Leo run the show themselves, serving up homemade pizza, spaghetti, sandwiches, hamburgers and the like. English, Spanish and French are spoken, and the service is friendly and attentive. A rare and delicious option here is homemade natural yogurt, which is used for real fruit sorbets and other hot weather treats to cool you down. Full bar service is offered, too, with both national and international liquors. Public restaurant hours are 11:30am - 8pm Wednesday through Sunday. **Rates:** $20 single, $25 double, $5 each additional person up to four, all plus applicable taxes. Low weekly and monthly rates available. $5pp for campers. Laundry service available. They also have other houses and *ranchos* for rent in the area. Fax 788-8351 or call/fax 788-8210 and leave a message for "Soluna". E-mail: solunacr@yahoo.com. They are located about 200 meters north of the *pulpería*, on the road going along the west side of the river. Look for their sign on the right side of the road, where their driveway descends into the property.

El Coco Lindo – Secluded and quiet, yet close to the coastal highway, this small business forms a somewhat self-contained complex that can serve as a base for exploring the area. There are two wooden cabins, a restaurant and bar, and a nice round swimming pool for keeping cool. Also set between a little-traveled road and the river, there are lots of tall trees, colorful ornamental and flowering bushes, banana and ginger, and some serious bird life. There is a quaint walking bridge from the property over the river to the main road through Ojochal, so the 'central' part of town is only a short hike away. There is also lots of lawn area to enjoy, and everything is kept green and vibrant. The 100-foot coconut palms provide lots of shade while the tall hibiscus hedge shields the lot from the road. The two cabins are set well away from the restaurant for privacy. They are very spacious, and have some real character. You cross the wide front deck and enter the bedroom through a nice wooden door with a small stained glass window. The open-beam loft ceilings help the hot air escape, as does the fan. There is both a double and single bed, night stands, and nice lamps. The screened windows are very large to maximize air flow, and have colorful curtains for privacy. The fully tiled baths have hot water showers and big mirrors. The cabins each have a kitchenette in one corner equipped with a refrigerator, stove, sink, counters, dishes and even a coffee maker. The restaurant and bar are located in a soaring *rancho* with a real thatched palm roof. There are two seating levels with tables, plus bar seating. There are also bamboo couches and hammocks for lounging, reading, etc. The unique decorations have a funky twist: mobiles, paintings, horse saddles and colored lights are some of the off-beat features. It's very breezy in the open-air space, and there are fans, too. Near the restaurant in a wide lawn area surrounded by colorful foliage is the moderately deep pool, with its own concrete deck with lounging furniture and umbrella tables. The restaurant serves an eclectic mix of Swiss and European dishes, plus some International standards. The European fare is augmented by a locally famous roast chicken, fish filet, filet mignon, and other choices. The prices range from $4-8 a plate. Full bar service is available, including cocktails and mixed drinks. Coco Lindo has happy hours Friday through Sunday from 4:30 – 6:30pm, with 3-for-2 drink specials. General restaurant and bar hours are from 11am to closing (up to 2am) daily except Wednesdays. Spanish, English and French are spoken by the owners. *Rates*: $35 double includes tax. Low season discounts. Special weekly and monthly rates. All the local tours can be arranged. No phone number yet, so e-mail cafdrig@vtx.ch. Web site: www.cafdrig.com.

El Perezoso Hotel – This French country style B&B has seven charming rooms set high on a verdant mesa 300+ feet above the Pacific. Guests can admire the 270-degree panoramic view from the spacious swimming pool at the edge of the bluff, surrounded by green lawn, flowering plants and palm trees, or look back at the Fila Marguerita mountains 1,300 meters high in the clouds. The hotel lives up to its name (the sloth, or 'lazy one'), encouraging . . . well, laziness and relaxation. The hotel was purchased by some folks from England in 2001, and the two couples did some renovating and sprucing up before reopening the small hotel. The single building is a study in European country style, complete with rounded French doors and windows, and flowering vines creeping up the outside walls and tile roof. The basic concrete structure is nicely accented with local hardwoods, and the two 'towers' jutting up from the first floor are an attractive and pragmatic architectural touch. A covered, tiled and furnished patio runs the length of the hotel on the ocean side, turning west into a separate lounging and dining rancho with tiled floors, nice wicker furniture and hammocks. Very cozy and cool. Lounge and patio furniture around the pool reinforces the sedentary atmosphere. The seclusion here is nice, with the sounds of birdsong and the distant crashing of the surf to soothe your brainwaves, and not much else. The sunsets are spectacular. The seven rooms have high vaulted hardwood ceilings, fancy door handles, ceiling fans and tiled showers with hot water. Five rooms have private baths, while two share facilities (and can be rented as a suite). The rooms have all the furnishings: double and single beds, night stands, closets, chairs, small dressing mirrors with cabinets, and nice decorations including colorful wall hangings and touch-sensitive lamps. An attractive, rustic outside staircase leads up to one of the 'towers' that makes a private penthouse room. The views from its balcony are the best at the hotel, from the forested mountains out to the Pacific and up the coastline. It has a louvered glass window and front door, with French doors out to the wooden balcony. The owners speak English and some French as well as Spanish, and cook up a complete breakfast as part of your stay here. *Rates:* $70 double for one of the tower rooms with private balconies. $60 double for the standard rooms. $55 double for one of the rooms sharing a bath. $15 extra for a third person in the same room. Supplementary charges on peak holidays. Group rates available. Lunches and dinners are available upon request. Local transportation is available to guests. Sodas, beer, wine and spirits are available to guests. Laundry and tours are also available. Fax USA (435) 518-8923, e-mail elperezosocr@yahoo.com, or check out their Web site at www.elperezoso.net. They are located about 2.5 kilometers above the highway in Ojochal.

Jardín Tortuga – The 'Turtle Garden', a German-owned restaurant and lodge a short distance from central Ojochal, is a verdant little hideaway where one can relax in privacy while enjoying the natural environment. The park-like grounds, a full hectare's worth, are an extensive garden developed from former pasture area. Besides oranges, avocados and lemons, there are mango, star fruit, guava, guanabana, banana, grapefruit, papaya, bread fruit and many other exotic fruit trees. More than 300 types of plants, flowers, ornamental shrubs, and medicinal herbs have been planted throughout the property as well, creating a very lush and colorful environment. Turtles and crayfish can be spied in the small ponds on the property, while large iguanas doze in the trees. Birdwatchers and photographers are particularly thrilled here. On the lower level past the stream and pond are tall palms and other shade trees leading across a more open area to the banks of a wide river where lizards sun on large boulders. There is even a small wading hole fed by a waterfall. The buildings consist of the owner's quarters, the restaurant, and three unique guest cabins. The two *ranchos* are two-story structures made with a mix of rustic and modern styles, with round wooden beams supporting hardwood second floors, thatched palm roofs, and concrete floors and walls on the first level. The ranchos are spacious with large screened windows. In the first one there is both a double and single bed, a table, a desk, a night stand, a closet area with hangars, a full bath with tiled shower, a large mirror and a huge window. The second cabin has an outside entrance to the second level, and benches on a small covered patio. The furnishings are similar to the first cabin. The third guest cabin is only one story, with a standard metal roof and more modern construction materials. It has a nice private, shaded area out front with a concrete table and benches. On the back side of the property, among the grass and shade trees, is a small cabina with two single beds and a wooden deck. All the cabins have private baths. The restaurant is set on the edge of a shallow rise over-looking the lower half of the property. It is housed in a *rancho* with and extended wooden deck, and the location is very tranquil with the sound of the river and birds wafting through the air. The food is a combination of Italian and Costa Rican fare, with several specialties being baked in a custom-built wood-fired oven. The meals are healthy and the prices reasonable. ***Rates:*** $15 single, $25 double, $5 each additional person up to four. Low season and group discounts. Camping is also available at low rates. English, German and Spanish spoken. Laundry, transportation and tours are all available. E-mail direct: theturtlegarden@yahoo.com.

El Mono Feliz – Another choice in Bed & Breakfasts is this quaint little place hidden away near central Ojochal. All five rooms are housed in the original home of the former owners, and is now completely reserved for guests. The new owners (2004) are from the Netherlands, and can host your stay in a variety of languages: English, Spanish, German, French and Dutch. The nicely finished guest house is of all concrete construction, with nicely tiled floors and polished hardwood detailing. The spacious covered terrace and kitchen area has a nice furnished sitting area, several tables for dining, a TV with DirecTV and a DVD player, and a nice stereo. Also available is a significant book collection with choices in several languages. This is where most of the guests hang out and socialize. There is lots of room for everyone. The kitchen is fully equipped, and available for use by guests. For accommodations there are three rooms with private baths, while two rooms share a bath between them, like a suite. The fully furnished rooms have nice double hardwood beds with fantastic spring mattresses, tiled baths and showers, and very attractive original artwork on the walls and even some tiffany lamps in some of the rooms. All the beds have very nice linen and quilts, and each room has at least one nighstand and a closet. Surrounding the guest house are over two acres of well-landscaped garden, with many fruit trees. The owners live in a house behind the pool, so there is always help near at hand. The back of the property leads down to a stream and wide river, with lots of shade and grass. There is a large pool right next to the guest house with its own gazebo and plenty of lounge furniture and hammocks, even a barbecue. The property is very quiet and private. Full bar service is available for guests. *Rates:* $45 double, breakfast included. Kitchen privileges for lunch and dinner. Low season and group discounts. Laundry service and transportation available. Phone 573450078 (Netherlands). E-mail info@elmonofeliz.com. Web site: www.elmonofeliz.com.

Club Fred Adventure Lodge – Set high on a ridge overlooking the mouth of the Terraba River and the grand Pacific beyond, this distinctive bed and breakfast focuses on aquatic tropical adventure. The multi-story lodge, built solidly and softened by tropical wood fixtures and accents, has five nice rooms with private tiled baths and a special exotically finished Bamboo Room. All the rooms are fully furnished, and finished with nice ceramic tiled floors for coolness and style. The rooms have tiled verandas to take advantage of the spectacular views of the river, island and sea, and there are lots of cool breezes to keep away the heat. The long pool in the back of the lodge facing the ocean is ideal for laps and deep-water running, or just keeping cool in the summertime heat. If you want to feel like you're on top of the tropical world, take a short climb up to the lookout tower for especially stunning panoramas of the surrounding landscape. In keeping with their theme of "where the adventure begins", they offer several exciting tours. You can take a kayak trip down mild rapids and through primeval mangroves, go snorkeling in the islands of the Ballena Marino National Park, or hike through the jungle to a large waterfall and swimming hole. For the more adventurous among you, a kayak tour exploring coastal caves is offered. Kayaks can be rented independently as well, and other tours can be custom-tailored to suit your personal thirst for excitement. As part of your stay, you can also take advantage of the deep water running classes, or the open invitation to Fred's guests to begin their day early in the morning with a jog through the village and down the local country roads before the day's heat begins. They have come across white-faced monkeys and scarlet macaws on some of these jogs. The pace is comfortable and relaxed. Afterwards, a dip in the pool and a healthy breakfast. ***Rates:*** $45 double standard, $55 double for the exotic Bamboo Room. All lodgings include a full breakfast. Weekly and monthly rates are available. Your host will be glad to drive you to one of the many fabulous restaurants in the area in the evening. He can be contacted in Costa Rica at 307-0289, or (360) 676-5726 in the US. E-mail tanner_fred@hotmail.com. For more info check out their web site at www.clubfredcr.com. Closed May - November, when the entire lodge is available as a vacation rental.

La Cascada – Carlos Lopez and his wife Elida own and manage this picturesque *finca* up against the mountains on the east side of Ojochal which adjoins an exceptionally strong waterfall. One rustic cabin is ensconced in the forest next to a rushing river, while two rooms are available in the owners' former house next to a small *ranchito* with a thatched palm roof. The *ranchito* provides a dining area for those who do tours here, complete with a pet toucan and green parrot. The richly landscaped property, 1-1/2 hectares worth with over an acre of colorful gardens, runs from the rough gravel road down to a scenic river and powerful waterfall (hence the name), where both guests and visitors can romp in the shallows and enjoy the jungle scene. The cabin is extremely secluded and quiet, near the waterfall, with birdsong and the rushing river providing the auditory backdrop to the tranquility. The cabin has two stories, with lots of space. It has double beds, a private bath, a furnished living area, lights and fans, wooden balcony, and complete facilities for cooking, including a refrigerator. It's built on a huge boulder right off the river – very cool (and private). The two rooms were added to the former owners' house in 2004 after they moved into their new home next door, and includes full kitchen priveleges. ***Rates:*** $35 for up to 4 people. Telefax 788-8351 (message phone, Spanish only), or just show up. To get there, take the road across the river above the plaza in Ojochal, and then follow the hand-painted signs. It's about 3 km. above the town. Carlos offers tours into the primary forest for guests and non-guests alike for $25pp including lunch, highly recommended by the locals (see hiking section). The tour takes you not only to the waterfall, but up to a great lookout point where you can see the Pacific, and past huge old rainforest trees full of thick vines. There are many animal spottings on these tours, such as glimpses of peccaries, monkeys and wild turkeys. To arrange a tour (if you are not staying there), call Carlos' brother 'Lalo' on the local radio system (who does many of the local horseback riding tours).

Other Lodgings: El Ultimo Refugio (not reviewed).

FOOD SERVICE

Restaurante Exo-Tica– On seven rustic polished wooden tables and three outside umbrella tables on the main road in Ojochal, one can enjoy some of the best cuisine in Costa Rica. Here you can sample heavenly French and International cuisine, served by one of the sweetest hostesses you will ever meet, all at very affordable prices. The restaurant opens at 11:00am Monday through Saturday, and you can partake of all of their culinary wares during the lunch hours. No matter what your schedule, I highly recommend a visit. The lunch menu is built around light American and Tex-Mex styles, and includes sandwiches, salads, and vegetarian dishes (like Quiche Lorraine). During the high season they offer daily specials as well. To wash it all down they have an extensive cocktail menu, all made fresh to order. Although their lunches are notable, it's their dinner menu that deserves the highest marks. To give you a sampling: Thai seafood pot in coconut milk, Thai peanut chicken, banana-curry fish filet, ginger chicken, garlic shrimp, choice beef filets with exotic sauces – the list goes on, and there is nothing here not worth a try. All the recipes were created by a Belgian chef, Marcella. The dinner courses are served with crisp vegetables, jasmine rice or potatoes of the day, and freshly baked French bread. To start off, appetizers include 2 different types of ceviche (Coast Rican classic and Tahitian), 2 scrumptious salads, and a delicious Vietnamese ginger soup. Full bar service is available for diners, of course, including champagne, aperitifs, French, South African and Argentinean wines, and a full complement of the standard liquors, plus that list of cocktails I mentioned earlier. Most of the to-die-for desserts are prepared by Dulce Lucy, the super-sweet co-owner and hostess. The extensive dessert menu — worth a trip here in and of itself — includes such indulgences as mint velvet pie, Tiramisu, key lime pie, and Canadian sugar pie to name a few. This is one of the best dining events I have ever had the pleasure of experiencing, period. French, English, Spanish and some German are spoken here. The prices at the restaurant are comfortably low, ranging from $4 – $9 for most of the main dinner courses. Special orders for the bakery (Repostería Dulce Lucy) can be taken at the restaurant. The ambience is accented by a small fountain, almond trees, and flowering bushes walling off the light road traffic. Hours are 11am - 9:30pm, Monday through Saturday. Call 369-9261, or e-mail ahead at dulcelucy2000@yahoo.com.

Pizzería Dos Gringos – Around 200 meters above the soccer field in Ojochal you can dine at the locally famous pizzeria and restaurant. The owners Rick and Bobbie Gauthier have renovated and enlarged the restaurant and relandscaped the grounds to create an even more attractive dining establishment. The large patio out front, highlighted by bamboo columns, is enclosed by a low stone wall and ornamental plants, and boasts a nice fountain and nice tile work. The river can be heard only 20 yards away cascading towards the sea. It's all very breezy and comfortable. The separate bar, made from a solid slab of polished Corteza hardwood, looks out over the flower and herb garden in the back, and hosts live music on occasion. The cushioned bamboo chairs and padded bar stools make drinking and dining here a very comfortable experience. The food? Well, the regular menu includes pizza made from fresh dough — thin or thick crust, with real mozzarella and parmesan cheeses – traditional sandwiches you'll be familiar with, avocado and chicken salads, real homemade sausage, rotisserie chicken, chicken wings with your choice of sauces 'from mild to wild', guacamole with chips, and even nachos. They bake their own breads, too, and offer American style desserts like homemade chocolate cake. They offer special meals and deals, like all-u-can-eat pizza Wednesdays for under $4, and weekend snack-and-beer specials for $2. They have soft drinks, draft and imported beer, several different wines, regular fruit juices, great coffee and full bar service to wash it all down, including a full range of cocktails, of course. They have satellite TV with English or Spanish programs to keep you entertained while you wait for your meal on big color TVs in the bar, or you can watch them prepare your meal in the kitchen, designed just for that purpose. They are so proud of their clean and professional operation that they'll give you a kitchen tour (time permitting, of course). The price range is low for this type of restaurant: $2-4 for most lunch and snack items, and most of the pizzas are under $10. During the high season, they have karaoke every other Saturday, and occasional open-mike jam sessions – bring your guitar or harmonica. Normal restaurant hours are 11am – 11pm daily. No matter what your schedule or tastes, there's definitely something for you at Dos Gringos. And if Spanish is not your strongest language, no worries — the owners are 'Gringos', manage the place themselves, and can help you with not only the food choices but local information as well in English, German and even French. They have take-out, too. If you need more information before you visit, e-mail rgauthier59922@yahoo.com.

Chez Elle – This very French restaurant near central Ojochal specializes in fantastic French crepes in a tranquil, social environment. Five hardwood tables with nice linen tablecloths are widely spaced on the wide covered terrace of the main restaurant behind a two-story building, which houses the owners' rooms and a really comfortable,

European style lounge on the second floor. Set well off the main road in Ojochal, the restaurant looks out past a small fountain and over a green belt to the tall trees lining the wide river that winds through the town. There are candle lamps set out on the table for romantic evening dining, and the loudest sound you'll hear is the light jazz or classical music playing in the background. The extensive menu is made up mostly of over twenty types of crepes, both 'meal' type of meats and such to sweet dessert crepes that will blow your mind. They offer Florentine, seafood, cheese, smoked, Hawaiian, and vegetarian crepes. The sweet options include ice cream, caramelized fruit, and flambé. Various French sauces are made from scratch from fresh ingredients and local produce. All the fruits are from local vendors or even neighbors, including mango, pineapple, water apples, oranges, lemons, papaya, etc. How about omelets? There are five kinds: cheese, herb, onion, bacon, and plain. All are served with a nice side salad. Incredible as it may seem, most of the crepes are under $3 each, some as little as one dollar! I suggest getting several. Also served is a kaleidoscope of seafood dishes, with you customizing the plate. Seafood options include Clams mariniere, marinated fish filet, tuna tartare, shrimp in capers sauce, and more. You can even choose a different sauce: curry and cream, garlic butter, or green pepper aioli. Shellfish (shrimp, lobster, clams, crab, mussels, oysters) is available in platters of individuals, batches or mixed, with your choice of sauce. All dishes are served with green salad or ratatouille, and potatoes. Prices range from $4-$9, with $5 being the average. Daily specials of French cuisine are offered in the evenings. Full bar service with cocktails is available. They have a menu in English, and the owner speaks some English and fluent French (of course), as well as good Spanish. Regular hours are 8am to 10pm daily except Sunday. As of 2004 the owners opened a very cool European/Bohemian style lounge on the second floor of the house. Very cool. One can relax on the long balcony outside, or enjoy inside seating on padded sofas and chairs with coffee tables and such. This is a real bar, with blended drinks, cocktails, national and imported liquors, and even games to play with your friends. Hours are 5pm till ???, every day except Sunday. For more information e-mail chezellecr@yahoo.ca

Other Dining Options: Hotel Villas Gaia, Rancho Soluna, Restaurante El Guaraná, Boca Coronado, Iguane Café, Rancho Terraba.

TOURS AND OTHER SERVICES

Flying Dutchman River Tours – Explore the longest river in Costa Rica and largest mangrove forest by either *panga* or kayak with the most versatile river tour service of the Playa Tortuga / Ojochal area. A dynamic, multilingual and photogenic river guide is put at your service, and all tours can be offered in English, Dutch, German, French and Spanish. The various motorboat (*panga*) and kayak tours will take you into the grand Río Terraba to Puerto Cortés as you explore the many faces of this waterway of wonders in a safe and comfortable manner. Visit crocodiles and caimans in their natural habitat, while iguanas and monkeys hang out in the trees along the river. Watch kingfishers, woodpeckers and myriad other exotic water fowl as they go about their daily business in the towering mangroves and surrounding marshes. These tours offer many excellent photo opportunities. One option is to get dropped off at Isla Garza beach to swim or explore some more before returning to your launch point at the new Terraba Marina. The *panga* tour runs $35pp and lasts around 4 hours. A more tranquil tour is to do the mangroves by kayak. Flying Dutchman has newer kayaks for you to get even closer to the natural wonders of the Terraba River Basin. You will be dropped with your kayaks and guide deep in the mangroves where you can start your 3-hour downstream journey. A more demanding expedition is a 6-hour plus journey starting from Palmar Sur farther upstream on the river. You will be transported to the top of the delta where your adventure begins with 200 meters of mild rapids. As you progress downriver you will see mountain ranges, rice fields, reed islands, mangroves, and abundant wildlife including white-faced capuchin monkeys. Park and play as much as you like. Other tours and opportunities offered by the Flying Dutchman and Hotel Posada Playa Tortuga (the tour's home) are Lalo's Horse Tours, Skyline Express Ultralight Tours, Frank Scott Wildlife Photo Tours, scuba diving and snorkeling, and deep sea fishing. They plan to open a fishing camp in 2005 as well. Call 384-5489 direct, or e-mail ptortuga@racsa.co.cr. Or just stop by Posada Playa Tortuga (see LODGINGS above). Web site: www.hotel-posada.com

Mystic Dive Center / Licorera Feliz – With a large office in the modern shopping center in Playa Ventanas, just north of Playa Tortuga, this full-service PADI-licensed operation offers recreational diving and instruction in English, French and Spanish. Just around the corner from the dive center in the shopping center, the same French Canadian owner runs **Licorera Feliz**, where one can stock up on snacks, drinks, and even exchange U.S. dollars. The dive operation specialize in diving and snorkeling trips to Caño Island outside of Drake Bay and the islands of Ballena Marino National Park just a few kilometers up the coast. All the excursions include all new, modern equipment, the services of an experienced dive instructor, a healthy lunch, and all applicable park fees. All the safety equipment is available including oxygen kits, and your friendly dive instructor is fully certified in rescue techniques and first aid. The groups are always small (4-10 people) allowing for very personal attention. Trips to Caño Island are all day affairs leaving at 6:30am, while jaunts to the nearby Ballena Marino National Park take up only a morning or afternoon. Courses are available from the basic 'Discover Diving' for those who have never dove but would like to try it (without getting certified), to 'Advanced Open Water' certification. Snorkeling trips can be arranged separately or with divers. Rates start at $80pp for a 2-tank dive in the park plus $10pp for equipment rental. Diving at Caño Island costs $145pp for a full day of diving. Snorkeling trips run only $45pp (Ballena) or $80pp (Caño Island). Simple boat tours, with hikes on Caño Island, are available as well. Travelers checks and VISA are accepted as well as cash. Call Kumari LeFebvre at 788-8636 direct, or e-mail mysticdive@yahoo.com or info@mysticdivecenter.com. Check out their web site at www.mysticdivecenter.com for photos and more details. In the liquor and specialty store one can find a nice variety of items that many travelers seek. There is a wide selection of good wines, imported beers, champagnes, and both national and international liquors. They have cigars and cigarettes, a great selection of imported cheeses, some excellent chocolate, and even some health food products. If it's a party you want to throw, they've got your supplies. They accept credit cards, too, and will take your U.S. dollars -- to pay for your purchases, of course (they'll exchange dollars for colones, too). Whether staying in the area or just passing through, Licorera Feliz probably has something you need. The air conditioning alone is worth the visit!

Ojochal Internet Café – This business and communications center in Ojochal is set up to give you the best Internet service possible in the southern zone of Costa Rica. The five late-model computers with 17-inch monitors are arranged on new computer desks spaced well apart for both privacy and comfort, while the direct satellite service avails you of instant access to the digital world unhampered by phone line limitations. If you are not completely versed in computerese, the owners and their cyber-wise children are all fluent in the often obscure computer languages, so help is always available for every level of user. The powerful air conditioning in the insulated rustic building keeps you cool while the aroma of freshly ground coffee adds a perfect touch to the European café ambience. It's always clean, cool and quiet inside the varnished hardwood building. The French owners, fluent in English and Spanish as well as their native tongue, offer hot and iced coffees, a full range of espresso drinks, and hot chocolate and teas. Chocolate covered coffee beans can be washed down with a fantastic juice drink from Argentina on their back porch, which is a very nice open-air environment for reading, socializing, or just waiting for a computer, the world beat music enhancing your experience. They also do business graphics, web design, and low cost web hosting. Regular hours are Mon-Fri 8am to 5pm, and Saturday 8am-1pm. Web site: www.ojochal-internet-cafe.com, e-mail ojochal_internet_cafe@ hotmail.com.

HIKING AND CAMPING

There are two cascades and waterfalls up in the mountains above the little town of Ojochal, one of them bordering the property of La Cascada (see above), and both of which are fairly close to the highway. The 10-meter cascade at La Cascada is really nice, and can be visited during the day for a minimal cost by those not staying in their cabins. Carlos, the owner, also offers 4-hour hikes through primary rainforest ending at the two-tiered waterfall with its natural slide, for a relatively small fee.

The beaches of Playas Tortuga, Ventanas, Piñuelas, Ballena and several more to the north towards Bahía and Uvita are beautiful to visit and/or camp on and are easy to get to, all of them having access roads off the highway with signs at the exits. Camping is available at Rancho Soluna (see above) at bargain rates, and for the few dollars they charge you get bathrooms with hot water showers at your disposal. Their riverside location is nice, too. Rancho Terraba, just south of Playa Tortuga between the highway and Terraba River, offers budget camp sites as well.

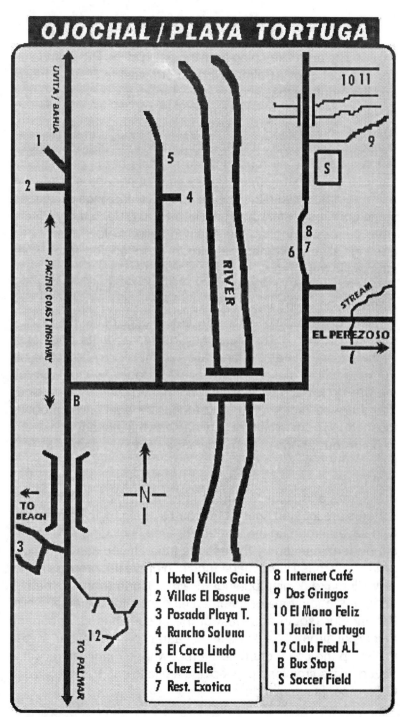

OJOCHAL / PLAYA TORTUGA

1 Hotel Villas Gaia
2 Villas El Bosque
3 Posada Playa T.
4 Rancho Soluna
5 El Coco Lindo
6 Chez Elle
7 Rest. Exotica

8 Internet Café
9 Dos Gringos
10 El Mono Feliz
11 Jardin Tortuga
12 Club Fred A.L.
B Bus Stop
S Soccer Field

OSA'S BACK DOOR

The area stretching from the basin of the Río Grande de Terraba just above Palmar Norte, northwest to Playa Tortuga and the mouth of the same river, and southwest down to Sierpe and the northeastern corner of the Osa Peninsula, is known as the *Valle de Diquis* (Diquis Valley), named after the indigenous people formerly populating the area when the Spanish conquistadores came. The most notable aspects of the area are its flatness — almost perfectly so — its vast banana and African palm plantations, and the bizarre enigma of the once ubiquitous stone spheres (*esféras*). The Sierpe and Blue Estuary Rivers have their own appeal, more fully detailed below. As of this printing, a new international airport is scheduled to be constructed in this area.

The town of Palmar is located right at the foot of the river canyon to the east from which flows the Río Grande de Terraba, at the base of the southwestern edge of the Talamanca mountain range. It is here that the *Costanera Sur* (Pacific Coast Highway, or PCH as I abbreviate it in this book) branches off from the Inter-American Highway (IAH) to follow the shore all the way up to Jaco Beach in the north, and eventually beyond. There are still some of the mysterious *esféras* laying around, those round granite balls of varying sizes that nobody can seem to figure out (theories from ancient indigenous games to E.T. flight path markers have been proposed -- see the book *Atlantis In America* for some anthropological and archaelogical history of the area and some fascinating theories). Two of the largest spheres are located right off the road at the park in Palmar Sur, with several more in the immediate area, including next to the airport terminal and by the antique train. If you can somehow divine how these were made (and can prove it!), drop me a line — we'll make a mint together. Palmar Norte (north of the big bridge) is a fairly major commercial center for the area, while Palmar Sur (south and west of the bridge) has an important municipal airport. As far as tourist attractions in Palmar, forget it. Go up the coast or out to Sierpe, whose road was recently paved. If it's time for a pit stop and a bite to eat, Palmar will do. Otherwise, just move on.

SIERPE

This small town on the picturesque Río Sierpe is the entry point to the extensive wetlands of the lower Diquis Valley and Delta of Terraba, the largest mangrove reserve in Central America. It is also the primary departure point for those heading out to Drake Bay (see next section), so if you are heading to the Osa you may end up traveling through this small river town to arrive at the Osa Peninsula through its northern 'back door'. Towering mangrove trees line the banks of the Sierpe River and its tributaries as it meanders its way out to the Pacific Ocean, where it empties into the sea just a few miles north of Drake Bay and the Osa Peninsula. The Sierpe River and its environs house crocodiles, caimans, monkeys and hundreds of species of birds, including rare varieties of tanager, heron, trogon, kingfisher, etc. There is also fantastic fishing throughout the year. The town has a general store, public telephones, and several boat docks, serving as the major port and supply hub for the lodges and community of Drake Bay.

Getting to Sierpe is easy. It is approximately 17 kilometers south of the IAH, a drive of around 15 minutes. The road was well paved in 2004 to Sierpe -- it's now one of the best in the country. The road passes through Palmar Sur and then past large agricultural plantations. A taxi can take you there from Palmar Norte or from the airport in Palmar Sur, and there is also regular local bus service between Sierpe and Cortés, passing through Palmar on each run. There is also another road to Sierpe from the IAH, the entrance being around 9 km. south of Palmar and 1 km. south of the Río Culebra along the Interamerican Highway. This road passes right by where the new airport is going to go, then past the road to Veragua Azul, by Eco-Manglares Lodge, then crosses a narrow suspension bridge and connects with the main road to Sierpe just two kilometers north of the town. Many tours are offered by the hotels and lodges of Sierpe, including local river tours by day or night, river and lagoon kayak trips, fishing trips on the rivers or out at sea, bird watching, horseback riding, Caño Island, Violin Island, Drake Bay, Corcovado National Park, diving, a local Indian cemetery, and more.

LODGINGS

Estero Azul Lodge – North American owners Gary and Patricia Van Kirk have without a doubt the classiest lodge in Sierpe, established now for over a decade and completely renovated just a few years ago. The property encompasses several acres, including primary riverside forest, and is beautifully landscaped and maintained with grass, fruit trees, almond trees, and tropical bushes and flowers. There are trails through the forest next to the lodge — bird watching is excellent. There is an abundance of iguanas, squirrels, parakeets and other wildlife. They hang bananas to attract the many species of birds in the area, as well at the monkeys. They actually have a pet orphaned howler monkey named Emma which they saved from certain doom, two talking parrots, plus white-faced and squirrel monkeys that still roam the property after being rehabilitated and set free here. The young howler is tame enough for you to pet. They have their own lighted dock on the river – very nicely done — and even a hydraulic dry dock. The two duplexes are independent cabins a few dozen meters away from the restaurant, arrived at by lighted concrete paths through deep green lawns. The recently refurbished rooms are extremely spacious, all wood construction, with polished hardwood floors, night tables, desks, attractive original artwork, fully tiled private baths, and a large fully screened and furnished porch area for protected lounging. There is hot water in the showers, electrical outlets, large screened windows with nice curtains, and ceiling fans. The 'Honeymoon Suite' is a private, luxurious 2-bedroom cabin with all the extras. Teak walls, television, air conditioning, bottled water dispenser, bamboo lounge furniture, and a huge bath are just a partial list. It has a real bath tub (hot water, of course), and lots of elegant, classy touches. The restaurant, bar and lounge are top shelf. Downstairs is the open-air breakfast terrace and juice bar, while upstairs is the lounge and formal restaurant, exquisitely decorated and very comfortable. The food at the guest-only restaurant is top shelf, being prepared by Patricia herself — an experienced gourmet chef — when she is at the lodge. Emphasis is on the local river fish and seafood, though meats, chicken, rice dishes, pasta, and salads are also served. Definitely some of the best meals you can get in the area. Prices are reasonable. *Rates:* $65-85 per room for up to 4 people. Laundry service is included, and both a hair dryer and iron can be loaned to guests. The lodge has their own boats available for many exciting tours, especially sport fishing. Unique tours into the Osa rainforests, waterfalls and nearby Laguna Chocuacu, teeming with wildlife, are offered directly by the lodge as well. All other tours can be arranged with English-speaking guides. Phone (520) 455-9333 in the

USA, 786-7422 in Costa Rica. E-mail esteroazul@hotmail.com. Web site: www.samplecostarica.com.

Eco-Manglares Lodge -- Located around 2 kilometers before you arrive in the town of Sierpe, this lodge on the banks of the Estero Azul, a wide waterway that feeds the Sierpe River, is both convenient and secluded. You arrive by a road which branches off the main thoroughfare to the left, cross a funky metal suspension bridge (take pictures), and you're there. The restaurant is located at the entrance on the right hand side, and the independent cabins are set above a greenbelt that borders the river itself, a few dozen meters away. The lodge is personally managed by the owners, a partly Italian family who moved here decades ago. The expansive lawn is interspersed with fruit trees, coconuts, and decorative plants, with a stone pathway leading from the restaurant to the cabins. The lodge has its own private dock, and trails in the forest behind the buildings for guests to check out the surrounding flora and fauna. All the cabins are independent structures with private baths, raised above the ground, with rustic wood construction and their own private decks. The tiled bath has a hot water shower, there are covered light fixtures, night tables with lamps, and even a bug zapper. There is a lot of white cane used in the cabinas, and the beds are made of beautiful mangrove wood. There is an extra table, a rocking chair, curtains and indoor plants. The big screened windows provide ample ventilation. All cabins have a double and single bed. English is spoken, both a hair dryer and iron are available, laundry service is available, and parking is right on the property. The full-service restaurant serves real Italian food, including pizza and pasta dishes, and all varieties of seafood. Also on the menu are salads, steaks, chicken, sandwiches, ceviche, and desserts. Breakfast (included with lodging) and all meals are also served to the public until 9pm. Even if you are not staying here, the restaurant is worth the visit. Large and spacious inside, outdoor dining on a large lawn closer to the river is also available. Eco-Manglares has its own boat for river tours, and can arrange any and all of the other local tours, or trips to Drake Bay, Caño Island, etc. *Rates:* $30 single, $40 double, $10 each additional person, all including breakfast. Group discounts available, as well as full board packages, and tour packages of several types. Phone 786-7414 or telefax 786-7441 for reservations. E-mail ecosiepa@racsa.co.cr. Web site: www.ecotourism.co.cr/ecomanglares.

Veragua River House – The friendly Italian owner Ven has created a wonderful, tranquil place to relax by the river in privacy just a few kilometers outside of Sierpe. South along the gravel road from the previous lodge, several acres of beautiful park-like grounds right on the peaceful east side of the Estero Azul are yours to enjoy. Tall hedges of hibiscus along the semi-private road afford ample privacy, while wide lawns dotted with tall fruit and ornamental tree provide lots of shade on the two huge lots by the river. Birders will feel right at home, with tons of exotic species flocking around the property with its various ecosystems. Eagles, scarlet macaws, toucans, kingfishers and many rare wetland species can be spotted. The main lodge and owner's house sit up on a small rise next to the river, with a nice concrete path to their own covered dock. You can lounge around in front of the house on the wraparound covered porch, or step down to the lighted dipping pool surrounded by tall plants for private bathing. To one side of the house is a large stone courtyard with an brick oven and large barbecue, the lodge's orchid collection hanging nearby. Inside the spacious house are a large pool table with a good stereo, a very nice lounge area, and a screened dining area off the kitchen, all on nice terra cotta tiles. Upstairs is another lounge area and a guest room and bath. All the construction and furnishings are very stylish and comfortable. The main bungalow is close to the house, with its own screened-in furnished porch. It has two bedrooms and one nice bathroom with tiled floors, a hot water tiled shower and white cane walls. The nice varnished cane ceiling keep things cool. The bungalow is fully furnished with a closet, night stands, lamps, tables, etc. The other three bungalows are on the far side of the property with a long lit path off the road leading to their marshside location. They all have terra cotta tiled floors and a deck looking out over the riverside marsh, and are equally well furnished and appointed. The bath and large hot water showers are fully tiled, with nice mirrors and sinks. A full breakfast is included, and other delicious homemade meals are available. The primary style is Italian, with other international meals being cooked up by the owner himself and his wonderful Tica wife. He bakes his own breads, and makes pizza in the brick oven outside. Barbecues of fish and meats are a good call. Both indoor and outdoor games are available (croquet anyone?), in addition to the pool table -- my personal favorite. ***Rates:*** $50 double with breakfast (discount with this book if you mention it when making reservations directly). Laundry, transportation, tours, phone and fax available. English, Italian, French and Spanish are all spoken. Ven has his own motorboat for river tours, and also rents a house with four kilometers of beachfront (wow!) on Isla Violin at the mouth of the Sierpe River. Call or fax 786-7460, or e-mail veragua@racsa.co.cr.

Hotel Oleaje Sereno — This simple two-story hotel on the banks of the Sierpe River, right in the town of Sierpe, is a good choice as either a one-night stopover on the way to Drake Bay or as a destination in itself. Just west of the center of this very small town, these modern lodgings are built like a typical roadside motel in the U.S.A., but with a bit more class. The parking area in front and landscaping were all redone recently, and a fenced parking lot was added across the street for those with cars. More improvements were made around the restaurant in 2003, which went through a significant expansion. All ten renovated rooms have nice desks, night stands with lamps, a closet area, ceiling fans and air conditioning. Both gauze and thick curtains over louvered glass windows ensure privacy, while a water pitcher and glasses are set out to help you quench your thirst. The spacious tiled baths have very large mirror and thick towels, while both the showers and sinks have hot water on tap. The decor is surprisingly modern for this area. The upstairs rooms have a view of the town and river, with the perpetual armadas of lilies floating downstream. All rooms have both a double and single bed. There is also a separate, newly renovated *casita* available, with four separate rooms and air conditioning. The bathroom is shared among the four rooms. English is spoken by the manager at the store El Fenix in town. Parking is available free to guests moving on to Drake Bay for a few days, or to people not staying at the hotel for only about $2.50/day. The hotel has its own boats for any kind of tour, including fishing, crocodiles (day or night), Caño Island, Corcovado, etc. A special tour of Isla Violin at the mouth of the Sierpe River, with its mangroves, beaches and extensive bird life, is also available. Their modern, well-outfitted boat has capacity for 25 people with lifejackets, an indoor head in a full cabin, and a strong inboard engine. A bilingual guide accompanies all aquatic tours. Other land or water transportation can also be arranged. The restaurant serves a variety of international dishes, especially seafood, in an open and relaxed environment. There is both inside and outside seating, with concrete umbrella tables right by the river. Offerings include 4 breakfasts, *casados*, chicken and rice, whole fish, sandwiches, filet mignon and various shrimp and fish specialties. Extra points awarded here for the linen tablecloths and fresh-cut flowers on the tables. Full bar service is also available. **Rates:** $30/room, for up to 3 people. $15pp for the rooms in the *casita*. Discounts for groups of 6 or more. There is a phone available, and laundry service (paid for by gratuities). Bicycles are available for rent. Call 786-7580 or fax 786-7311 for reservations. E-mail oleajesereno@racsa.co.cr, web site www.oleajesereno.com

Hotel Margarita – This small Tico-run hotel on the west side of the soccer field represents your low budget option set away from the hubbub of the central area, next to the elementary school (with the musical sound of children playing at recess times). Two buildings connected by a covered concrete walkway house a total of 18 rooms, most with shared bathroom facilities. There is a long bench on the front porch of the building for watching the day go by, or a soccer game if there's one happening. There's plenty of seating for you and your friends. The hotel is only a block and a half from the river, and only two blocks from 'downtown' Sierpe. There is secure parking right next to the rooms, and a public phone right on the corner. Lots of birds in the big trees around the hotel add some life to the surroundings. The rooms with shared baths run down the length of one hallway and up another adjacent to the owners' quarters. The restrooms and showers are located next to a large sink with a mirror for guest use. The rooms are decent in size, with fans and good ceilings. Some have a table and chair. The rooms with private baths are in a separate building with a wide furnished patio out front. They have tiled floors and baths, with hot water showers. There are several potted plants (and some laundry) hanging around the buildings for a touch of décor. Everything is kept very clean. **Rates:** $7 for a room sharing baths, or $12 for the rooms with private baths, both for up to 3 people. Telephone use (there is a charge for their phone), and messages accepted. Call 786-7574 if you speak Spanish.

Other Lodgings: Río Sierpe Lodge, Mapache Lodge, Sábalo Lodge.

FOOD SERVICE

Centro Turístico Las Vegas – This small group of businesses started primarily as a waterfront restaurant in central Sierpe, then added an internet café and some rooms. The well-established and popular **Marisquería, Restaurante y Bar Las Vegas** was recently renovated and expanded in 2003, adding more tables and space, and an *al fresco* terrace overlooking the docks and Sierpe River. They had planned to expand even more in 2004, adding a meat and fish grill. The restaurant has a special counter area for tourist information, wth brochures and maps and such. The open-beam loft ceiling is made of varnished hardwoods in an attractive pattern. The nicely tiled floors lead to a long bar of polished hardwood where you can order up almost anything imaginable, and meet some of the locals. The bar has a snack menu in addition to all the national and imported liquors. A good stereo is always going (they have lots of CDs of music in English), and fans keep the air moving along with the fresh breezes off the water. The view of the river is great, and you can watch boat traffic, crocodiles, and even monkeys cavorting on the other side. The menu is more than ample, with both all the Tico standards and international dishes. Breakfasts of omelets, pancakes and bacon and eggs are listed with *gallo pinto* and other typical Tico choices. They serve fish filet many ways (in Creole sauce even), chicken, seafood, beef, pork, spaghetti, salads, and even fast food. On the same menu one finds Filet Mignon, Smoked Pork Chops, Garlic Shrimp, Bolognese Spaghetti, Chef's Salad, ceviches, sandwiches, and homemade refried beans. They have all the juice drinks, of course, and desserts as well. The service is fast and friendly. Prices are very reasonable, with a sandwich and fries going for around $3, and typical lunch and dinner plates (*casados*) getting an average of $4. Breakfast is really inexpensive, and even the Butterfly Jumbo Shrimp is only about $8. Next door there is a new **Internet Café**, with several new machines and lots of space. The computers are pretty fast, especially for this area. Across the street they were planning on putting several rooms for those staying overnight. They have their own boat for taxi service out to Drake Bay, customized inshore fishing trips, or local aquatic tours. The restaurant is open daily from 6am till 10pm, with the bar staying open till at least midnight. Take-out is available.

Other Dining Options: See Pizzería Piccola de Osa at Eco-Manglares Lodge, and Restaurant Oleaje Sereno (at the hotel), as their restaurants are open to the public. Other options are Restaurants El Ankla and Blue Marlin.

THE OSA PENINSULA

The world-famous Osa Peninsula, one of the most biodiverse places on the entire planet, has been described as "the most biologically intense place on Earth" by no less an authority than National Geographic. The main feature of the Osa is the 42,000-hectare Corcovado National Park, home to almost 400 known species of birds, 140 species of mammals, 116 species of amphibians and reptiles, over 500 species of trees and more than 6000 species of insects. The park protects endangered species such as the jaguar, puma, crocodile, tapir, poison dart and golden frogs, and the harpy eagle. The beaches of the Osa are also major nesting sites for several varieties of sea turtle. If you want to really *experience* a lowland tropical rain forest in its most pristine and natural state, yet also enjoy the tropical beach environment, the Osa Peninsula is definitely the place to go.

The east side of the Osa Peninsula is bordered by the Golfo Dulce (Sweet Gulf), an incredible marine paradise where humpback whales, whale sharks, three species of dolphins, and schools of tuna come to breed and play. The unique ecosystem here provides not only an ideal environment for aquatic mammals, but also for world-class fishing, with giant snook and snapper routinely hauled in by sport fishermen and locals alike. There are also some excellent surf breaks for those looking for the 'perfect' wave. Whether you visit Drake Bay on its northern base, Corcovado National Park in its heart, the gulf and Pacific coastlines around its southern end, or a combination of all these exciting and picturesque areas, the exhilarating beauty and energy of the Osa will leave an indelible impression upon your psyche.

There are many ways to get to the peninsula. Both SANSA and NatureAir fly in to Puerto Jiménez and the Drake Bay area every day. During most of the year, there is a very good passable road between Rincón and Drake Bay. A ferry leaves daily at 11:30am from Golfito on the other side of the gulf to Pto. Jiménez. Buses from San José run directly to Puerto Jiménez from the Transportes Blanco bus office near the Atlántico Norte terminal in San José (257-4121), as do buses from Ciudad Neily in the south at 7am and 2pm daily. If you are coming down by car, make a right at the "Servicentro Chacarita" gas station about 32 kilometers south of Palmar in Chacarita on the IAH (watch for the large green signs on the road just before the turnoff). 42 kilometers into the hilly, rainforested base of the peninsula along the paved road, you will descend from the mountain ridges into the quaint little town of Rincón, right on the shores of the Sweet Gulf (*Golfo Dulce*). From here it is just 35 kilometers to the primary town on the Osa Peninsula, Puerto Jiménez.

DRAKE BAY

Named after Sir Francis Drake, who once moored here for a spell and, as legend has it, buried a rich treasure somewhere along the coast in the area, this wide bay and the coastline to its south on the Pacific is one of the most picturesque spots in Costa Rica, where lush lowland rain forest flows down verdant mountainsides to meet the warm, rolling surf of the Pacific Ocean. The bay itself lies at the base of the Osa Peninsula, home of the world-famous Corcovado National Park. Caño Island, a land and marine biological reserve famous for pre-Colombian spheres, world class diving, and excellent sport fishing, can be seen from the shore. The most common way to get there is by water from the town of Sierpe, where there are many taxi boats available. The trip down the Sierpe River is breathtaking as it meanders its way towards the Pacific among giant mangrove forests. There is also a good gravel road winding straight though the rainforested mountains of the peninsula, leaving from the east side of the Osa Peninsula on the Golfo Dulce just south of the town of Rincón at the Rincón River, and arriving at the beaches of Drake in about an hour and a half by car (4-wheel-drive only in the winter months). Once you get to the tiny village of Agujitas in Drake Bay, however, you can only travel by foot, horse or boat, unless you are going out to the Los Planes area around four kilometers inland, which now has a decent gravel road. The road from Rincón to Agujitas can also be hiked in about 6-1/2 hours by those hardy enough to try it, though you could probably catch a ride, or the collective taxi and/or bus which operates much of the year. The buses going to and from Pto. Jiménez will drop you off at the Río Rincón where the road begins (there is a covered bus stop). It's a beautiful trip either way. A much quicker and easier option is to take a flight from San José in the morning. SANSA and NatureAir are now providing daily service most of the year to the area, and there are frequent chartered flights as well arranged by your destination lodge. Both boat launches and cars finish the trip into the resort area. This option usually gets you to Drake Bay by around 9am, which gives you plenty of time to do a tour your first day in the area (call ahead to your lodge to make arrangements).

In the tiny hamlet of Agujitas (Drake Bay's 'town'), there is really not much to do except relax, swim and enjoy the environment. There is a small public *soda* with basic Tico meals (closed Sundays), several *pulperías* with all the basics, and a disco once every week or two on Saturday nights for some nightlife activity.

An incredible variety of tours are available from the wilderness lodges of Drake Bay and the surrounding area, which is the primary attraction here, this area being famous for its eco-tourism. Sport fishing, diving, snorkeling, hiking, Corcovado excursions, trips to Caño Island, bird watching, waterfalls, night tours, dolphin and whale watching, horseback riding and even a canopy tour are offered. Wherever you stay, the staff at your lodge can make arrangements for any of these tours. In addition, within an hour's walk along the shoreline path towards Corcovado are Río Claro and Playa San Josecito. Río Claro has great surf offshore, a hidden waterfall ensconced in rainforest, and kayak rentals for cruising the river (during high season). Playa San Josecito, a bit further south along the coast about two hours from the border of Corcovado National Park, has a wide sandy beach and fantastic snorkeling right off shore in reef-protected shallows. Drake Bay and the Pacific coastline of the Osa is a hikers' and beachcombers' paradise, and one could spend many days in this area (or longer) without running out of exciting things to do.

LODGINGS

The accommodations in this area range from very good to excellent and, now that public electricity has finally arrived in 'inner' Drake Bay, fans and lights are standard features. Most of the 'outer' Drake Bay lodges have generators, solar, or hydroelectric power. All but one of the lodges mentioned below are all located right on or near the beach, providing the soothing backdrop of gently rolling surf for your daytime adventures and nighttime dreams, and almost all of them have their own boats for both transportation and tours, and can make arrangements with others if they don't. The vast majority of the lodges have owners and/or managers fluent in English. The few that don't can at least communicate in basic English. Some can speak several languages. Note: This is one of the most popular and heavily promoted spots in the southern zone for tourists, so if you are coming during the high season it would be best to call or e-mail ahead for reservations, as most of the lodges fill up at this time. The accommodations listed below appear in order by location starting from about a kilometer east of the village of Agujitas, on the gravel road coming in from Rincón (see above), then heading west towards outer Drake Bay. The lodgings in outer Drake Bay and south to Corcovado National Park are described in the following section. It would be best to read both sections, and check out the web sites, before making a final decision about where to stay.

Pirate Cove / Caño Divers – The location of this attractive adventure lodge is both convenient and scenic, set on the ocean side of the infrequently used gravel road on its own private point above the mouth of the Drake River, forming a picturesque, idyllic little cove as it empties out of an estuary into the bay. The small lodge is currently composed of four cabins and three private rooms. The colorful landscaping is being continually crafted around the natural exuberance of tall palms, almond trees, vibrant bromeliads, and old fruit trees with huge epiphytes clinging on their trunks and branches. With the ancient jungle palms and scattered rainforest trees, the overall effect is one of primeval splendor. The lodge building houses the kitchen and the spacious dining deck, where several long tables provide guests with not only healthy meals, but an nice river and ocean view. The four cabins are connected by a raised wooden walkway with a green rope railing – unique in the area. The triplex with large private rooms is situated at the far end of the complex. All the cabins have their own deck with hammock, two beds with orthopedic mattresses and nice linen, large screened windows to keep the bugs out while letting the sounds of nature in (the birds, frogs and cicadas are very active here), and deliciously thick bath towels. Two of the cabins have been expanded and completely renovated. They are much larger than before, have both a double and two single beds, beautiful varnished floors and detailing, a spacious furnished deck, and fully tiled baths. The rooms in the triplex are much a bit more spacious than the cabins, with varnished hardwood floors, wide private decks looking out over the rivermouth and bay, and nice furnishings and detailing. The rooms have fully tiled private baths, too. Both the renovated cabins and the rooms have instantaneous gas hot water heaters. The food? Well, the words 'bland' and 'meals' will never be used together here, with the European resident co-owner directing the cooking. Basically a 'Euro-Tico' mix of lively dishes, the emphasis is on quality and flavor to pique your palate. Dinner is a 3-course affair. The homemade breads and pastries are excellent, and the desserts worth seconds. English, Italian, Swiss, and German is spoken. ***Rates:*** $47pp std cabins, $58pp rooms and deluxe cabins, full board (beer and sodas extra). Several lodging/meals/tour packages are available, even custom packages (see their Web site). The emphasis here is on diving Caño Island, and Pirate Cove is a PIRA resort (PIRA stands for PADI International Resort Association). Their two custom dive boats – both over 30 feet, fully equipped and covered – are perfect for the area, with powerful 4-stroke engines. The lodge is located about a kilometer before the town of Agujitas on the main road from Rincón. Call 234-6154 or 834-1226, fax 253 0344. E-mail erlane@racsa.co.cr . Web site: www.piratecovecostarica.com.

El Mirador Lodge – Situated on three hectares well above the road at the eastern corner of the bay's sandy beach, this rustic lodge owned by Antonio Vargas and his family is Drake Bay's only real budget option. Lots of fruit trees, flowers and ornamental plants add character to the wide lawns around the combination dining deck and owners' house, and the guest rooms nearby. There are chairs and hammocks on the evergreen lawn for relaxing outdoors. There is an organic garden on the property where composting and permaculture methods are extensively utilized. Above the small complex, at the end of a nice path that winds amongst a pineapple garden and flowering plants, there is a new lookout rancho on a high ridge for enjoying spectacular sunsets, with panoramic views of the bay, island and mountains. The rustic triplexes and two private cabins that house guests are built almost completely of bamboo and wood. The two triplexes have long benches and counters running along the length of their covered decks for lounging, reading, etc. The large screened windows and wide doors let the breezes flow, and all the rooms have concrete private baths.

One private cabin is located between the triplexes, while the other is down in the private entrance, with it's own carport and surrounded by tall trees. Both have private baths. At the main lodge building there is a long common deck with both bar and table seating where all can enjoy the views. Meals start out with an international breakfast, with very healthy portions of typical Tico fare for lunch and dinner with seafood and occasional international dishes mixed in. Much of the produce comes from their property, from the organic garden which keeps expanding through the years. The meals are very good, and one is never left hungry. The atmosphere here is very open, friendly, and hospitable, as befits a family-run business. They have their own motorboat for most excursions, including dolphin tours, and will be happy to arrange any tours that they do not offer themselves. Some English is spoken by the family. *Rates:* $40pp includes all meals and natural drinks. Transportation and a cell phone are both available. They also offer camping in a sheltered area or on their lawn for $5pp. Call 387-9138, 356-4758, or 836-9415. E-mail info@mirador.co.cr, Web site: www.mirador.co.cr.

Albergue Jade Mar — Jade Sea Lodge offers seven comfortable lodgings right off the road above the beach in 'central' Agujitas. One long building houses five private rooms, with an outside shower, nice green lawn and ornamental plants. They added a private wood cabin in 2003, and a spacious rental house as well for couples and groups. They have a separate dining rancho with its own large kitchen. Doña Martha Pérez and her family run the small *cabinas* themselves, so this is another place you can mix with the local Ticos. Doña Marta speaks some English, so communication is no problem if your Spanish isn't up to snuff. The spacious rooms are built in typical style for Costa Rica, concrete floors and half-walls with varnished wood making up the rest of the structure. Each room has a private bath with a commodious shower, and opens onto the common porch with long benches, the view looking through the trees to the bay and ocean beyond. Each room is furnished with a double and/or two single beds and a small table, and has its own hammock on the porch. The private cabin sits between the dining rancho and rooms, with its own views of the bay, surrounded by ornamental plants and flowers. The secluded house has two large dormitory-style bedrooms, a full kitchen with breakfast bar, a living room, a covered and tiled outside patio, and a great view of the forest of the property. House residents share two tiled showers and bathrooms. The dining and lounging rancho, attractively built with various hardwoods, sits about 30 meters from the rooms along a concrete path, and is surrounded by trees, flowers and lush foliage. It has five large tables, catches lots of breezes, and has a bay view through the trees. Meals are cooked by the family in the dining rancho, and feature typical Tico home cooked fare with plenty of seafood, including shrimp dishes, with lots of veggies, fresh fruit, and salads. **Rates:** $45pp full board during high season, sodas and beer extra. The house rents for $40 per couple (no meals included). Discounts for students (with proof), and groups. Low season discounts apply. Another option here is to pay only for lodging, and find your meals elswhere. With this option, lodging in the rooms is $20pp per night. The family has their own boat for almost all the area tours including both Sirena and San Pedrillo in Corcovado, and for aquatic transportation as well. There is 24-hr. security and parking right next to the rooms for those who come in by car. Don Rafa will pick you up himself in Sierpe by boat if you call in ahead ($15pp each way). They have a small office at the lodge, so communications aren't a problem. Phone direct 384-6681, 845-0394, 822-8595, or 786-7591. Fax 786-6358, attention "Jade Mar". E-mail info@drakebayjademar.com, web site www.drakebayjademar.com.

Rancho Corcovado — This lodge right on the beach in the village of Agujitas is managed by the large González family, a perfect place to immerse yourself in the local culture while taking advantage of the beautiful setting of the bay. The beach is wide and inviting here, and the main *rancho* is only a few steps from the shore. A wide green lawn, decorated by ornamental plants and flowers and shaded by tall coconut palms and other tall trees, spills out onto the beach from in front of the *rancho* where small waves perpetually lap the sandy shore. There are two sets of rooms, one just off the beach in the shade of the hill and the other on top of the low ridge with sweeping, panoramic views of the bay. There is also a new cabin with four single beds and a private bath. English is spoken by two of the family members, so if your Spanish is less than perfect you won't be lost. There is a lot of privacy, especially up on the ridge, yet you are close to everything. The beach here is especially calm and nice for bathing. The standard rooms have double beds, single beds, or one of each, with up to 3 per room. All have private baths with showers. There is a long tiled deck running the length of the buildings, with a wide railing, lounge chairs and a table for gazing at the bay and distant coastline (this is one of the best views anywhere). The construction is rustic style, with plenty of room to move around. The food in the large private *rancho* restaurant is typical Tico with options, such as pasta, fresh fish, meats, ceviche, salads, etc. all complimented by fresh fruit grown right there on the property (papaya, pineapple, mango, oranges, etc.). Clients can request certain meals, based on availability. There are large hammocks out under the palm trees on the beach for relaxing after a satisfying meal. The family will provide their own English-speaking guides for their tours in the area, all of which are done themselves with their own launches (they have 4 boats, one with a capacity of 16 persons). They also have their own horses for tours to local waterfalls and rainforest, plus a tour to the Sierpe River mangrove forest. They can also rent kayaks. *Rates:* $45 a day per person full board. Also available is camping right on their grassy lawn by the beach for those with their own equipment for $6 a night, which includes use of nice tiled bathrooms. Call 241-0441, 786-7059, and/or 350-4866.

Jinetes de Osa / Costa Rica Adventure Divers — Set just above the shoreline on the west side of the bay, this North American-run resort specializes in the various water adventures available in the area, notable scuba diving. Facing east from an optimum site just above the black sand beach on the bay, the sunrises are absolutely stunning from here. The small beach-front retreat is encircled by tall coconut palms, mature almond trees (ideal for viewing scarlet macaws at close range), tropical fruit trees, and many varieties of ornamental and flowering bushes. It's only a short walk along the beach to either the local *pulpería* or the Agujas River. The main dining area and cozy bar is a two-story structure all done in varnished hardwoods with nice new tile work, and has hammocks and a dart board upstairs. The furniture and bar are all beautifully finished local hardwoods as well. The three daily meals are comprised of fresh baked breads and tropical fruits complementing a tasty cuisine of locally caught seafood or the chef's special of the day. A really nice touch is complimentary coffee service every morning delivered right to your door. The guest rooms have high ceilings, private tiled baths with 24-hour hot water showers (most rooms), varnished hardwood or ceramic tile floors, ceiling fans, nice curtains covering large screened windows, a table and chair, wooden shelving, and ample space to move around. There are newer rooms added in 2003 with bamboo chairs and tables, more spacious bathrooms with finer finish work, and upgraded furnishings. They are all located along the side of the hill looking out over the picturesque bay. Each room has either a double bed or both a double and single bed. All rooms have a nice porch out front, either varnished hardwood or tiled. Costa Rica Adventure Divers is an on-site dive center taking advantage of the close proximity of Caño Island, and the only PADI-certified facility in the southern zone. Jinetes offers a wide range of professional underwater services for the recreational scuba diver, from professional instruction to guided scuba excursions with PADI-certified instructors and dive masters. They have their own fully-equipped boats with emergency oxygen, including a new one in 2000, a custom-made 30-footer. The diving rates are very reasonable for the area. They offer underwater still and video camera rentals to capture those special, unique aquatic moments that you can relive again and again long after your Costa Rican vacation is part of the past. *Rates:* From $45pp dbl. full board low season, $75pp dbl. high season (alcoholic beverages and sodas extra). Discounts are available for larger groups and extended stays. In the U.S. call (800) 317-0333; e-mail crventur@costaricadiving.com; Web site www.costaricadiving.com. In Costa Rica call 826-9757 or 236-5637.

Aguila de Osa – Casual elegance with a tropical flair. This luxury complex is set high above the water facing the rivermouth and the bay, with their own attractive pier and support buildings below on the river. Lighted concrete paths lead up the high ridge, with thousands of ornamental plants, fragrant flowering bushes, fruit trees and grasses blending with much of the original indigenous flora. Construction is all to the highest standards, with much attention to detail like the natural stone finishes on the retaining walls and cabins. The main lodge building is a soaring *rancho* near the water with lots of ceiling fans, beautiful hardwood tables, an attractive bar, good stereo, and a small gift shop. Fresh cut flowers adorn the furniture, and all is kept immaculate. The standard rooms all have hand-carved wooden doors, ample screened windows, lofty vaulted ceilings, ceiling fans with lights, brass fixtures in the fully tiled baths with 24-hour hot water, queen-sized bamboo beds, night stands, reading lamps, closet, and even original artwork decorating the walls. Each room has its own furnished deck out front with spectacular views and a varnished hardwood bar for sitting, writing, etc. Deluxe cabins have huge bathrooms with sunken tubs, skylights, more closet space, and larger rooms with lounging areas of rattan furniture. The independent, private "Honeymoon Suite" has a wraparound deck next to a huge stand of bamboo. Aguila prepares some of the best food in Drake Bay, if not the southern zone, and many people staying elsewhere come here for dinner. Experienced chefs in gourmet styles are brought in every year to train and work with the cooks here to create masterpiece meals designed to please even the most demanding palate. Dinners always begin with appetizers and a little socializing. Red and white wines are placed on the table while the meat, seafood and vegetables (mostly organic, locally grown produce) are brought out for the family-style dining. The flower arrangements, candles and beautiful china add classy touches to the setting. And your health is virtually guaranteed, with a $20,000 water purification system employed to keep things clean. Totally complete bar service is available, with any number of exotic cocktails to choose from. And ordering is no problem, as both English and Spanish are spoken fluently here. *Rates:* Lodging and meals during the high season (including wine with dinner) run $160 single and $250 double standard; $270 double for a junior suite; and $300 for a full suite. Additional persons are $125 each, while children 4-12 get a 50% discount. Lodging and tour packages available and encouraged. The hotel does all its own tours – the full panorama available – and even has its own dive shop, custom dive boat and fishing fleet, and IGFA-rated gear in their own sport fishing shop. Phone 296-2190, fax 232-7722, or e-mail reserve@aguiladeosa.com. Web site: www.aguiladeosa.com.

Drake Bay Wilderness Resort — Spread out along its own peninsula on the north side of the Agujas River, this North American and Tica run resort is one of the largest in the area, established back in 1986. Over fifteen years of TLC have molded a magnificent garden environment with bougainvillea, hibiscus, mature fruit trees, bamboo, and wide lawns with hammocks, benches (and even a swing) sloping down to the water. There is a natural whirlpool at the end of the 5-acre property on the point, and a chemical-free salt-water swimming pool with 'Fort Drake' lounging deck and great views near the dining rancho and bar. The standard ocean-level rooms are in triplexes of concrete and varnished hardwoods, very spacious units with tiled baths, 24-hour hot water showers, and beautiful murals on the walls. They were all recently remodeled, expanding their private verandas and adding special features like *cara tigre* posts and upgraded ceramic tile. A queen and single bed, night stands and benches for your luggage round out the furniture, while ceiling fans, screen doors and shuttered and louvered windows keep both the air flow and lighting controllable. There are also larger and nicer luxury suites and secluded honeymoon suites available. The previous tent lodgings have been upgraded to fully enclosed cabañas, with lights, fans, shelves, reading lamps, private decks and double door entries. The restaurant is large, screened, and has a view of the bay, with lots of interesting pre-Columbian artifacts and mounted insects to check out. The meals are buffet and cook-to-order breakfasts, complete and healthy lunches, and delicious multi-course dinners, with a mixture of seafood and meat dishes prepared in a variety of international styles, always served with crisp salads and homemade breads fresh from the oven. All the water is purified here as well. The comfortable and attractive bar and dining lounge, located amongst the accommodations along the shore, has checkers, chess and dominoes for gamesters of all ages, and free coffee 24 hours a day. Also offered is free daily laundry service. *Rates:* $95pp standard, $65pp for the private cabaña option, and $125 for the luxury rooms and honey-moon suites, all full board. Lodging/tour packages available (encour-aged). Major discounts for children 16 and under. Low season rates negotiable. They do all their own tours, with 6 boats and several guides handling everything including scuba diving, sport fishing, interactive dolphin/whale tours (with digital video option), bird watching, mangrove river tours and 1-day trips to Sirena in Corcovado. Mountain bikes are also available, perfect for a trip to Rancho Mariposa, their private butter-fly farm in Progresso. There are kayaks available or a free canoe for river explorations. Internet is available in the evenings, and they have full communications at the lodge. Call direct 770-8012 or 382-0147 cellular, or 256-7394, or fax 221-4948. E-mail info@drakebay.com; Web site: www.drakebay.com

La Paloma Lodge — Welcome to another class act of Drake Bay. Set on 14 acres on a cliff above the northwestern end of the bay, seven cabins and four rooms give you an option on how to best enjoy your stay in the jungle. Not only the grand central *rancho* but all of the lodgings have panoramic ocean views. The beautiful and immaculately landscaped grounds — complete with arched trellises of hibiscus flow-ers — attract many native bird species. Winding stone and concrete paths lead to all the buildings through the abundant garden flora and to the large blue-tiled pool and stone patio area with a wooden deck and umbrella tables and chairs where you can enjoy the spectacular vista up the coastline and out to Caño Island. The combination dining area and lounge is housed under a thatched-palm *rancho,* which has com-fortable couches with coffee tables, a small library, reading lamps, charts and posters, a long deck with benches and chairs looking out to the spectacular sunsets, and table seating for up to 30 guests or so, all finished with varnished hardwood and floral patterns that reflect the relaxed ambiance of tropical elegance. The separate kitchen serves a delectable variety of fantastic dishes, with fresh fish, shrimp, and chicken specialties featured, all cooked with gourmet quality and served in sev-eral courses with salads, vegetables and desserts. Both the food and friendly service deserve my highest marks. There is also full bar ser-vice, the crowd usually gathering to socialize before dinner. The rooms are perched on a rise above a long hibiscus hedge, and are primarily of hardwood construction with sliding French doors opening onto a private furnished deck with a view. The split-level cabins are all unique, but their common features include lots of space both downstairs and in the sleeping loft, nice tiled baths with their own gas water heaters, wide furnished decks with hammocks, roll-up blinds, full screening, fans and varnished hardwood floors. The loft is reached by a spiral stair case leading to either double or single beds with comfortable mattresses. All the accommodations have 24-hour electricity and hot water. A special treat is to stay in one of two Sunset Ranchos, set out on separate points with fantastic panoramic views of the Pacific and northern coastline. *Rates:* Full board rates (bar drinks excluded) are $115pp for the rooms, $140pp for the cabin, with discounts for groups of 3 or more. Call or e-mail for the Sunset Rancho rates. Low season discounts apply. Phone messages are accepted, and laundry service is available. La Paloma has a substantial staff of English-speaking guides, and do almost all the tours and transportation themselves for their guests. They have arguably the best dive boat in the area, and their tours to Caño Island for diving and snorkeling are superb. They also offer free use of kayaks, boogie boards, and snorkeling equipment. Call ahead at 239-2801, or e-mail at info@lapalomalodge.com; Web site: www.lapalomalodge.com

Cocalito Jungle Lodge – Nestled in the heart of virgin rainforest, this very secluded jungle lodge brings you adventure just getting there. About half and hour from the Drake Bay area, this ecological retreat with an open, friendly atmosphere gives you an opportunity to experience first hand the magic of this magnificent reserve which connects to Corcovado National Park border just a few kilometers away. See the agrarian village settlement of Los Planes and hike private trails teeming with wildlife to refreshing waterfalls and rivers, or just hang around in a hammock in the botanical gardens where the owners have carefully selected a variety of flowers, fruits and nuts to tempt the local wildlife. Majestic scarlet macaws, toucans, parrots, hummingbirds, mot-mots, trogons, morpho butterflies, and mischievous capuchin and howler monkeys are among the frequent visiting diners. Coatis, kinkajous, and maybe even wild cats can be spotted right from your deck. The surrounding wildlife refuge is home to many endangered species including the jaguar, black panther, puma, ocelot, jagarundi, tapir, golden frog, and harpy eagle. The lodge has four comfortable bedrooms as well as camping facilities. The restaurant specializes in traditional dishes prepared with the organically grown fruits, vegetables and herbs in season. *Rates:* $65pp accommodations with 3 meals included. Camping $45pp with meals. All tours available. For reservations call (519) 782-3978 in Canada. E-mail BerryBend@aol.com. Web site www.costaricanet.net/cocalito.

FOOD SERVICE

There are no independent restaurants in the Drake Bay area

outside of a little *soda* on the beach, so if you're camping or day trip-
ping and not booked into one of the lodges you'll have limited choices
of where to eat. The lodges officially offering restaurant service to non-
guests include Jinetes de Osa, La Paloma Lodge, Aguila de Osa, and
Cocalito Lodge, all of which are located on the western side of Drake
Bay, and all of which serve excellent meals (see above). If you go out
beyond the inner bay, meals will get to be hard to find, until you get to
Poor Man's Paradise out in Playa San Josecito. This is not to say that
other resorts and lodges do *not* offer restaurant service to the non-
guest public, just that they have not indicated this to me as part of their
standard services. Wherever you are at the time, just ask, and if they
won't serve you, they'll probably let you know someone close by who
will. Don't expect to get anything cheap, though. If you're going low
budget, stock up at a *pulpería*. Or fast.

TOURS AND OTHER SERVICES

The Original Canopy Tour – Jinetes de Osa is the host of the
newest Original Canopy Tour. Now people of all ages can safely experience the rainforest canopy via rope and cable in Drake Bay. The tour
features nine platforms, six traverse cables – with one spanning over
210 feet (70 meters) – and a 65-foot (21 meter) observation bridge.
Guest safety is a high priority as a fully trained bilingual guide takes
you deep into the rainforest to observe tropical wildlife in its natural
habitat. You can see two species of monkey, coatis, sloths, and hundreds of species of exotic bird life. The resplendent rainforest of the Río
Agujitas basin offers many natural thrills. Observing the forest canopy
of this rich and biodiverse area is facilitated by the finest gear available,
including Petzl and PMI. Some of the rope used is actually specially
designed for The Original Canopy Tour. Former President Jimmy Carter,
well into his 70's, completed an Original Canopy Tour in 2000. Children
of all ages are welcome. There are several tours available daily. Times
are flexible, starting in the morning and ending in the early afternoon.
Rates are $55 for the basic tour including transfers to and from your
inner Drake Bay lodgings. (Guests at the outer Drake Bay lodges pay
$5 each additional round trip.). Other guided tours available here are
horseback riding and hiking to the Agujitas Waterfall. Contact **Jinetes
de Osa** (see their information under LODGINGS above) for more information and reservations.

Corcovado Expeditions -- Corcovado Expeditions Tour Operator and Guiding Service is owned by three Costa Rican naturalist

guides who each have over 7 years of professional guiding experience on the Osa Peninsula, including Corcovado National Park and Caño Island Biological Reserve. The staff has completed certification courses on natural history and local ecosystems taught by the University of Costa Rica, the National University of Costa Rica, the Neotropica Foundation, the University of Florida, the Organization of Tropical Studies, the National Institute of Learning and more. They have personally guided expeditions for Artic Jungle Films' Exploring Horizons (a Discovery Channel production), National Geographic, Green Tracks, University of Costa Rica, National University of Costa Rica, The National Scientific College, Wisconsin University, Penn State University, Pepperdine University, Chicago North Park University, the Washington Times, the Tico Times, Central American Weekly and many more. Their office is located on the west side of the bay, near the end of the public road, right in front of the beach. The office is a small square wooden building, painted and signed, and raised up off the sand with a concrete front porch. The office serves as not only a tour operator, but also as an agency for lodgings, taxis, domestic plane flights, and more. If you are unfamiliar with the area, they can help you get oriented, and set you up with a place to stay. Their primary focus is local aquatic tours, with bilingual guides who have many years of experience working as tour guides in Drake Bay and around the southern zone. Some are trained as biologists, others environmentalists, and some in eco-tourism. Here are some examples of their tours: Trips to Corcovado National Park (by boat) at both San Pedrillo at the edge of the park, and Sirena, the largest station in the middle of the park on the ocean; Caño Island trips for snorkeling, hiking, or both; mangrove tours; and overnight guided trips to Corcovado at Sirena. They can also take you horseback riding, guide you to hidden waterfalls, and help you search for elusive poison dart frogs, or wild jungle cats. Rates are very reasonable. Day trips to Corcovado run only $50 to $75, while overnight trips are $120 per person. Snorkeling trips to Caño Island are $55. English is spoken, from pretty good to totally fluent, by all the guides. Phone 818-9962 or 833-2384 or 833-2648. E-mail corcovadoexpeditions@hotmail.com, or info@corcovadoexpeditions.net.   Web   site: www.corcovadoexpeditions.net.

Other Tour Options: See the description of the lodges for exclusive tours of their own properties, and/or excursions with their own boats and guides. You can also ask about a night tour by Tracie. The local diving specialists are Caño Divers (at Pirate Cove) and Costa Rica Adventure Divers (at Jinetes de Osa).

HIKING AND CAMPING

As mentioned above, this area is a hiker's dream come true, with multitudinous habitats, isolated pristine beaches, and all the rainforest you could hope for. The public trail along the shore from Agujitas will give you plenty to marvel at as it winds its way along the coast from the little village, through the resort and lodge areas around the outer bay, and south down the stunning Pacific coastline all the way to the Corcovado National Park entrance at San Pedrillo 3-4 hours later depending on your clip. You'll pass thousands of towering palm trees, hear and see scarlet macaws and multitudes of other birds, hike around volcanic rock formations, and skirt the rainforest that tumbles down to the sea. Three types of monkeys are common. The lodges are all right on the coast, and each have varying property sizes that consist primarily of primary and secondary rainforest, so wherever you're staying you can check out their exclusive trails, cascades, rivers, etc. You can also head inland to a place called Los Planes, also on the border of Corcovado. I recommend a visit to Río Claro, where you can lay on a nice sand beach, get some good waves, or swim about 100 meters up the river and hike to a hidden waterfall.

Another great option — although it's not exactly hiking — is a visit to Rancho Mariposa in Progreso, a butterfly farm, working ranch and miniature zoo owned by Drake Bay Wilderness Resort (see above). Besides the hundreds of butterflies in all stages of development, you can see peccaries, agoutis, a toucan, wild turkey, macaw and other rainforest creatures up close. You can also hike up into the forest above the pastures and ranch buildings. There is a nominal charge, and they'll rent you a mountain bike for the trip at the lodge in Drake Bay. They also have kayaks for short trips up the Agujitas River, free to their guests. La Paloma has kayaks, too.

I personally recommend the hike from Rincón de Osa on the Sweet Gulf through Rancho Quemado to Progreso and finally Drake Bay. I've done it myself. Not only do rides often show up, but the scenery is spectacular. I saw a coatimundi on the road on one of my trips, and heard howler monkeys nearby on several occasions. If you're up to it, it's a great way to get to Drake (though I wouldn't miss the trip down the Sierpe River, either).

Not many people camp independently in this area, but this is definitely an option. The beaches between Drake Bay and San Pedrillo at the border of Corcovado are beautiful (see below). Rancho Corcovado and El Mirador Lodge in Agujitas, and Poor Man's Paradise in Playa San Josecito, offer facilities for campers and individual meals if needed. Camping at Rancho Mariposa is $20pp. Other lodges may do this also, though it isn't part of their standard services (This isn't what you would call a 'low-budget' vacation area). I recommend at least one night in one of the lodges for a nice break, especially for the great food. In any case, you could make a complete ring around the Osa Peninsula starting or ending here, which would be quite an intense, exhilarating adventure.

DRAKE BAY AREA

TO
ISLA DEL CAÑO

N

Drake Bay

Rio Agujas

Rio Claro

Road from Rincon

Playa San Josecito

TO CORCOVADO

1 Pirate Cove / Cano Divers
2 El Mirador Lodge
3 Jade Mar Lodge
4 Rancho Corcovado
5 Corcovado Expeditions
6 Jinetes de Osa / Canopy Tour
7 Aguila de Osa
8 Drake Bay Wilderness Resort
9 La Paloma Lodge
10 Cabinas Las Caletas
11 Delfin Amor Ecolodge
12 Corcovado Adventures
13 Marenco B & R Lodge
14 Punta Marenco Lodge
15 Bahía Paraíso RF Lodge
16 Guaria de Osa
17 Poor Man's Paradise
18 Proyecto Campanario

DRAKE BAY – CORCOVADO

The following lodgings are located between Drake Bay proper and Corcovado National Park. They are all situated along the shore as one heads out from Drake Bay along the Pacific coast, south towards the ranger station at San Pedrillo. The secluded setting, natural environment, and wonderful views are fabulous, and well worth a hike along the long-established and well-maintained coastal trail. The accommodations are listed in the order of their appearance as you head south along the coast.

The only facility available outside of the lodges is a small *pulpería* in Playa San Josecito where hikers and campers can get a cold drink or stock up on supplies. There is a road that, after going out to Los Planes from Agujitas, turns into not much more than a wide trail that ends at Playa San Josecito. It is currently only passable by foot, horse, or maybe motorcycle in the summer. It's best to either hike out to this area along the scenic coastal trail from Drake Bay, or arrange transportation through your destination lodge.

Cabinas Las Caletas — For those looking to escape from the hectic pace of the city to a place of rest, relaxation, tranquility and peace, Las Caletas is for you. The small family atmosphere is conducive to releasing the pent-up stresses of modern life and soaking up the tropical ambiance. The cabins and owners' house are perched atop a steep ridge right above a small private cove, with expansive views of the Pacific and the coastline north of Drake Bay. Careful landscaping highlights the natural setting, though electricity is available in all the rooms through noiseless solar panels and a water-driven turbine. The forest slopes gently down to the lodge itself, and vegetables and fruits are grown on the property, The owners are a Tico and European couple, who strive to make your stay with them as tranquil as possible. Las Caletas only entertains a few guests at a time, maximizing both attention and privacy. The library, dining and lounge areas – recently expanded with the addition of tables, lounge chairs, and more deck space — are on the first floor of the main lodge, as well as one of the rooms. The ample deck is used primarily for relaxing and reading, and also a manicured lawn right out front for soaking up the rays, all with fantastic panoramic views. English, Spanish, Swiss, German and Italian are all spoken. The 3 daily meals are a mix of European and Tico styles, with vegetables and fresh fruits coming from the property itself. There are three options at Las Caletas: a room in the main lodge with a private bath, rooms in a two-story duplex with private baths and their own decks, or a completely private, secluded cabin far above the main lodge.

The duplex has a magnificent pattern of variegated hardwoods, and beautiful tiled baths were added. They come with beds both upstairs and downstairs, two hammocks on the upstairs deck, and a downstairs porch. The secluded private cabin is arrived at via a stone-lined gravel path, and surrounded by a wide lawn with secondary forest rising up at the edges. It has both a double and single bed on the second floor, with a living and lounging area downstairs, and a private bath. It also has its own ocean view. **Rates:** The room in the lodge is $50pp full board, and a room in the duplex or private cabin runs $60pp double, $55pp triple, and $50pp for 4. All prices include applicable taxes. All natural refreshments are included, with beer and sodas being extra. Both laundry and phone service are available, including an international credit card phone. David and Yolanda can make all local transportation arrangements for you right from the lodge. They have sea kayaks and snorkeling gear for the use of their guests at no extra charge. Las Caletas will pick you up in their own launch if you make arrangements ahead of time. To make the necessary reservations, call them at 381-4052 telefax, or 826-1460. E-mail: info@caletas.co.cr. Web site: www.caletas.co.cr

Delfin Amor Ecolodge — Dolphin Love Ecolodge is a secluded, eco-conscious haven whose emphasis is on guided interaction with the incredible abundance of marine life in this pristine aquatic haven in the Pacific around Drake Bay and Caño Island. A research foundation of both volunteers and professional researchers has been established to help with the study of these playful creatures, and the tours and information they currently offer have been covered by international media such as the Discovery Channel, Animal Planet and the Travel Channel. The property itself consists of roughly 10 acres of hilltop gardens on the point in the Las Caletas area just outside the bay, with secluded sandy beach just below the lodge and about 5 acres of private rainforest as a backdrop. They have an extensive heliconia garden, with over 25 species, and the lodge structures minimally impact the scenery in keeping with their natural philosophy. The dining and common is a high *rancho* with hardwood floors and a large outside deck, an open-air structure with colorful murals. They carry an impressive book and video library for guests to peruse, including videos of their tours. Pet macaws and parrots attract wild cousins for chat sessions while monkeys, parrots, and even occasional ocelots can be seen in the rainforest behind. New in 2004 is the 'Harmony Room', an open-air covered platform with yoga mats, hammocks, a ping pong table and even a hanging mirror ball. This new space is reserved primarily for quiet activities such as reading, relaxing and yoga (instruction available). The six spacious cabins were totally renovated in 2003 with tiled floors and new private baths that are nothing less than spectacular. The aquatic theme is fantastic, and unique in the zone. Half walls give way to screened windows all around, with curtains to ensure privacy. The rooms have two large double beds with carved headboards, comfortable mattresses and very high quality sheets, with shelving and a small cabinet for personal items. All the cabins have stunning, unique murals painted on their outer walls. The food is primarily vegetarian with fresh fish almost daily, caught by the staff from right out front and prepared a variety of ways. Lots of vegetables and greens, too. They even have a smoker for much of the fresh fish they bring in, which enhances the already excellent fare, whipped up by their resident 'pirate chef'. *Rates:* $140 single, $85pp double, $75pp triple and $65 quad full board (sodas, beer and wine extra). Group discounts available. VISA and M/C accepted. The dolphin and whale tours consist of cruising out on the ocean in their own fully-equipped launch — with stereo, hydrophone and individual seats, and accompanied by a biologist — and interacting with the marine life. These tours -- available to non-guests -- are interspersed with guided tours to Corcovado, Caño Island, and all the other attractions of the area. Call 847-3131 direct, or e-mail info@divinedolphin.com. Web site: www.divinedolphin.com.

Corcovado Adventures Tent Camp — Well off the beaten path, you can get a bit closer to nature and the rolling surf of outer Drake Bay, and away from the central cluster of lodges, at this tranquil home of the original tent camp style of accommodations in southern Costa Rica. 50 acres of jungle property, about half primary rainforest, ends abruptly at the edge of the Pacific among wide lawns, fruit trees and tall palms. Bordered on the east side by a cascading creek and freshwater pond and on the west by secluded beaches along a winding coastal trail, the small collection of 17 tent-huts and support buildings sits right on the shore of volcanic rock formations and sandy beach, their front yard being one of the best snorkeling spots on the Osa's coastline. The buildings were all renovated in 2003, and some more landscaping was done to further enhance the environment. All is backed by a forested ridge from which descend troops of monkeys daily for bananas and play. There is a large rancho with a thatched-palm roof and tiled floors for dining and lounging, a separate row of communal baths and sinks with bamboo siding adding the tropical touch, and a separate building with the office, staff quarters and large kitchen. There are hammocks hanging on the fruit trees around the tents for guests, and a couple in the *rancho* as well. The top-quality walk-in tents are set on large wooden platforms and covered by heavy tarpaulin roofs, giving them lots of protection as well as privacy, and each have their own deck facing the sea. They have double and single beds, a night stand with shelves, and several chairs for the deck. There are 5 full baths with 8 sinks for the 8 tents. Environment-friendly solar panels and a hydroelectric pelton wheel power the kitchen, *rancho* and bathrooms. Candles are provided for your tent room. The meals are a mix of fresh-caught local fish and meats, with optional vegetarian choices if you prefer. There are always lots of fresh veggies and salads, too. A great feature for the adventurer is a whole myriad of FREE stuff for the exclusive use of guests here: kayaks, snorkeling equipment, canoes, surf boards, boogie boards, and even fishing equipment. There are free snacks as well, and free laundry service. The camp does most of its own custom-tailored tours, including inshore fishing and Caño Island tours, with Tico guides fluent in English and with many years of experience guiding tourists in this area. ***Rates:*** $55pp full board during high season (sodas and beer extra). Multi-day packages are available. They can pick you up either in Sierpe or at the Drake Bay airport in Progresso. Call or fax direct at 241-4678 or 396-2451, or try 384-1679. They also monitor marine radio ch.16. E-mail info@corcovado.com. Web site: www.corcovado.com.

Marenco Beach & Rainforest Lodge — First opened in 1982 as a biological research station on about 200 acres of pristine coastal rainforest, Marenco long ago surpassed its original goals of simple conservation and local education to incorporate ecotourism at its best. The property now encompasses over 1,500 acres. This is your classic eco-lodge on a grand scale, with four hectares of professionally landscaped grounds set aside high on a ridge looking out to the Pacific for the small group of lodge buildings. The rest of the extensive property is primary and secondary rainforest set along five kilometers of breathtaking shoreline, with well-maintained and marked trails (in English) winding through the enchanting, densely forested ridges above literally bursting with wildlife. There are 8 guest rooms in two buildings, 17 private cabins, a large rancho housing the private restaurant and bar, a separate office with a semi-public phone, fax , internet, and a few additional support buildings. The restaurant serves a delicious mix of Tico, American and European dishes from menus — prepared by a professionally trained chef — in a traditional thatched-palm rancho with lots of hardwood, lattice, weaved palm, white cane, bamboo and live plants. A few elegant touches are added like double linen tablecloths, linen napkins, and candlelight dinners, all enhancing your enjoyment of the breathtaking panoramic views. A special feature: buffet breakfasts! (Hey, it made *my* morning!). The rooms and cabins all have private baths with tiled showers and private hardwood decks with ocean views, with some also looking into or over forest with monkeys often coming by to check out the guests. All are fully furnished, and have either 2 single beds or a double and single bed. The cabins have high thatched-palm roofs and lots of space. Electricity is provided from 5pm to 11pm daily for the lights, fans and outlets, though they'll turn it on for you during the day if necessary. How about daily maid service? You bet. English is spoken by almost the entire all-Tico staff, with some speaking German or Italian as well. Marenco is designed and run as a somewhat more structured resort lodge than some of the other accommodations in Drake Bay, and it's levels of service and professionalism reflect that approach. **Rates:** Lodging from $75 per night and meals $30 per day. Definitely call or e-mail ahead for daily rates appropriate to your situation, and for reservations. Just about every possible tour is available, from self-hikes for every level to scuba diving at Caño Island. Credit cards are accepted. In Costa Rica call 258-1919 or fax 255-1346. USA 1-800-278-6223. Europe 1-305-908-4169. E-mail: info@marencolodge.com, web site www.marencolodge.com.

Punta Marenco Lodge – Set at the edge of their own wildlife refuge spanning over 500 hectares (~1,300 acres) of mostly primary rainforest, this small lodge owned and run by the Miranda family sits on top of a high bluff overlooking the Pacific Ocean. Rio Claro National Wildlife Refuge (formerly known as Marenco Biological Reserve) augments another 116 hectares of private reserve near Corcovado National Park, affording guests of this mid-priced eco-resort access to one of the most expansive tracts of pristine lowland jungle in Costa Rica. The beachfront here runs for several kilometers, with the lodge buildings spread out on the ridge among well-tended lawns and rock-lined pathways. The naturally abundant wildlife can be seen and especially heard all over, with scarlet macaws and toucans dominating the bird scene. The views from the lodge and ten private bungalows are exceptional, with Caño Island visible just offshore right out in front. The spectacular sunsets occur right behind the island part of the year. The nice landscaping, very open with scores of fruit trees and carefully placed ornamental plants and palms, accents the very natural environment. The bungalows are tall *ranchitos* with real thatched-palm roofs, traditional structures with a 'jungly' feel. However, comfort is not sacrificed as they are all screened in, allowing for fantastic air flow, and stay very cool (guests sometimes ask for blankets). A nice double bed plus an extra single bed or bunk beds are complemented by nicely finished rustic wooden and bamboo furniture. The private decks have love seats or rockers, hammocks, and great ocean views. The fully tiled bathrooms have nice sinks and large colorful mirrors. Lots of privacy is afforded by thick curtains, palm siding on the deck, and surrounding plants and shrubs. Electricity is provided from 5pm – 10pm every night, and each bungalow has plenty of lighting. The split level lodge building, used primarily for dining, is a huge *rancho* that houses the kitchen, family quarters, and the guest dining room. The open-air, bilevel dining terrace has colorful tablecloths on several tables with padded rustic chairs. The food service is family style, with a mix of Costa Rican and international dishes. The multi-course dinners offer chicken, fish, pastas, vegetables – but not much rice and beans, despite the Tico ownership. Vegetarians can be accommodated upon request. There is basic bar service available with meals. All the local tours can be arranged directly by the resort. **Rates:** $55pp full board (sodas and alcoholic drinks extra). Packages available for 2-4 nights, with or without tours. Low season and group rates. Laundry service is available. English is spoken by the owner/managers and some of the staff. Call 222-3305, or 222-5852 telefax. E-mail ileptamarenco@yahoo.com. Web site: www.puntamarenco.com

Bahía Paraíso Rain Forest Lodge -- This beachside lodge, located on what it claims to be 'the best tropical beach in Costa Rica', does have a fantastic location between tall verdant ridges jutting up from the beach and the deep blue Pacific Ocean. The sandy beach is absolutely ideal for swimming and snorkeling, with lava rock formations forming a protective ring around the picturesque little cove. Cruise ships stop here to allow their passengers to take advantage of the stunning tropical scenery, do tours of Bahía Paraíso's botanical gardens, lookout ridge, and private rain forest, and snorkel in the cove. Other lodges even do day tours with their own guests at this beach. The grounds are well landscaped and immaculately maintained, with bright green grass, coconut husk rings around flowering bushes, palms and almond trees on the shore, and tall shade trees throughout. The Tahitian-style open-air restaurant has a high thatched-palm roof, and is set behind a wide manicured lawn dotted with colorful ornamentals and palms. The formal guest lodgings are located off to one side of the restaurant, a rectanglar concrete structure housing two levels of accommodations. The four standard rooms, on the sides and back part of the building, are spacious, fully tiled rooms with private tiled bathrooms. They have nice varnished wood bunk beds with good mattresses (one has a double bed, too), night stands with lamps, a pinewood closet with hangars and shelves, ceiling lights, strong floor fans, and screened lattice windows with roll-down shades. The two 'superior' rooms facing the beach have their own private patio with leather rockng chairs and hammocks. They are much larger, and have both double beds with varnished headboards and two sets of bunk beds. They have all the amenities the standard rooms have, plus enough room inside to do yoga. The tent lodgings are spread out on a large shady field right off the beach. The tents are actually two-room affairs, with a 'living room' and 'bedroom', set on concrete pads with their own furnished patio. The widely-spaced tents have 2 or 3 single beds each, a night stand with a lamp, and share very nice fully tiled bathrooms. Meals here are primarily International style, with pastas, sandwiches, fish, chicken, beef and pork. A full range of breakfast choices are available, and the multi-course dinners include soup or salad and dessert. Non-guests pay $5 for breakfast and $8 for lunch or dinner. All the local tours are offered directly by the lodge except diving. They have their own sport fishing outfit ('Just Fish'), too. Fluent English is spoken by the staff, and full electric service is provided till 10pm. Rates: $87.23pp Superior, $75.60pp Standard, and $58.15pp for the tents. All 3 meals and natural drinks are included, as well as free use of kayaks and snorkeling equipment. Low season discounts. The $7 camping fee gets you hiking and bathroom priveleges (if you eat at the restaurant). Phone 538-1414, e-mail info@bahiaparaiso.com. Web site: www.bahiaparaiso.com.

Guaria de Osa — Named after the magenta-purple colored national flower of Costa Rica, Guaria de Osa is a rainforest-ocean retreat and ethnobotanical gardens embedded in a nature sanctuary. The setting is exhilarating, with aromatic ylang-ylang trees filling the air with fragrance. Over 100 species of exotic, native and endangered tree species bloom in the neighboring creek. A myriad of ancestrally cultivated ethnobotanical treasures and wild medicinals from South and Central America are being cultivated, as well as culinary and herbal gardens in permaculture models. The primary steward of Guaria de Osa is Jonathon Miller W. a young ethnobotanist and conservation biologist with 12 years of experience in the conservation of tropical rainforest and the preservation of indigenous plant knowledge. He is the Director of The Osa Foundation/Grupo Osanimi. Nestled just off the beach, Guaria de Osa's main lodge building, the Lapa Lapa Lodge, is a tall wooden structure made from 90% naturally fallen trees. The grand three-story structure has rising cloud-burst eaves, fanned Maloca-wood rafters, a majestic observatory cupola and an uninhibited open central space, resembling Taoist-style architecture. The first floor is beautifully tiled; the second is made of exotic purple heart wood. The Lapa Lapa Lodge was built to hold retreats, workshops and conferences in areas such as hatha yoga, tai chi and meditation. The acoustics are perfect for music and dance. The Observatory Cupola is up one story, crafted from an assortment of rare woods. The panoramic vistas from here are absolutely splendid. The Green Dragon Lodge and La Choza Lodge are both two-story guest housing with private baths, a shared bathhouse, and nice balconies surrounded by flowering vines. All meals are prepared with the utmost of care using fresh, natural local ingredients. Vegetarian menus are offered. Crystal clean water comes from a spring that gushes right from the rocks above the lodge. A solar system furnishes evening lighting. 3% of all proceeds from guests benefit rainforest conservation projects. Guaria's staff and guides are ethnobotanists, naturalists, conservation biologists, permaculturists, yoga instructors, masseuses, etc. They act as skilled guides for Corcovado excursions, bird-watching, scuba diving, herbology and ethnobotany walks. Rates: In addition to Sentient Experientials' Calendar of Special Events (definitely see their web site at www.Guaria.com), they offer individual lodgings at $65pp; children up to age 5 are free; youth ages 6 to 10 are half price. This includes lodging, 3 meals with vegetarian options, tax, tips for Guaria's staff, and the donation to The Osa Foundation/Grupo Osanimi's rainforest conservation projects. Group discounts. Lodging only is $40pp. Camping available. Meals available separately. Work/study/volunteer rates available. E-mails: info@Guaria.com or sentient@experientials.org. Phone in the USA (510) 235-4313, fax (510) 215-9840. Web site: www.Guaria.com

Poor Man's Paradise -- It is! But it isn't. *'Huh?'* Definitely a verdant tropical paradise, this secluded patch of heaven is a place suitable for travelers of all income brackets, not just the 'poor man' (or woman, for that matter). Originally homesteaded by the Amaya family 30 years ago, a portion of this 60-acre *finca* was converted to a resort in 1992 to provide a living for the large Amaya clan. This isolated and peaceful locale is situated along 1/4 mile of the sandy-shored Rincón de San Josecito, just 2 hours by foot from the southern entrance to Corcovado National Park at San Pedrillo. The beachside portion of the property is dedicated primarily to the resort and family residences, with some more land given over to small crops and fruit trees. The bulk of the land is primary and secondary rainforest, with springs, creeks, waterfalls, and lots of wildlife, with several trails to choose from. The resort area is nicely landscaped and maintained, with neat shrub-lined paths. There are several lodging options available here. Thirteen rooms, most of them built or refurbished fairly recently, have tiled private baths and decks with an ocean view. The rooms are beautifully finished and furnished with dresser drawers, a closet, a mirror and either a double or two single beds. There are also two-story *ranchos* with open-air lounge areas below, complete with hammocks, tables and chairs. The communal bath facilities have nice tiled floors and showers. The 10'x12' tents are protected by their own bamboo houses and provided with wooden decks and chairs, with real beds inside. The nice dining rancho is spacious and comfortable, and there is a new separate bar for lounging and socializing. The dining area has lots of nice tables, is attractively decorated, and has several indigenous artifacts on display and a few souvenir items for sale. The meals include a lot of fresh local fish and shrimp in addition to chicken, fresh vegetables, rice, beans and corn, salads, real Tico desserts and plenty of fresh fruit. Breakfasts include gallo pinto, pancakes, omelets, etc. Fluent English and German are spoken here. *Rates:* Camping is $8pp/night, with meals available for $7-$9 each. The large tent/bamboo shacks are $40pp/day full board with shared bath. A private room or cabin with private bath is $60pp/day. All prices add tax. Discounts for groups. Laundry service is available. Free activities include hiking, swimming, and exceptional snorkeling. Tours include guided hikes to Corcovado or a pre-Columbian cemetery site, deep-sea fishing, horseback riding, cave tours, and night hikes. Call or fax 786-7642 in Costa Rica, or 383-4209. In the USA, call toll free 1-877-352-1100. See their web sites at www.poormansparadiseresort.com and www.mypoormansparadise.com. E-mail poormansparadise@cheqnet.net.

Campanario Biological Station — This working biological field station, conservation and education center, and ecotourist lodge, was founded in 1990 by teachers and ex-Peace Corps volunteers wanting to contribute to global conservation in a personal and significant way. The Station protects a spectacular forest and coastal area within walking distance of Corcovado National Park, and is a model for nature-based sustainable living. In this isolated locale less than an hour's hike from the San Pedrillo station of Corcovado, you find yourself in a dream-like corner of paradise. Small waves splash onto a sandy shore with lava rock formations jutting out towards the sea, while a small river cascades down from the verdant ridge past the field station and across the sand. The main building is a two-story concrete and wood structure housing the field station, kitchen, dining and lounging areas and student dorm rooms. In addition to this field station, there are also separate individual tent cabins, each with its own private bath. Steps to the field station lead up to a wide patio in front of the spacious dining and reading area, with several chairs and hammocks to facilitate appreciation of the view out to Caño Island. Many books, field guides and other educational materials can be found in their extensive library. The student work stations are set up in another part of the building, near the shared bath facilities which are very nicely finished with ceramic tile. Upstairs are the student/resident sleeping quarters, which are comfortable dorm-style accommodations with a large wooden deck out front, with writing tables, chairs and hammocks to appreciate the view and breezes. The tent cabins, located up on a ridge far above the station, are canvas rooms on large wooden platforms, with deck chairs on their private porches. A high roof covers each tent cabin, and the intelligently designed private open-air bathrooms are very nicely tiled. Each tent cabin is bordered on three sides by a tall hedge of hibiscus and other ornamental plants to provide privacy. The rest of the property is dedicated to Nature, with well-maintained trails leading to a waterfall (this hike is included with your free guest tour) and marked stations with educational information about the flora and ecosystems. Around half the 70-hectare property is primary rainforest, ~35% secondary forest, and the rest is regenerating "successionary" forest. Solar power is provided for the basics. Other tours and transportation can be arranged. The food is served buffet style, with an emphasis on vegetables, fresh fruits, salads and a nice mix of seafood, meat and chicken dishes. There is always plenty. English is always spoken by at least one of the staff or volunteers. Rates: A 4-day, 3-night package including a rain forest tour, a mangrove tour, and a tour to Corcovado National Park runs $394pp all-inclusive. Discounts for families and other groups are available. Call 258-5778 for reservations, or e-mail campanario@racsa.co.cr. Web site: www.campanario.org

Other Lodgings: **Drake Bay Treetop Resort** is a small, friendly lodge in the Las Caletas area, between Cabinas Las Caletas and Delfin Amor Ecolodge. The upscale **Casa Corcovado** sits right on the border of Corcovado National Park.

CHACARITA – PTO. JIMÉNEZ

As you go south from Palmar on the IAH, after about 32 kilometers you will come to a large gas station called "Servicentro Chacarita" with the word WELCOME painted on the roof above the pumps. It sits on the corner of the intersection bordering the only road going into the Osa Peninsula (there is a set of big green signs just before you get to this spot with '**Puerto Jiménez**' as one of the towns listed). This stretch of road, paved to **Rincón** and then graded gravel road to Pto. Jiménez, has multiple panoramic vistas, lots of towering rainforest, lowlands with cattle pastures and rice fields, and very few people. Fortunately or unfortunately, there is very little tourism infrastructure until you get to Pto. Jiménez (see that section), but now there are several places to stay and eat that are worth checking out. It's a breathtakingly beautiful area, especially along the paved road along the forested ridges. The real estate prices are some of the lowest in the country, especially for ocean view and beach front property (contact me directly if you'd like some more information), and tourism is just beginning to happen here.

I have broken this section down into three even smaller areas based on both geography and available accommodations and activities. Please take the time to read through these sections, at least to get a better idea of what the main part of the Osa is like.

CHACARITA – RINCÓN

The paved road in from the Interamerican Highway was recently patched and even partially resurfaced a couple of years ago, so don't fret about making that turnoff at the gas station in Chacarita to follow the "Puerto Jiménez" signs. It's a fantastic drive -- just take it slow. There is one nice place to stay just west of Los Mogos, and a luxury hotel scheduled to open near Rincón. The first one, established now for several years, I present to you below.

Suital Lodge – Three private cabins and an attractive mountain-style lodge are set amidst park-like grounds surrounded by towering primary rainforest on this 28-hectare property that stretches from the main paved road down to a secluded pristine beach on the Sweet Gulf. Over fifty fruit trees of mango, lemon, guava, banana and more dot the 10 acres or so of open land that is utilized for the lodge and cabins, while mostly primary rainforest makes up the rest of the property, with around five kilometers of wide, clearly marked trails wind around the *finca* and down to the shore. The main lodge and owners' quarters, set atop a small rise at the end of the gravel road, is a tall two-story European style structure modified to accommodate the tropical climate. It has nice ceramic tiled floors in the common areas downstairs, with the rest of the structure made of finished local hardwoods, including purple heart wood. The small family – a Tico man and Swiss woman with their young daughter – have their sleeping quarters upstairs, while two rooms are available on the first floor where the living room, kitchen and dining rooms are located. The rooms share a nice tiled bath with a large tiled shower, and each have both a double and single bed, large windows with wooden shutters, nice ceiling fans, and plenty of shelving. The three private cabins lower down are surrounded by fruit trees and ornamental plants. Cicadas sing in the surrounding forest as you walk up onto the private decks with comfortable leather rocking chairs. I am reminded more of Europe or North America when I see these strong, sculpted and well-finished structures, a quiet, comfortable place to relax. Each cabin is set up the same way, with both a double and single bed on hardwood frames under real ceramic tile open-beam roofs. There is plenty of space for luggage, and a brass ceiling fan with lights keeps the air flowing. Two heavy wooden shutters open the smaller windows, while a massive weighted half-wall swings into the cabin to reveal a small bar open to the veranda. The bathroom is exceptionally well done, with beautiful tile and hot water showers. Slightly above the cabins is a soaring *rancho* with a thatched palm roof and excellent modern lighting for reading, lazing in a hammock, or socializing. The owners prepare breakfast and/or dinner by request, baking their own breads for morning meals, and offering both Tico and international evening meals at low prices. They'll also prepare a box lunch for their guests (additional charge for meals). Free coffee and natural juices are available anytime to guests, at no additional charge. ***Rates:*** $30 single, $45 double for the cabins; $20 single, $36 double for the rooms in the lodge. Low season discounts. They have their own kayaks for rent, which can be launched from their semi-private beach cove. Call direct 826-0342. E-mail suitalcr@hotmail.com. Web site: homepage.mac.com/suital/

RINCÓN - LA PALMA

After about 42 kilometers along the main road you will descend into the picturesque town of Rincón de Osa, the terrestrial gateway to the Osa, which sits right on the shores of the far northwestern corner of the Golfo Dulce (Sweet Gulf). Just before you get there, you will be treated to one of the most spectacular views in southern Costa Rica, a broad panoramic vista looking out over the gulf to its far southern shores and the mountains in Panama over 60 kilometers away, and over to the peninsula on one side and the mountains of the Piedras Blancas extension of Corcovado National Park on the other. It's breathtaking. You may want to stop and take a photo, or dine at the quaint little restaurant there (see first description below). Beware of the locals, though. . . . Relax – it's a joke! I live in this area.

There is really very little infrastructure for tourism in Rincón as yet, though the potential is tremendous. Maybe that will change by the time you read this (the upscale hotel should be opening soon). Regardless, the first *real* town you will come to after Rincón, about 11 kilometers farther south, is the small farming community of La Palma, which has the second largest town on the Osa Peninsula. La Palma is not only the departure and return point for Corcovado National Park through its eastern entrance at Los Patos, but also has a beautiful sand and coral beach (Playa Blanca). A **Guaymí Indian Reservation** is located on the border of Corcovado (but much closer than Los Patos to the town), with its own primary rain forest and handicrafts for sale, though it's quite a trek to the tiny village and you really need a guide. The town of La Palma has public administrated phones, several stores, and taxi service for those on foot. No less than seven buses a day pass through La Palma going to and from Pto. Jiménez during the high season. Cheap accommodations and meals can be had here in the three *cabinas* and several *sodas* in the center of town. The bus stop is one of these places, located right near the corner where the main road turns left coming in from Rincón (there is a small sign indicating Pto. Jiménez). The only really nice lodgings in La Palma itself are just outside of town. See below for a description.

Cabinas y Restaurante Ventana Al Golfo -- *'What a view!'*
That is the first thing that will hit you as you drive up to this small but very attractive restaurant on the side of the road above the magnificent Golfo Dulce and the little town of Rincón. This is an ideal place to get some R&R from your road trip into the Osa Peninsula, and also enjoy some quality food and drink at low prices. You may even want to spend the night in the nice rustic private cabins ensconced in the gardens and forest behind the restaurant. The owner of this family-run Tico business learned both English and cooking skills in the United States, where he has spent several years. He and his wife and daughter run the restaurant, and he has a 4wd pickup that can serve as a taxi and tour vehicle. The property has a total of about 6 acres, while an acre or so is dedicated to the restaurant, parking lot, gardens and cabins. There are hundreds of pineapple plants, lots of ornamental shrubs and heliconias, and wide green lawns around the restaurant. Monkeys and sloths are regular visitors, and toucans and scarlet macaws can be seen every day in the surrounding forest. Mot-mots, cuckoos, laughing falcons, trogons and tanagers are all very common here. The secluded private cabins are set above and behind the restaurant area, and one can be driven right up to (in the summer at least). They are built on stilts above the forest floor, and made almost completely of rough-cut wood. They both have nice balconies, with a unique veranda of sliced *cara tigre* trees, which is also a feature of the restaurant. One cabin has walls of various varnished hardwoods – very nice. Both cabins have wood framed beds with headboards, closets, big showers, screened windows with curtains, and double beds (two in the larger cabin). They both have a view of the water through the trees, and are engulfed in birdsong in the mornings. There is excellent security as the family lives right there in the restaurant. The menu consists of a mix of typical Costa Rican plates plus many international standards like pastas, burgers, sandwiches and steaks, with seafood usually available cooked several ways. The owner learned to cook not only in the States, but also at one of the luxury lodges in the area. Both the coffee and the French fries are excellent. They have all the standard fruit drinks, of course, and most sodas, plus cold beer. Prices range from $2-3 breakfasts, to lunches and dinners of $3-5. They serve delicious homemade desserts, too, made from squash and fruit grown on the property. Many locals make it a point to stop here on their trips through the area. Tour services offered by the owner include Drake Bay trips, tours of Cabo Matapalo and Carate, and 4wd taxi service to anywhere in the area. Possible boat and kayak tours are seen in the future. ***Rates:*** $10pp. Group discounts. Meal, lodging and tour packages available. Phone 837-2169.

Osa Palmas -- Perched up on a ridge rising up from the flatlands of the La Palma area, this new Tico-owned ecolodge is a great place for getting off the beaten path and experiencing secluded rain forest. The huge family finca has over 270 acres, with around 38 acres preserved as primary forest. The huge open-air rancho with the restaurant and one guest room is built on the edge of a bluff with a panoramic view of the lowlands, gulf, and mountains. Massive tree trunks hold up the structure, with more rustic style construction adding to the country theme. There are lots of nice wood and glass-topped tables on the spacious tiled floor, and some rustic lounge furniture on the spacious balcony. The long curved bar has stools for visitors, and a large TV and stereo. There is a really nice mural on one wall, and some excellent textured stucco work on two others. Tucked up in the peak of the rancho is a special couples' suite, with fantastic 360-degree views through wide screened windows, polished purple heart wood floors, and a private tiled bath. The two main rooms, up on a separate ridge near the rancho, form a duplex of very spacious, comfortable accommodations. The two rooms are separated by a high concrete wall (sound barrier), with the rest of the construction of wood. The main rooms has nice tiled floors, and there is a private covered balcony with great views and a couple of chairs to enjoy them. Each room has two double beds with a long shelf behind them, and a small closet in between. The vaulted ceiling has a large fan, and there are desk lamps near the beds. The copious bathroom has a massive tiled shower that has a screened wall looking out to the view. There are also three rustic cabins built on the highest and farthest ridge behind the other rooms, backed by thick rain forest. The lodge is expanding, with ultimate goals that include a small lake for fishing, and a swimming pool for children and adults, a total of 15 cabins, two canopy platforms, and a butterfly farm. The restaurant serves a wide selection of international dishes, from a menu in both English and Spanish. They serve a wide variety of snack foods (chicken wings, gazpacho, ceviche, chef's salad, etc.), and dinner entrees such as chicken in red wine, garlic mahi-mahi filet, marinated pork ribs, and grilled beef tenderloin. Their pizzas are fantastic. Lots of excellent desserts and full bar service are available. Prices are reasonable. *Rates*: $35pp for the standard rooms, and $50pp for the lookout room above the rancho, with all three meals included. A bewildering variety of tours are available, most of them on or from their property. The list includes several hikes (birding, rain forest, plants), aquatic tours (fishing, dolphin and whale watching, kayaking), tree planting, cow milking, night life, and more. Cultural tours are also available (local farms, indigenous reservation, etc.). Web site: www.osapalmas.com.

HIKING AND CAMPING

La Palma is generally visited by the backpacking set, who typically begin their trips through Corcovado from Carate after a night in Puerto Jiménez, and exit through the Los Patos station on this side of the peninsula, hiking out to La Palma in the morning. Some of them do it in reverse, starting from La Palma and hiking the 12 km. or so to Los Patos, which involves crossing the river about 27 times, then continuing on to Sirena on the Pacific. Hikers coming from Drake Bay through San Pedrillo can exit here, too, after passing through Sirena (I hear that the Los Planes station is closed), or vice versa. There are several stores to buy provisions right in the center of town, and an *almacén* (literally 'warehouse', but more of a large general store here) about 50 meters north of the intersection — you can't miss it — where you can get rope, hardware, sheets of plastic, etc., as well as groceries. That's where we usually shop, and buy construction materials. The owners' son William Jr. speaks good English.

Camping can be nice at Playa Blanca, 2 km. directly towards the gulf from downtown La Palma. Rincón is not really set up for it, as there are residences on the beach side of the road. Like I said, most of the hikers and campers that come through here are Corcovado-bound. The other types of campers that come to the Osa are surfers, who head directly to Cabo Matapalo, which is also exceptionally beautiful (see that section).

LA PALMA – PTO. JIMÉNEZ

As you cruise down the gravel road through the flats of the Osa Peninsula near the Golfo Dulce, there isn't all that much in the way of tourist facilities. There are generally more cows, chickens and African palms than people, and the towns are *very* small. However, if avoiding the tourist traps and rubbing shoulders with the local people – or just getting a secluded beach on a river or the gulf all to yourself – is your 'thing', then the following lodgings are something you want to check out. They appear in the order you will come across them going south on the road into the Osa, some ways after leaving La Palma.

Garzas Doradas – Located on the main road to Puerto Jimenez outside of the hamlet of Amapola, this budget tourist complex built on over 50 acres of former agricultural and pasture land offers lodgings, food service, and a soccer field. There is a long driveway leading to the restaurant and rooms, with a full-sized football field (for you Brits out there) where local matches are played. The rooms are set near the restaurant, hidden among the tall foliage. The rest of the property is made up of secondary forest and open fields, with around 10 acres of primary rain forest, and a small fish pond. There is plenty of room to park next to the restaurant and cabins. The restaurant is very large, and open-air structure with a wide main dining area and separate bar and secondary dining room. There is a nice brick barbecue area with a wood-burning stove. The restaurant décor is rustic but nice, with varnished *cara tigre* posts, quality wooden tables and chairs, and a painted and polished concrete floor. The L-shaped bar serves a full range of liquors, both domestic and imported, plus mixed drinks and some basic cocktails. The menu consists of typical Costa Rican restaurant fare. They have rice dishes, spaghettis, shrimp platters, fried chicken, ceviches, sandwiches, fish filets, steaks, and pork chops. The food is always prepared fresh to order. Prices are very low, ranging from $2 to $5 for lunch or dinner plates. The rooms are located in three separate cabins scattered among trees, tall shrubs, heliconias and fruit trees. They are all rustic construction of concrete and wood. Two are private one-room cabins, while one is a two-room cabin located off the driveway into the complex. All the rooms have double, single and/or bunk beds, shelving, a fan, screened windows with curtains, a high ceiling, a big mirror, and a full private bath. The largest cabin is primarily for groups, with lots of beds and its own kitchenette for preparing your own meals. There is great security as the owners' house is right behind the restaurant, and there is always staff present. A swimming pool with its own attached bar was in the plans as this book went to print. **Rates**: $10pp high season. Low season and group discounts. Laundry service available. Transportation can be arranged. Restaurant hours are 10am till late daily. No phone or internet here, so just show up. Look for their large black sign next to the cyclone gate on the west side of the road near the town of Amapola.

Köbö Farm & Lodge – This large agricultural and ecological farm, located just 300 meters off the main road near the previous business, boasts 75 acres of primary rainforest, plus over 40 acres more of secondary forest, pasture land, and cultivated areas. Several other lodges in the area (Neotropica, Osa Palmas, etc.) bring their guests here for 'agri-cultural' tours. The name of the lodge means 'dreams' in the native Guaymí language. Newly established as an ecotourist lodge, the farm focuses on demonstrating healthy and sustainable agricultural and animal husbandry methods, besides providing visitors with the excellent opportunity to witness sustainable development first hand, and even partake in its fruits. They have banana and cocoa groves, myriad varieties of fruit trees, medicinal plants, edible herbs, and even hardy tropical lettuce. They have cattle, pigs and chicken – all raised organically – where they get their own milk, cheese, eggs and meat. They even make their own chocolate. A river passes through the working ranch, which has a corral, sugar mill (they extract it from sugar cane), tool shed and the lodge. There are several trails on the property, some going through the primary rainforest where you can see monkeys, sloths, coatis, toucans and scarlet macaws in abundance. Other trails wander through their extensive gardens and cultivations. The lodge is a spacious 2-story building fabricated primarily of indigenous hardwoods. It has massive posts of *cara tigre*, and lots of teak wood. The first floor is tiled with a nice pattern, while the second floor is all wood. Downstairs is the kitchen, dining room, living room with television, and a full bath. The upstairs has a wraparound deck that accesses the six guest rooms, plus another fully tiled, spacious bath with a hot water shower. The guest rooms are simple but very clean, with double or single beds. The meals here are typical Costa Rican country dishes, served family style in the dining room. The meals feature organically grown vegetables and fruits from the property, using home-grown herbs and spices, and augmented by homemade breads and desserts. They serve wonderful fruit drinks, and excellent *authentic* hot chocolate. Tours are available to non-guests, and include cow milking, garden tours, rain forest treks, and gold panning. Guests can walk the property solo, or hire an English-speaking guide. **Rates**: $35pp includes all three meals, natural refreshments, and access to the hiking trails. Low season and group discounts. Laundry service available. Transportation and other outside tours can be arranged. Phone 351-8576. E-mail osalero20@hotmail.com. Web site: www.kobofarm.co.cr.

Cabinas El Titi -- Far from the maddening crowd, these new rustic country lodgings provide tourists the rare opportunity to experience life on a typical Costa Rican *finca*, and engage in a little cultural exchange with young adults and country children. The owners Enrique and Alba (a school administrator) are simple folk who decided to turn their property into an eco-tourist attraction. There are around 50 acres of forest on the property, the rest given over to tall shrubs and open fields. Many animals can be spotted in the secluded forest, like coatis, monkeys, armadillos, anteaters, and more. One of the main attractions are the squirrel (titi) monkeys, as this *finca* has more than the average number. Of course there are lots of scarlet macaws, toucans, and other exotic bird life to be seen as well. You can sample fresh fruit from their many trees, or ride their horses through the private forest or down to the beach only a few kilometers away. Hiking is abundant on the large property, either alone or with one of the family. The lodgings are really basic, modeled after the traditional wooden homes built by the settlers here decades ago. Construction was still going on when I visited. They have central dining area, with a bar and picnic tables, on top of a rise. There are two private cabins near this structure, which share a bathroom. The other two cabins are two-story structures, both of them very secluded. They are set on top of small ridges, surrounded by secondary forest emerging from the former pastureland. The all-wood cabins have sleeping rooms both upstairs and downstairs, with wood slat beds and cushions. They do have full electricity and lighting. Basic but comfortable, much better than camping. The food here is classic *campesino* style cooked up by the family, with lots of vegetables and fresh fruits. ***Rates***: $20pp includes three healthy meals and natural refreshments. Transportation and tour services are available. You can drive right in on the private road all the way to one of the cabins and the family's home, which was the original dining room. The *cabinas* are located between the towns of Amapola and Cañaza. Look for the entrance just after a small metal bridge on the west side of the road. The short private road crosses a shallow river, and dead-ends at their property. Call 360-7048 (Spanish only). Pager 224-2400 'Enrique Segnini Saballo'. E-mail titiosa@hotmail.com.

Sombra De La Lapa Artist Retreat — Located 15 minutes north of Puerto Jiménez, above the town of Agujas, and situated on a 120-acre private rain forest reserve, this artist retreat acts as both a workshop area and private home for Michael H. Cranford. Michael is an accomplished artist living on the Osa Peninsula since 1999. He works mostly in acrylic paint and air brush. His work is both realistic and surrealistic, with major influences by M.C. Escher and Christian Reese Lassen. His paradisiacal and beautiful space is now available for single artists, writers, photographers and musicians who would like to expand their creativity with pristine rain forest and the enchanting Golfo Dulce as both their background and inspiration. The facilities feature a 3000 square foot home, boasting three large bedrooms, two kitchens, a Jacuzzi tub, and two large workshop areas. Forty acres of primary forest directly behind the retreat house, as well as panoramic views of the calm deep-water gulf where dolphins and whales breed and play, set the mood for releasing your creative juices. A birders' paradise with daily visits by toucans and scarlet macaws, monkeys and other wild mammals can also be spotted regularly next to the house – they have even been known to pose for painters. Michael is also available to instruct in acrylic medium during your stay at Sombra de la Lapa. If you need a break from sedentary pursuits, hiking opportunities include one full mile of private trails, as well as day trips to a secluded waterfall. Reservations are required, with a minimum stay of three days. The minimum 3-day package includes 3 hearty meals per day and natural beverages for $375pp. Longer retreats are available at lower rates, with a maximum 8 people. Transportation can be arranged from Puerto Jiménez, and tours in and around the Osa Peninsula. Group pricing and additional discounts available. Phone 378-3013 or, if you are already in Pto. Jiménez, stop in at Juanita's Mexican Bar and Grille in Pto. Jiménez and ask the bar tender to get a hold of Michael (Michael is a part owner of the restaurant, and also has several samples of his work hung there to check out or even purchase). E-mail miguelincr@hotmail.com. Web site: www.michaelincostarica.com.

Jardin de Aves -- Garden of the Birds is a working farm, wildlife refuge, and jungle reclamation project founded by North American John Reid. He has stocked caimans, fish, shrimp and even clams in the two ponds on the property, and reforested a greenbelt with native trees to become additional habitat for future generations of indigenous creatures, like the endangered squirrel monkey. Located between the towns of Agujas and Sándalo at the Río Terrones bridge, the twenty-five acres of fruit trees, primary and secondary forest, working pastures and wildlife trails offers something for everybody. The atmosphere is laid back, family style, and not just another jungle lodge scene. There are four unique cabins, a rental house (formerly the owner's house), and a common cooking and dining area with a smoker, barbecue pit, tables, and hammocks. John has a corral and barn for his 12 horses, which you can observe being trained and cared for. The land around the buildings is extensively landscaped and well maintained, while the gardens full of an incredible variety of fruits, herbs, and vegetables. Monkeys can be spotted frolicking and scarlet macaws can be seen nesting in a grand old Ceibo tree. The four unique cabins are built primarily of local hardwoods in a stunning variegated pattern, with beautiful hardwood furnishings. The beds have firm box spring mattresses, and the amenities include nice brass porch lamps. The Bobo Cabin (or 'Love Shack') sits right above the creek near a small cascade, and is reached via an enchanting wooden bridge. It has a king-sized bed in a large room, and a private bath. Monkeys, toucans and macaws can all be viewed (and heard) at close range. The screened porch provides an intimate view of the wildlife. The two-story Tepsquintle Cabin, built high on stilts surrounded by dense brush and tall forest, has unobstructed jungle views on a secluded site washed with the sounds of Nature. Two other cabins are available. All the cabins have either patios or decks, lights and fans, and all are very private. The rental house has three bedrooms, a fully equipped kitchen, and a small swimming pool. Optional meals are comprised of a mix of Tico and international fare featuring fresh garden produce and dairy products from both the lodge and nearby farmers. **Rates**: $20pp for the regular cabins, or $45 double for the Love Shack (Cabina Bobo) with continental breakfast; $175/week for the house. Work/stay volunteer programs available. Meals available upon request. Laundry service available. Very inexpensive camping is also a possibility here. John's specialty is adventure tours around the Osa, with river and ocean kayaking, remote camping, sport fishing, jungle hiking treks, night tours, birding tours, beach or mountain horseback riding, snorkeling and bike rentals offered. His emphasis is on multi-day expeditions, with expert local guides and all equipment supplied. Package and group rates available. Stop by on your way in, or call 735-5676. E-mail safariosa@hotmail.com. Web site: www.safariosa.com

Bosque de Río Tigre Sanctuary & Lodge — Located right on the southern branch of the Río Tigre just outside of the tiny town of Dos Brazos, this 31-acre private reserve is a naturalist's and bird watcher's paradise. The view from the 2-story lodge looks out over the river to the opposite hillside cloaked in rainforest, and is shaded by tall trees on three sides. Basically, you are smack in the middle of secondary rainforest here. By some stroke of good fortune, this particular location is blessed by a constant flow of tropical bird life and troops of monkeys. The lodge itself has four guest rooms on its second floor — none sharing a wall — and lots of windows and open areas looking out over the river and into the surrounding forest. The upstairs guest area is all hardwood construction, with large hammocks hanging in between the comfortable rooms and shared bath. The downstairs houses the kitchen and lounge area with a beautiful bar of varnished hardwood, and has an extensive library on the wildlife and environment of Costa Rica. A separate open-air cabin is available, surrounded by trees and lush foliage, and equipped with its own private bath with sink, flush toilet, and shower. The meals here are varied and flexible according to your needs, from typical Tico to North American 'rustic gourmet', with fresh fruit juices in abundance and afternoon snacks. There is always a complementary thermos of coffee waiting for guests every morning. There are many activities available, including guided treks through the rainforest, forays into Corcovado National Park, gold mining, bird watching, horseback riding, and both river and ocean kayaking (see a description of their tours in the Pto. Jiménez section). Liz and Abraham, the owners and your hosts, are experienced naturalists who enjoy introducing their guests to the flora and fauna of the neotropical rainforest. An absolutely fantastic one-day hike led by Abraham, and one that can be done in place of a multi-day Corcovado trek, leads from the lodge here to Luna Lodge in Carate on the other side of the Osa, meandering through pristine primary rainforest as it skirts the southern edge of the national park. For those who don't like to stray too far from the lodge, there are trails through the rainforest on the property itself, as well as a 50-foot waterfall and a breathtaking look-out point just a short hike away. **Rates**: $88pp double occupancy full board (high season), including 2 sodas or beers per day, or $110pp with a 4-hour guided birding tour. Discounts for children, groups of 8 or more, and in low season. Great lodging/tour package rates. Separate birding tours available without lodging (see TOURS section). To book your stay fax: Costa Rica 735-5045 (to "Liz Jones, Dos Brazos") or call 735-5725 (messages), or e-mail info@osaadventures.com; Web site: www.osaadventures.com. Driving in directly with a rental car is not a problem, all the way to the lodge in the summer, and almost all the way in the winter.

Río Nuevo Lodge -- Another newer lodge for the area, this one is located at the end of a long road traveling deep into the mountains of the Osa. A few kilometers north of (before you arrive at) Puerto Jiménez, there is an entrance that branches off the main road and takes you through pastures, forested hills, some agricultural land, and scattered homes. At the end of this journey you arrive at a couple of small houses and, after braving an impressive suspension bridge over a deep gully, the attractive idyllic complex of this lodge. Perched high on a finger of land between two branches of the river, the lodge centers around a soaring thatched-palm open-air *rancho* with wide polished hardwood floors and nice views of the surrounding forested ridges and the river below. The large kitchen takes up the back side, where much of the excellent typical food is prepared on an old-fashioned wood burning stove. The rancho has a large dining deck with three long wooden tables, and a small table with cushioned chairs. There is also a lower lounging deck, with hammocks, a couch, chairs, and railings of *cara tigre* cross sections. Guests can take advantage of the presence of books, a guitar, and a small television. Lighting and power is provided by solar panels. In front of the lodge building, the land slopes down to the junction of two streams, where most people cool off in the wide swimming hole. The tranquil sound of flowing water is ever-present. The eight guest cabins are actually tents set on wooden platforms, with canvas roofs to keep out the sun and rain. They each have two single beds, and two chairs on their small private decks. The collective baths, two restrooms and two showers in one square building, have nice walls of whole white cane. Gravel paths lined with river stone and torches lead to all the buildings, and lush landscaping surrounds the complex. There are fruit trees, ornamental shrubs, flowers, and vetever grasses. Across the river gullys are walls of rain forest, where all four species of monkeys can be spotted, as well as a number of exotic bird species. One of the nice features of this lodge is the opportunities for extended hiking in primary rain forest. They have several trails to choose from for all levels of ability, including treks to waterfalls, gulf view lookout spots, and intense hikes all the way across the peninsula to Río Oro or Carate. You can also take a night tour, go horseback riding, or rent a mountain bike. English is spoken both at the lodge and at their office in Pto. Jiménez. *Rates*: Lodging only is $17 plus tax per person. Full board rates (3 meals and natural drinks) run $43pp double plus tax. All rates include round trip transportation from Puerto Jiménez, if necessary. Besides their own tours, other area tours like snorkeling at Caño Island and multi-day trips into Corcovado National Park can be arranged. They have a nice office in downtown Pto. Jiménez, next to the Restaurant Carolina. Call 735-5511 or 735-5411. Web site: www.rionuevolodge.com.

PUERTO JIMENEZ AND VICINITY

This tropical frontier port town is the primary destination for people coming into the Osa. It is the largest community on the peninsula, and the only one with private phone service. Therefore, it is the major transportation and communication hub of the area. The office of Corcovado National Park is located here, as well as a bank, post office, emergency clinic and municipal dock.

Being near the heart of the peninsula, Puerto Jiménez (or just Jiménez to us locals) is home to scores of breeding pairs of scarlet macaws, which can be seen every day flying through town or squawking in the trees. It is an excellent base for exploring the Golfo Dulce, too, with its amazing marine life. Many possibilities exist for the adventurer here, including sport fishing, horseback riding, swimming, boating, or just hanging out and hearing the stories. It used to be a lot like the Old West around here just a few years ago, with everything that entails. There used to be a lot of gold changing hands, brought in by the local miners who were pulling it out of areas deep in the peninsula, and local Ticos would come into town on their horses for shopping, drinking and what-not (some of the expat locals, too). The streets were only paved a few years ago. Most of this is pretty much past, though. The local atmosphere is still very laid-back, with shorts and tank tops the standard attire, and 'Let your hair down and enjoy' the predominant attitude.

For those seeking the core experience of primary lowland rainforest, this is usually the launching point for these types of excursions. Tickets to the park are sold at both the Corcovado Park office and Osa Natural, a private tourist information office with bilingual staff located on a corner in 'downtown' Jiménez, which is all of three blocks long. There are also guided tours to other privately owned stands of primary rainforest around the Osa, some right on the edge of the park (see below) — in other words, you don't *have* to go into the park to see virgin jungle with all its birds and animals, contrary to popular belief. The mangroves of **Río Platanares** just outside of Jiménez are a kayaker's and birder's paradise, and the **Cabo Matapalo**, **Dos Brazos** and **Carate** areas have literally thousands of hectares of untouched rainforest, spectacular waterfalls, and fantastic beaches to explore. Dos Brazos, 12 kilometers north and west of Jiménez on the **Río Tigre** (Tiger River), is the old center of the gold mining industry in the peninsula, before the park was formed, and the old mining tunnels and even the not-so-old miners themselves can be found nearby, and you can even pan for gold (and find some) right on the river just outside of town.

Read the "Osa Peninsula" section above for bus schedules from San José and Ciudad Neily to Pto. Jiménez. Buses leave for Jiménez from the Transporte Blanco station in San Isidro twice daily, at 6:30am and 3:30pm. There is also a minibus that goes between Escondido (just north of La Palma) and Pto. Jiménez twice a day. That makes a total of *eight* buses a day coming into and leaving from Jiménez during the high season. Getting there by land is not a problem, especially since the road into the Osa is now totally patched and resurfaced. SANSA and NatureAir fly in daily also (check their schedules from the airport in San José). The ferry leaves Golfito at 11:30am every day for Jiménez, and the Golfo Dulce Express can get you to Jiménez from either Golfito or Zancudo Beach three days a week (inquire at Café Net El Sol).

LODGINGS

Agua Luna – These clean and modern rooms right on the gulf are very popular among those who want the convenience of being in town, the backdrop of mangroves full of bird life, location on the water, and all the modern conveniences. The two buildings are actually bordered on two sides by water, in front the Sweet Gulf with the town's municipal pier and concrete walkway along the shore, and in back a small estuary. You can see the forest-clad mountains rising above the beaches on the other side of the gulf, and catch the breezes right off the water. You are at one far edge of town, so traffic and noise are minimized (unless the restaurant has a disco night, which happens once a month or so). It is reminiscent of a beachside motel in North America, with a tropical ambience. The building closest to the pier houses the hotel's office and six of the fourteen rooms. It is surrounded by a low concrete wall and wrought iron, with a large gate for cars to come in to the parking area. There are many attractive, mature shrubs and trees within the walls. A tiled, furnished and lighted terrace runs the length of the building in front. These deluxe rooms are very spacious, built with heavy concrete walls, tiled floors, and wood panel ceilings. All the deluxe rooms have a telephone, bench, shelving, color T.V. with cable, glasses for water, refrigerators, night stands with lamp, hot water showers and baths, and air conditioning. They have either two double beds or one full and one single, with the towel and sheet arranged nicely for your arrival. The bathrooms are huge in these rooms, with built-in bathtubs to boot. A large sink and mirror are provided, and the ample window looks right into the mangroves. Huge glass picture windows look out towards the gulf from the bedroom, with both light and heavy curtains for privacy. The other building is just a few meters down the road, and boasts a large covered and fully furnished terrace out front with a secure entrance and many potted plants and a faux well. The rooms have the same sound-deadening, heavy concrete construction. They are lined up on either side of a nicely done hallway through a glass door, providing more security and privacy than the other rooms. The back rooms have a view directly into the estuary. These rooms have cable TV. The standard rooms are similar to the deluxe rooms but lack refrigerators, hot water, bathtubs and telephones. **Rates:** $55 double for the deluxe rooms, $40 single, plus tax. Standard rooms are $45 double, $25 single, also plus tax. Discounts during low season, and for groups of 10 or more. Laundry, transportation, phone and fax messages, and all the local tours are available through their nice office, which has maps and guide books to check out. They have an associated restaurant and bar just up the road by the same name. Call 735-5394, call or fax 735-5393, or e-mail agualu@racsa.co.cr.

Cabinas Marcelina — These attractive rooms are located at the far end of the 'downtown' area on main street, across from the Catholic church. They are owned by a member of one of the oldest families in the area, Lidiette Franceschi B., and offer comfortable lodgings at low rates. The rooms are housed in two concrete buildings behind the owner's house (and well away from the street) with a small office around the corner. They form an 'L' facing a wide lot of lawn, shade trees and some fruit trees, along with lots of attractive and colorful landscaping. There is a new *ranchito* near the rooms, with a thatched palm roof and plenty of furniture for lounging. If you have a car, there is secure parking on the grass near the rooms. The older rooms in the long building were renovated and expanded in 2002. A concrete porch with chairs and potted plants runs their length, which also serves as a covered walkway for the rooms. Two additional, larger rooms were added to make a total of eight, all of which now have hot water showers on tap, TV's (upon request), and tiled floors and baths. Even the window guards have been custom made to fit the new, improved style of the remodeling. All new furniture was purchased, and the beds – typically two doubles in each room – have very nice box spring mattresses and new linen. At least three of the rooms have air conditioning. All the rooms have nice fans, night stands, lamps, shelving, and an area for your luggage. They are simple, clean and comfortable, definitely a major step above the standard budget lodgings of the town. Secure parking is available right inside the lot on the grass in front of the rooms. *Rates:* $25 double standard, plus $3pp for breakfast. The rooms with A/C are $35 double. Laundry is available, and some English is spoken. The family owns a large *finca* near Playa Platanares, and offers an exclusive tour that combines beach, forest and mangroves. They have made the property into wildlife refuge, Preciosa-Platanares Wildlife Refuge, where you can take a tour on horseback through several eco-systems. The beach part of the tour goes to Playa Platanares, from which you can observe a large part of the Golfo Dulce, along with all its abundant shoreline flora and fauna. This is considered the nicest beach on the entire Osa Peninsula for sunbathing and swimming. There are pelicans, frigate birds, sand pipers, and lots of interesting crabs here. You can spot four species of mangroves in the wetland portion of the refuge, where crocodiles mix with monkeys and numerous bird species. Their secondary forest has three species of monkeys and other mammals, as well as many birds of prey and butterflies. The three-hour tour can also be taken on foot. Call or fax 735-5007 for both the lodgings and the tour, or just show up.

   Parrot Bay Village — Located on its own secluded beach, yet within walking distance of central Pto. Jiménez, Parrot Bay Village touts itself as a "luxury sportfishing eco-lodge". This small coastal resort, recently renovated by the new owners in 2001, is situated right on a beachside lot backed by a mangrove reserve teeming with wildlife. The sandy shore in front of the hotel is great for swimming, and the views across the gulf are fantastic. An open air cantina and restaurant is located right on the premises, also renovated in 2001. The grounds are wonderfully landscaped with a myriad of colorful flora, making for a garden-like setting. A volleyball court lies between the cabins the beach, and sea kayaks are available free to guests for cruising around the gulf or up the Platanares River nearby. Monkeys, alligators and dozens of bird species can be seen while cruising silently through the pristine local waters or, for you land lubbers, the footpaths through the croco-dile lagoon directly behind the lodge make the wildlife just as acces-sible. Even those who just want to leave the world behind may get some exposure to the jungle as both capuchin and squirrel monkeys can be seen frolicking in the trees above the cabins on occasion. For those interested in getting really intimate with nature, ask the staff when "feeding time" is at the adjacent crocodile swamp – just keep your hands in your pockets. The completely refurbished cabins are beautifully finished in tropical hardwoods, each having their own name and uniquely carved door. The spacious interiors have ceramic tiled floors, ceiling fans and private baths with real hot water showers, and are fully furnished with table and chairs. The carved mirror frames and in the bathrooms and reading lights are nice touches. Most of the cabins now have air conditioning, and several have outside showers. The single level cabins can accommodate up to four people comfortably, the two-story cabins can accommodate up to five, and the "Casa Delfin" can sleep up to seven. The latter is a private two story house set away from the cabins, also recently renovated and modified to accommodate guests (it was the office and staff quarters for the previous owners). The house offers a spacious living room with lots of windows, a master bedroom with A/C, an upstairs loft with two double beds and reading lights, and a full-length outside porch on the second floor looking directly over the volleyball court to the Sweet Gulf. The lodge also offers two special all-inclusive packages, one for sportfishing on their own fully rigged offshore boats, and the other for you eco-adventurers. *Rates:* $90 single, $110 double, $130 triple, $150 for a group of 4, and $185 for the Casa Delfin. Laundry service is available, as are Swedish massages by appointment. Call 735-5180 or fax 735-5568 direct, or e-mail at mail@parrotbayvillage.com. Web site: www.parrotbayvillage.com.

Crocodile Bay Lodge – This luxury sport fishing lodge located right off the gulf in Pto. Jiménez offers world-class fishing, top shelf accommodations and professional eco-tours. 44 acres of grounds are surrounded on three sides by tall forest and mangrove swamp, while wide manicured lawns and professional landscaping provide a colorful natural environment. Dozens of scarlet macaws can be seen feeding and frolicking in the trees every day, and monkeys abide on the property. Your first experience of the lodge is walking through hand carved polished doors into an air conditioned reception lobby where English-speaking staff help get you oriented. The white-tiled central lodge building also houses the well-stocked gift shop, attractive main bar (with a pool table) and commodious dining rooms, all of which are air conditioned for maximum comfort. Behind the main lodge is the large free-form swimming pool with a swim-up bar. Next to that is a unique hot tub built a dozen feet or so on top of a volcano-like structure, affording 360-degree views of the grounds. The 28 rooms are housed in two-story concrete four-plexes spread out around the lodge and pool area and connected by lighted concrete paths. The construction and furnishings are both top quality, with bright tiled floors, polished hardwood detailing, and classy tropical décor. There are two classes of rooms, all having either tiled porches or hardwood decks with rocking chairs and potted plants. All the rooms have queen sized beds, nice nightstands with brass lamps, a clock radio, a telephone, ceiling fans with lights, a writing desk, dresser drawers, a full closet, air conditioning and hot water on tap. The spacious bathrooms have either a tiled shower with bench seat or Jacuzzi bathtub and shower. The hardwood counters and huge dressing mirrors add a touch of class, and the large tinted glass windows have thick white curtains. All the rooms are very large and quiet. The thick bath towels are changed daily along with the bedding, and same-day laundry service is available. In addition to the guest rooms, there are two 3-bedroom houses available, with king sized beds, satellite TV, Jacuzzi bathtubs, full kitchens, and more. Crocodile Bay Lodge also has an air-conditioned conference center that can accommodate groups of up to 80 people. The meals here are prepared by a large kitchen staff guided by an experienced chef trained on international cruise lines in American specialties. Lunches include things like pizza, burgers, and grilled fish, while dinner is a multi-course event with a choice of main courses and desserts. *Rates:* All-inclusive sport fishing packages start at $2,395pp double occupancy for three days. Reservations required. They have their own large fishing fleet. They also have their own butterfly farm, and can arrange all the off-site area tours, including Corcovado National Park. Call (800) 733-1115 in the USA, fax (415) 209-6177. In Costa Rica call 735-5631. E-mail info@crocodilebay.com. Web site: www.crocodilebay.com

Cabinas Eilyn — Out on the southern edge of town going towards Cabo Matapalo, away from the bustle and traffic, these immaculate rooms are attached to the Tico owners' house for a more homey and personal environment. A great opportunity to practice your Spanish! Around 300 meters past the gas station heading south on the main road towards Cabo Matapalo, the well-landscaped front yard welcomes you with its simple tropical beauty, with a nice lawn and ornamental shrubs. Many birds are active in this area, including macaws and toucans, which visit often. The property is bordered by large empty lots, so there is very little distraction from the peaceful setting. Two large rooms are located to one side of the owners' house, and another room is in the back behind the kitchen and dining area. The very spacious rooms are marvelously detailed, with tiled floors and baths, varnished hardwood furniture, cathedral ceilings, tiled porch with lounge chairs, television, and night table. The rooms have either a double and single bed, or bunk and single beds, and can hold up to four people.

The back room is equally well finished and also has its own private bath across the porch from the door with a gravel floor shower that lets you bathe in private in the open air. "Gato" William and his family take particular pride in the comfort of their guests. Breakfast is a customized event with the family taking your request for an American or Tico style meal. *Gallo pinto*, pancakes, French toast, a fruit plate – they'll cook it up for you before your adventurous day on the Osa on the expanded tiled porch with large patio dining table. Laundry is also available. William has a 2004 fully equipped 4wd Toyota Prado taxi for up to 7 passengers (with A/C and stereo) and offers transportation and tours throughout the Osa Peninsula, Drake Bay and beyond, with totally flexible schedules and good rates. He can be your personal guide on various expeditions to places like Cabo Matapalo, Carate, Corcovado National Park, and Doz Brazos. He can also arrange other tours including off-shore sportfishing (both budget and top rated) and scuba diving. A public phone is right in front of the house on the road, and the family also makes their fax and computer available to guests. **Rates:** $40 double including tax, $3 for an extra person. Rate includes a full breakfast. They will also loan guests the kitchen facilities (donations appreciated). English is spoken by the owner Gato. Best to call 735-5465 or 735-5590 telefax a day or two ahead of time to secure your room. E-mail: cabinaseilyn@hotmail.com. Web site: www.destinostv.com/cabinaseilyn.

La Choza Del Manglar – Set far back from the road against mangroves behind a high wall of bamboo near the airport, this small hotel was purchased by a savvy entrepreneur and converted into a fabulous tropical B&B. Formerly '*Cabinas Los Manglares*', the hotel has undergone a complete renovation (2004) and dramatic improvements. The 4 acres of landscaped grounds, with concrete paths, fairytale bridges and splashing fountains, is surrounded on three sides by natural marsh and mangrove forest, and many birds and animals come by daily for the fruit hung out by the owners. Photographers love the place as they can catch monkeys, raccoons, huge iguanas, scarlet macaws, toucans and other exotic wildlife in their natural habitat only steps from their room. Hand-carved furniture was brought down from Nicaragua, and there are tiki torches, candles and colored lights at night for a spectacular ambience. There are six rooms in the main accommodations next to the restaurant, all lined up behind a covered, furnished patio with king-sized hardwood and leather lounge chairs. They are all concrete construction for quiet privacy, with nice rounded doors and framed glass windows with louvers. They have new orthopedic spring mattresses on hardwood beds with headboards, tiled floors, a writing table, nice candelabras and even candle holders for a romantic touch. They all have nice private baths with hot water, and air conditioning. Across a fairytale bridge through a patch of mangrove you come to the back of the property with wide lawns, ornamental bushes, tall coconut and almond trees, pineapples, and big old fruit trees. There are two private cabins and a duplex here available to guests, also completely renovated. The cabins have their own verandas looking out over totally private backyards on the mangroves, and really nice stone floors and baths – very cool. The huge open-air restaurant is an inspired, living work, with dazzling murals throughout by artist Michael Cranford, and hundreds of vibrant plants blending in with the artwork, creating the powerful feeling of being immersed in the jungle with a view out to the sea. It's awesome. The tables are also works of art with sandy beach scenes under smoked glass. The new bar – very classy and modern – has a dizzying variety of both drinks (the drink menu sports choices from the cheapest beer to French champagne – four pages worth!) and music. The main menu changes daily, featuring 3-4 main courses with soup, salad, and excellent desserts. They serve breakfast (primarily international and American styles) all day, and have a very extensive snack menu. The restaurant is open daily except Monday from 6:30am to 11pm or midnight, depending on the day. *Rates:* $35-50 single and $50-67 double, including a full breakfast of your choice. Group discounts. Laundry service available. They have their own English-speaking guides for tours, plus offer massage, manicures and facials. Phone, fax and Internet available. Telefax 735-5002. E-mail info@manglares.com. Web site: www.manglares.com.

Cabinas Iguana-Iguana – Set off the main road right at the entry point to Puerto Jiménez, this large, shady complex offers inexpensive lodgings and a full-service restaurant run once again by the original owners. Well-established mature landscaping surrounds the wide parking area and four buildings making up the hotel. There is a huge stand of bamboo and many tall shade trees where dozens of green, brown and multicolored iguanas love to hang out, including a mature banyan tree. Several coconut palms can be seen, and scarlet macaws often visit the tall almond trees to get a bit to eat. Most of the standard rooms are off to one side in one long building with a wraparound corridor, the others in a duplex near the town side of the property. The concrete and wood structures which house the rooms have large screened windows with curtains, tiled showers, bamboo shelving, and night stands. All of the standard rooms have private baths. The queen, double, single and bunk beds got new mattresses in 2001, and all the rooms have good fans. There are also three separate 'trucker suites' that share one bathroom off on the far side of the parking lot. The first set of buildings you actually come to when you enter the property is the office, which can help you arrange your itinerary in the Osa, and the large open-air restaurant and bar. There are several large tables in the restaurant and lots of seating on barstools at this, one of the more popular local watering holes. Behind the restaurant is the biggest smoker and barbecue in the area. The food is classic Tico fare, with all the standard options. Soups and salads are also available. The bar serves up a limitless flow of beer, shots, fancy tropical cocktails, and a full menu of bocas (snacks). They even have real draft beer on tap, a rarity in these parts. The restaurant and bar open at 5pm daily, and close when the last person has gone to bed. To cool off after a hot meal, they have a huge pool out back with its own rancho. Under the thatched palm roof you can get poolside bar service and lounge in a hammock while escaping the heat (during the summer season). For the adventurers among you, Iguana-Iguana can arrange guided tours of Corcovado National Park, or any other area tour. They will hook you up with only experienced, fully bilingual guides. ***Rates***: $10pp for the standard rooms. The 'trucker suites' go for $5pp. Camping is $5 per tent with bathroom facilities provided. Call 735-5158 telefax, or e-mail dosiguanas@racsa.co.cr.

Cabinas Bosque Mar – These twelve newer rooms (2001) are located near downtown Jiménez next to the old bank building, just around the block from the center of town yet well shielded from the noise. These rooms are among the very nicest for those on a tight budget. Walking in from the gravel road past a small *soda* on a open-air terrace, you enter a 2-story foyer of white ceramic tile. There are several rooms available off the wide central common area, and up the tiled stairs with nice *cara tigre* handrails on the left. On the second floor there are more rooms spread around an open second floor court area. There are an abundance of potted plants on the floor, on the stairs and hanging to add some natural vibrance. Upstairs there is a tiled balcony with several chairs for looking out over the road to the mangroves beyond. All the immaculately maintained rooms have tiled baths with hot water showers, adjustable ceiling fans, fluorescent lights, cable TV with CNN in English, shelving and nice sheets on newer beds. Some of the rooms have air conditioning. The owners live downstairs for optimum security and convenience. There is a phone for international calls right in the foyer, and the small eatery out front serves a wide variety of typical meals, as well as milkshakes and many cold drinks. There is also a small office on the first floor, where you can purchase T-shirts, post cards, and organic-based insect repellent. ***Rates:***

$8pp without A/C; $30 per room with A/C for up to three people. Low season, group and long stay discounts. Several tours are offered by the owner Jaco, who speaks some English, with his own boat and 4wd vehicle. Some of the tours available are dolphin watching, one-day Corcovado National Park excusions, both inshore and offshore sport fishing, and a boat trip up the protected mangroves of the Esquinas River in the northeast corner of the Sweet Gulf. For either accommodations or tours, telefax 735-5681 or 735-5102 (Spanish only).

Cabinas y Restaurante Carolina — Right in the heart of town on the main drag, these rooms are centrally located for those wanting both action and convenience. The open-air restaurant is very popular with the local expatriates living in the area, and it's a great place to meet other tourists and some colorful local characters, and get information on the area. Most of the rooms were recently built on the second floor of a small commercial building next to the restaurant, while several are located behind the restaurant in a small courtyard. The new rooms are set four on each side of a long covered corridor that terminates in a wide furnished veranda looking out over the bustling downtown area. All the floors are nicely tiled, and the construction is excellent quality with varnished pine walls. The newer rooms all have 2 or 3 beds on nice varnished wood frames with headboards, and glass night stands. The fully tiled baths have hot water showers. One room has air conditioning, and televisions were planned for some. They all have at least one fan, and the glass windows are huge with adjustable louvers. All the rooms are cleaned daily. The older rooms in the courtyard are well-maintained and spacious. Their private baths have exceptionally large showers. The restaurant, a landmark in these parts, has ample table seating up in a covered terrace raised two steps above the sidewalk at the two public phones smack in the middle of main street. The tables each have their own adjustable fan for comfort, and there is a large mural on the north wall. The front is open to the street, and one side to a narrow alley between them and a tourist business office on the first floor of the newer construction, the kitchen being in the back. Breakfast, lunch and dinner are served from 7am-10pm. Soups, salads, beef, pork, excellent seafood, rice dishes, pastas, ceviches and more can be found on the Spanish-English menu, all at reasonable prices. Specialties include chicken cordon bleu, fettuccine alfredo, filet mignon, and fish filet in ginger or garlic sauce (the mushroom sauce is excellent, too, especially with the French fries). Speaking of French fries, they're very good. All bar drinks are available, as well as German, Chilean and Italian wines. They naturally have all the fruit drinks available, and some desserts as well. *Rates:* $8-10pp depending on the room, and $30 per room with A/C. The business has two of its own English-speaking guides, and its own late-model taxi for transportation and tours anywhere in the country. Call 735-5696, or 735-5185.

Cabinas Jiménez -- Purchased by a North American couple in 2003 and completely renovated and remodeled, these comfortable rooms right on the water are located on the quiet side of town, near the main road as it enters Puerto Jiménez. John and Crystal came down on vacation one year, and decided to make their future annual visits 'paid vacations' by buying and operating these well-established accommodations. Nine rooms in two buildings and one spacious bungalow are grouped along around a 1/2 acre of shoreline, where constant breezes roll off the waters of the gulf, and one can see the boats and wharf bobbing in the distance. Stone and concrete paths lead to the rooms, the owners' house, and the private bungalow, with almond and palm trees providing lots of shade, and new landscaping recently added that is very pleasing the eye. The rooms are definitely a cut above. You can get a room with one double and one single bed, a double and two singles, or two double beds. All of them have air conditioning, hot water showers, a small refrigerator, and ceiling fans with lights. Guatemalan textiles are used for bedspreads and rugs, in vibrant colors and designs. The louvered glass windows have wonderful batik curtains in various Asian patterns, and all the rooms have magnificent natural scenes on the walls painted by a talented local artist. Besides the rich covers, the double and single beds have nice thick linen and new mattresses. The baths and floors are finished with attractive ceramic tile. Two of the rooms have private decks (one wood and the other tiled), while the rest have patios, all with new wooden lounge furniture. The private bungalow has some extra features like fully louvered windows for more air flow, butterfly and sea life curtains, and a large new wooden deck looking out over the bay. It has one double and two single beds, a table and chair, and two ceiling fans with lights. ***Rates***: The rooms are $30 single, $40 double, and $50 triple. The bungalow rents for $60 single or double, $75 triple, or $85 quadruple. Low season, group and long-term discounts available. Future plans include their own fishing tours and jungle treks, but in the meantime they can help set you up with all the local tours. Fluent English is spoken, of course. Phone 735-5090. E-mail cabinasjimenez@yahoo.com.

Cabinas The Corner -- These newer rooms between the main street in downtown Jiménez and the old bus station (now the office of the collective daily taxi to Carate) are an excellent budget option for those seeking clean rooms at rock-bottom rates. The two-story bulding was recently renovated. It has a small parking area, lots of plants out front in planters and pots, and excellent security with a big gate at the building entrance. The first floor has one of the rooms and the manager's home, with a tiled corridor in front. Up the stairs on the right are the other four rooms, these sharing a common bath. Tall trees on the west side of the buidling provide welcome afternoon shade. The downstairs room with the private bath is long and narrow, with nice tiled floors and three single beds. It has a floor fan and shelving, both a screen door and a thick pine wood door, plus a very nice bathroom with hot water. The upstairs rooms share a wide patio area with sliding glass windows along its entire length. The patio has wide benches, and a table with chairs. The rooms are all wood construction, with varnished floors and walls. Only two rooms share a wall. They are very clean, and furnished with night stands, ceiling fans with speed control, and both dark and thinner lace curtains over large screened windows. The upstairs shared bath is really nice, with rich dark tile on both the floor and walls, and sliding glass doors to the hot water shower. *Rates*: $6pp shared bath, $8pp with private bath. Low season and group discounts available. Laundry machines – including a drier – are available to guests, as well as a secure storage room. The owners run the collective taxi service to Carate, and the place to catch it is right by the rooms. Other transportation can be provided as well, for groups of up to seven people. Airport pick-up, tours throughout the peninsula, and more can be arranged by just walking across the street to their office, or calling them. Call 735-5328 for the rooms. Call 837-3120 or 834-1345 for the taxi service. Ask for Roxana (she speaks some English).

Other Lodgings: Cabinas Mariela, Pensión Quintero, Cabinas Thompson, Cabinas Katty.

*　*　*　*　*

The following establishments are located on **Playa Platanares**, a long sandy beach stretching for miles about five kilometers from the airport in Jiménez. The beach stretches from Punta Arenitas and the Río Platanares in the north to a jutting point in the south with some nice tide pools. There is a living reef just offshore, and lots of classic tropical beach scenery with coconut palms, almond trees, and tons of iguanas, birds and other wildlife. To get there, take the road on the back side of the airport (there are signs at the turnoff), and just follow it out through a little mangrove estuary and over a concrete bridge towards the beach. The road curves left just before the shore and runs behind several of the lodges, then curves back towards the beach and runs along the shore out to Playa Preci-Osa Lodge. The lodges appear below in the same order you will arrive coming from Pto. Jimenez. It's very secluded, and crowds are one thing you will definitely <u>not</u> find here. It's the nearest alternative to staying right in town, and only about 10 minutes by car (about 25 by bike) from central Jiménez. The lodges will be happy to pick you up if you need a ride in, though a taxi is only about $5. You could also walk from the beach in Jiménez at low tide if you don't mind getting your legs wet, and if you have a strong desire for unnecessary exertion.

Black Turtle Lodge -- This 3-1/2 acre beachside resort is the newest addition to the lodgings at Playa Platanares, established in 2003 by yet another set of North American ex-pats seeking a more harmonious existence. The grounds are beautiful, with fruit trees, towering shade trees, and well-developed gardens augmented by 9,000 shrubs and trees planted by the owners over the last two years. There is even a pond with frogs, basilisk lizards, and tilapia fish. Monkeys and other mammals come here to drink, plus hordes of birds. Ocelots, jagarundis, and jaguars have been spotted on the property as well. There are nice sand paths throughout the complex, with bamboo foot washes at the cabin entrances. There are both one-story and two-story wood cabins here, with the latter having private baths. The smaller cabins are open on all sides, with thick screens and curtains. They are fully furnished with bamboo, having night stands, closets, even a bamboo bed frame and light fixtures. They have Egyptian cotton sheets on the queen and single beds, skylights, fans, and a water pitcher with glasses. The two single cabins share a very nice bath house, which has two full baths with instantaneous hot water on tap. The two-story 'tree-house' cabins have two bedrooms and an open-air private bath, also with hot water on tap. The second story, with beautiful varnished wood floors, has a spacious, fully furnished deck – the view of the surrounding gardens and Sweet Gulf is spectacular. Reading lights, bamboo roll-up blinds, and vaulted wood ceilings are additional amenities. Out on the beach there is a private hammock platform, with a high roof, a foot wash, several extra large hammocks, and a big shower nearby. There is also a covered and fully screened yoga platform, equipped with soft lights, fans, and exercise mats and blocks. The dining and socializing deck is located on the first floor of the owners' quarters, where you can savor the fantastic flavors of the owners Jeff and Mary. Jeff was a private chef in upper Manhattan in his former life. The meals are so delicious here that many people ask for the recipes. Exotic dinners like red curry coconut mahi-mahi, garlic rosemary chicken with roasted root vegetables, and grilled dorado with caramelized onion balsamic cream reduction sauce (whew!) are the norm here. Mary is a magician with homemade breads and pastries. Even gourmets will leave the table sated and happy (see the food page on their web site for guest comments and recipes). Breakfasts and lunches include lots of fresh fruit from the property. For activities, there are kayaks, boogie boards, frisbees, games and books for guests to enjoy. You can get a free walking tour of the property, and all other local tours can be arranged from the lodge. *Rates*: $65pp and $85pp plus tax full board, depending on the cabin. Group rates available. Phone 735-5005, fax 735-5043. E-mail info@blackturtlelodge.com. Web site: www.blackturtlelodge.com.

Iguana Lodge – This beachside resort beckons you with a relaxing tropical atmosphere only a few steps from the fine sandy beach of Playa Platanares. The grounds are carefully landscaped to preserve the natural diversity, and many creatures are to be found in the surrounding foliage including lots of iguanas, scarlet macaws, toucans, parakeets, and other bird life, as well as some occasional monkeys, raccoons and coatis. Their four private cabins are two-story structures of shaped concrete and local hardwoods, very spacious, open and comfortable. The upstairs of the two original 'family' bungalows has a wide covered deck complete with hammock that boasts a spectacular view of the gulf and coastline across the water, a large double bed and single bed, ample shelving, fans and lighting. The first floor has another bedroom and a full bath, with its own private deck, making each bungalow a self-contained unit with lots of living space. The concrete and tile work are first class, and the commodious shower with seat and dressing area are a treat. The two larger bungalows are set up a little differently, with a queen and single bed upstairs. Each floor has its own bath, the downstairs with a large porch and the upstairs a wide wooden deck. Both levels have lots of space and very nice bamboo furniture. They also have a very impressive three-story, three-bedroom beach house for rent. The lodge building itself is a giant two-story rancho with a massive thatched-palm roof, the lower floor housing the spacious kitchen, reception area and guest lounge. The lounge area boasts an extensive book library and several board games. Their Japanese style bath house – unique in the southern zone – has gas-fired hot water to melt the stress away. Their split level 'hammock shack' on the sand is ideal for napping, reading or sunbathing. 24-hour 110-volt electricity is provided by solar panels, and all the rooms have hot water on tap. The food is gourmet quality, with an emphasis on fresh seafood caught locally. Dishes like Mackerel Dijon and grilled snapper pilapa with

Veracruz relish are the delicious norm, with fantastic desserts like mango mousse, key lime pie and pecan pie (probably the best I've ever had) to finish things off. Fresh baked scones, breads and pastries are standard fare, plus traditional American breakfasts. Banana crepes anyone? Awesome! And even morning coffee in bed . . . . Beer, wine and mixed drinks are available. Guests enjoy free use of both kayaks and boogie boards. *Rates*: $100pp full board during high season, half price for children under 12. The house rents for $330/night. Significant discounts during green season. All local tours can be arranged. VISA accepted. The owners of Iguana Lodge are proud supporters of both the marine turtle conservation project and the town library. Call 735-5205, fax 735-5436, e-mail info@iguanalodge.com. Web site: www.iguanalodge.com.

Pearl of the Osa — This hotel, restaurant and bar next door to Iguana Lodge is perfectly located for pleasant relaxation by the beach for either day trippers or overnight guests, situated on a full hectare (2-12 acres) of well-tended land. The large two-story building houses eight attractive, recently remodeled rooms upstairs and a full bar and great restaurant downstairs, all built with quality materials and a splash of style. The long U-shaped bar was crafted from rare Christopher Columbus and purple heart woods, and shows off its extensive selection of liquors in a carved hardwood and mirror display. There is an excellent stereo to keep the rhythm flowing, and personal attention by the staff. The 20m x 7m open-air restaurant faces the beach just a few dozen yards away from under the hardwood floors of the rooms upstairs, and the view past the beach front landscaping and out to the gulf is complimented by soft sea breezes. There are lots of strong yet decorative *cara de tigre* posts supporting the structure below and on the deck above. The food is an eclectic mix of Italian, American and Mexican styles. Hamburgers, pizzas, tacos, burritos, and club sandwiches are all available, with daily specials to boot. Lots of seafood can be found alongside French fries and tostadas on their "classic beach food" menu (a la California). All meals are made fresh to order, and there is a full selection of cocktails, beer, etc. available. The prices are very reasonable, ranging from $2 for snack plates to $5 for most main dishes. The rooms, all on the second story, are arranged in a rectangle, back to back and side to side with a wide wraparound hardwood deck for access. From the back side you look past thick *barrigón* trees to some secondary forest and pasture behind the property, with an abundance of bird life adding alto notes to the surf's basso symphony. The front rooms have an inspiring view of the gulf. Each room has its own private bath with a large shower. The large curtained windows let in the breezes with the help of ceiling fans inside, and electricity is provided by generator most of the day and in the evening for the lights and outlets. The double beds have real mattresses and wooden box springs for extra comfort. The hotel and restaurant are run by the owners of Iguana Lodge next door, North Americans who are always ready to assist you with your vacation plans and activities. Don't miss their pasta and salsa dancing nights here on Fridays, open to the public, with live music and lots of local color. *Rates:* $45-85 per room depending on the room you choose and the season. Laundry and transportation are available. Discounts for longs stays. To make reservations, call 735-5205 or fax 735-5436. E-mail info@pearloftheosa.com, Web site www.pearloftheosa.com. The restaurant and bar are open to the public from 7am to 8pm daily (later Fridays), so you won't go hungry (or thirsty) if you're doing a day trip to the beach here.

Playa Preci-Osa -- The most secluded of the accommodations on Playa Platanares, this European-owned and managed bed and breakfast offers comfortable private bungalows at very reasonable rates. The only lodge here located within a national wildlife refuge, the owners are dedicated to conservation and responsible ecological tourism, volunteering to have their land protected by law against large-scale development. They are major sponsors of the turtle protection program as well, which hatches over 10,000 baby turtles every season. The lodge grounds, encompassing around two acres of organized gardens and lush landscaping, is a wonder of vibrant life and color. There are more birds than most other areas, and one can spot butterflies, tree frogs, raccoons, coatis, possums, and monkeys. There is a half-kilometer self-guided trail through the gardens, and the lodge will provide you with a written pamphlet describing the various life forms you will encounter. They have bananas, yucca, lemon grass, vanilla, papaya, pineapple, chilies, avocados, and 20 different medicinal plants to see. The sandy paths are lit at night, so you might want to check out their frog pond after dark. The main lodge is a two-story building near the beach, with the second floor dedicated to a spacious dining and socializing area, open to the breezes with a view to the sea. There are lots of books in English, German and Spanish, and information on local wildlife. The 4 two-story bungalows are unique round structures made of concrete and wood, set well apart from each other among the gardens. Two have ocean views, while the other two have nice views of the grounds from the second floor balcony. You enter via a covered tiled porch with a foot wash. There are two single beds in the ample downstairs area, with a table and chairs, nice shelving, night stands, luggage racks, ceiling fans with lights, and night lights directly over the beds. The large bathroom is fully tiled, and has a nice mirror and attractive shell work on the walls. The second floor has a double bed and private veranda. There are some nice paintings on the walls for decoration. A full breakfast is included with your stay, featuring fresh fruit, eggs any style, toast and coffee or tea, and *gallo pinto*. Coffee is free all day to guests. Optional lunches are light and fresh. Dinners feature fresh fish, local vegetables, and other international meals prepared with herbs and spices from their garden. Dinners are organized with the guests in the morning, so custom diets can be accommodated. Pure potable water comes from their own well. Electricity is provided from 6pm till 10pm daily. ***Rates***: $40 single, $50 double, tax included. $10 each additional person up to four. English, German, Spanish and French spoken. Laundry service available. Free use of boogie boards. Bikes available for rent. All local tours arranged upon request. Phone 818-2959, fax 735-5043. E-mail playa-preciosa@web.de. Web site: www.playa-preciosa-lodge.de.

FOOD SERVICE

Pollosa -- Don't let the small size of this cool little eatery fool you – it's got good food, things you will find nowhere else in the Osa Peninsula. They have a wood-fired, glass-walled rotisserie where they roast wholesome, organically raised chicken and pork. The meat is first marinated, then basted with a special sauce to add a tasty flavoring. It's excellent. Carlos, the Tico owner, is assisted by his European wife, who whips up real potato salad and delicious homemade desserts. Besides portions of roasted chicken and pork, there is a good menu of other dining options. Salads include roast chicken (naturally), Greek (goat cheese, olives and mushrooms), and vegetarian. Spaghetti is offered with NINE different sauces and ingredients, like shrimp, octopus, bologna, and garlic. Sandwiches of tuna, chicken, pork and goat cheese are available. Desserts include tiramisu, three milks, chocolate mousse and fruit salad. Lots of fruit drinks and shakes are available. The prices are very reasonable. A whole roasted chicken is only $6. A portion of roast chicken is less than $2, and comes with tortillas and your choice of two great sauces (for sale separately as well). Their large salads run around $4, as does their spaghetti. Sandwiches are only around $1! All the food is available for take-out, and is perfect for beach picnics or jungle treks. You can get whole, half or ¼ chickens with tortillas and sauces to go. The goat cheese is made by them on their ranch with the milk from their own goats, which are also raised with organic foods. All the food is healthy, well-prepared, and filling. Many of us locals buy here, especially the guides and sport fishermen who are taking groups of tourists out. For regular diners, there is both indoor and outdoor seating on several tables, with fans inside and breezes outside on the covered patio. Regular hours are Noon to 9pm daily except Saturdays. They are conveniently located right next to Cabinas The Corner, around 50 meters off the main street. Phone 735-5667.

Il Guardino -- This new Italian restaurant, the only one in the Osa Peninsula, is owned and managed by Italian immigrant Giulio and his Tica wife Cecilia, long-term residents of the area. Giulio was born in Genova, Italy (as was the classic pesto sauce), and brings his intimate knowledge of Italian cuisine to share with us in this very attractive restaurant in central Puerto Jiménez. There are actually three separate dining areas here: in the front yard under thatched palm roofs, inside on varnished wooden tables with woven bamboo place mats, and in the private back garden surrounded by tall trees and lush foliage. All the fantastic wood work, including the unique and artistic bar, was hand crafted by Giulio himself, who owns a furniture business. There is a sushi bar as well, located inside across from the bar. The main reason to come here, though, is for the food. Range chicken is raised organically especially for the restaurant, as are many herbs and spices. I'll walk you through the extensive menu (which comes in Italian, English and Spanish). Specialties on the first page include seafood lasagna, Milanese eggplant, and Mexican salad. The next two pages are primarily pasta dishes, including meat ravioli with Porcini mushroom sauce, spaghetti with fresh tomato and shrimp, trenette with pesto sauce, tricolor penne pasta with broccoli cream, and tortellini with sweet cream and ham. Most of the pasta is made from scratch, of course. They have several salads (including both palm heart and snail), and antipasto. Other dishes listed are barbecued pork ribs, beef tenderloin with garlic and rosemary, grilled chicken breast, and grilled lobster with lemon-butter sauce (my mouth is watering). You can't have a real Italian restaurant without pizza in my mind, and so they do – seven different kinds. You can make your own, too, with additional ingredients like sweet corn, zucchini, and palm heart, besides all the standard toppings. The prices are very reasonable, with the average main course costing $5, and large pizzas for only around $7. To help you digest the rich fare, the bar has a full range of domestic and imported liquors, including Italian wines and liquors, various beers brands, and even a cocktail menu. Sake or green tea? No problem. The separate sushi menu is available in the evenings, and served with authentic bowls, plates and utensils bought just for this purpose. If you'd like to order ahead of time, call 735-5129. Hours are 10am – 10pm daily during the high season, 5pm - 10pm low season. Take-out available. Fluent English, Spanish and Italian are spoken.

Jade Luna Restaurant -- Barbara Burkhardt trained as a chef in two prominent New York schools, including the New York Restaurant School, then went on to work all over the United States for 20 years, perfecting her culinary skills. After falling in love with a Costa Rican man on vacation one year, she ended up settling in the Osa Peninsula and fulfilling an ambitious dream of hers: opening her own upscale restaurant. Her and her husband Marcos have adopted 'Casual fine dining at its best' as their motto for this tropical gastronomic adventure, found just outside the town of Puerto Jimenez on the road to Playa Platanares. Open from 4-9pm Monday through Saturday, the new restaurant (opened in July 2004) specializes in grilled and Cajun pan blackened seafood, chicken, steak, chops and burgers. There are a wide variety of other dishes, put up on a daily 'chalkboard menu' that depends on the availability of certain ingredients. They have a special refrigerator just to properly age their beef. You can start with items such as Greek Salad with goat cheese or classic Caesar Salad with hearts of palm, or dip into some conch fritters or lobster bisque. Entrée choices include Black Angus rib-eye steak with green peppercorn butter, and jumbo shrimp and vegetable kabob. How about a spicy Cajun pan blackened tuna steak? Check this out: Spiny lobster, pan seared with garlic and brown butter. Beef and fish burgers are served with steak fries or onion rings. There is always a homemade pasta dish on the board, and the desserts are incredible. You can finish things off with fudge brownies, hot caramelized pineapple, or one of their famous homemade ice creams and sorbets. Flavors include vanilla bean, mint chocolate chip, butter pecan, real coconut, coffee, mango, peanut butter and green tea. The ice cream is available every day from 11am on, and alone is worth the trip for sure. Dinner prices are as follows: Appetizers and salads run from $2-5, while main courses go from $10 to $15 for the most expensive (like fresh lobster). Burgers are around $5 each. The open-air dining room is surrounded by wide lawns and colorful professional landscaping. The terracotta tile floors are accented by arched openings and soft papaya walls. The custom-made tables and chairs are made of beautifully finished *cristobal* wood, with classy yet colorful place settings and dishware. Ceiling fans keep things cool, and there is some hand-crafted artwork and jewelry available in the next room. Phone 735-5739 for reservations.

Other Dining Options: Restaurante Agua Luna, Juanita´s, Iguana-

Iguana, Pearl of the Osa, Rest. Oro Verde, Rest. Carolina and several little *sodas* around town.

TOURS, STORES AND OTHER SERVICES

El Epicentro (The Epicenter) — Puerto Jiménez's first consolidated commercial complex in downtown Puerto Jiménez offers area residents and travelers with the largest variety of goods and services available in one convenient location, all adjoining one another in the center of town. Café Net El Sol (735-5718, -5717, -5719) is a combination Internet café and tourist information center, boasting six modern computers with high-speed satellite service about to switch to the newly available DSL Internet access via wireless networking. Telephone and fax services are also available in addition to tourist information and reservation services covering the entire peninsula for travelers interested in wildlife, kayaking, and horseback tours, sport fishing, accommodations, air, land, and sea transport, Corcovado Park information and reservations, tent rentals, sales of maps, postcards, and souvenirs, all with friendly English-speaking staff to help with your information and communications needs. The café is also the home of El Sol de Osa, the peninsula's first and only on-again, off-again regional newspaper (www.soldeosa.com). Open from 7a.m. to 11p.m. every day except for Christmas, Palm Thursday, and Good Friday. Juanita's Mexican Bar & Grille (735-5056) features a wide range of Mexican and seafood dishes on its evening menu as well as a variety of international dishes on its breakfast and lunch menu. With a laid back atmosphere, Juanita's always covers major sporting events on its two large-screen television sets. The town's favored watering hole among locals and visitors alike since its opening in 2001, Juanita's offers a wide range of exotic umbrella drinks and happy hour drink specials every day between four and six, and daily featured specials including our original Thursday night Crab Races. Open from eight till midnight (or later) every day except Christmas, Palm Thursday, and Good Friday. Friction Zero Concepts (735-5702), parent company to Café Net El Sol, offers business-to-business web site hosting and design services, business software development, networking solutions, point-of-sales computer systems, hardware sales, graphic art, advertising, and publishing solutions for area businesses. Osa Water Works (735-5702; www.osawaterworks.com) offers comprehensive alternative energy, water supply, water filtration and treatment, and pollution control engineering and installations for regional home sites and commercial and residential developments, offering a complete line of solar and hydroelectric solutions for residents of Costa Rica and Panama, as well as fossil fuel generators, batteries, and ancillary electronics. Oro Fino offers an assortment of fine jewelry, bracelets, chains, watches, and souvenirs, and offers a full-service jewelry repair service. Open from 8:00am till 7:00pm. Abastecedor El Trebol offers a variety of groceries and is open from 6:00am a.m. to 9:00pm daily. Stop in at El Epicentro to see where they fit on your Richter Scale.

Osa Natural -- This tourist information and reservation office, located across from the sports field between the post office and library, is a non profit project of Asomet Golfo Dulce, the Tourism Chamber of the Puerto Jiménez area. Many of the local tourism businesses organized themselves to form this office, which is in charge of the promotion of their respective services. Besides the specific services they offer in tourism, they have a full range of communication equipment: phones, fax, marine band radio, and three computers for internet service, which is open to the public (I use it myself quite often). If you are just arriving in the area, and need some information on what to do and where to go, this office can be of great help. The bilingual staff are generally young and friendly, and can give you specific information on lodges, hotels, tours, restaurants, and more, and even make reservations if you like. There is a series of tours and local packages that are very unique in the market. They offer both national and foreign tourists a variety of natural attractions in protected zones such as National Parks, Biological Reserves, Indigenous Reserves, Forest Reserves, mangroves, rivers, beaches, and the Golfo Dulce, which is surrounded by rain forest and a large variety of wildlife. If you don't want to talk to anyone, there are many brochures on a long table in the office, and lots of fliers and such on a big bulletin board advertising all kinds of tourist businesses. Any questions will be answered happily by the staff. The internet service is low cost, and they sell cold drinks if you're thirsty. The office is very comfortable, with air conditioning and ceramic tiled floors. Hours are Monday through Saturday from 8am till 6pm. If you are not yet in the area and wish to know more, they have an extensive web site at www.osanatural.com. To contact them, e-mail osanatur@racsa.co.cr, or phone 735-5440.

Osa Aventura — A friendly Irish bloke (Mike Boston) will make your adventure in the Osa an unforgettably fun and educational experience. Mike specializes in single and multi-day adventure tours to Corcovado National Park, Caño Island, and other interesting places throughout the Osa. He is a qualified biologists with many years of study, field and guiding experience, and residence in the tropics. His

specific expertise lies in mammals, reptiles, amphibians and crocodiles. Mike can set up your customized excursion into the wilds of the
nearby rainforests, mountains and beaches, tailoring the trips to suit
your particular interests, fitness levels and schedule. The flexible itin-
eraries can include hiking, scuba diving, horseback riding, kayaking
(this area lends itself well to this), boating and camping. You also have
the choice of staying in or near several beautiful lodges during the adventure. Some interesting options include one or multi-day bird watching tours, night safaris in search of crocodiles and other nocturnal beasts,
and waterfall treks to hidden spots deep in the peninsula. English and
Irish are spoken fluently. He can also provide tourist information and
lodging reservations in the area, especially for the Carate area. Call or
fax 735-5670, or e-mail mike_boston2000@yahoo.com or
info@osaaventura.com. Web site: www.osaaventura.com.

Bosque del Río Tigre Birding Tours — Although offering a
wide variety of educational tours and excursions, Bosque del Rio Tigre
specializes in birding trips on the Osa Peninsula. Birders are encouraged to bring their "want lists", and Liz and Abraham will enthusiasti-
cally help find those elusive species. The Osa Peninsula hosts over
400 species of birds and the site list for Bosque del Rio Tigre contains over
300 of those. Although the area surrounding the lodge is one of the best
birding areas in Costa Rica, trips may be arranged to many other locations on the Peninsula, each with it's own special mix of bird life,
including Corcovado National Park. The Rio Tigre area contains a wide
variety of habitats including riverside, pasture, scrub, lagoons, orchards,
primary and secondary forest, garden, flatland and mountain. The
grounds and surrounding wildlife sanctuary are maintained with birds in
mind. Of special note is an Orange-collared Manakin lek within a 15
minute walk of the lodge, a lagoon with nesting Boat-billed Herons and
on the hill across the river can be seen the Turquoise Cotinga. Of
course birders will see many of the common Osa Peninsula species
such as Chestnut-mandibled Toucans, Scarlet Macaws and several of
the 4 species of trogon. Other species of note which are often difficult
to see in other locations include Uniform Crake, Baird's Trogon, Marbled
Wood-quail, Fiery-billed Aracari, Scaly-throated Leaftosser, Oliveous
Piculet, Red-rumped Woodpecker, Golden-naped Woodpecker, and the
local endemic, the Black-cheeked Ant Tanager. This species is seen
on the banana feeders around the lodge for much of the year. During
certain times of the year the White-crested Coquette and White-tipped
Sicklebill are almost guaranteed to be seen. Some experienced tropical birders have sighted over 100 species in one hike around the lodge!
For those less inclined to walk and for those seeking the Red-breasted

Blackbird, Pearl Kite, Yellow-billed Cotinga, a scarce mangrove species or the Mangrove Hummingbird, Liz and Abraham offer a very popular roadside birding trip to Rincon. A trip to the Sirena Ranger Station in Corcovado National Park may be arranged to search for the Spectacled Antpitta, Red-throated Caracara, Great Currasow, and Crested Guan. For birders more interested in behavior, your guide will show you the local nesting, feeding and lekking spots for the various species. There is a complete site list on the Bosque del Rio Tigre website. Guiding for customized birding trips is priced at $7 per hour with a minimum of two people, $10 an hour for one person. An early morning birding tour is $25pp including breakfast. Fax 735-5045 (to "Liz Jones, Dos Brazos") or call 735-5725 or 383-3905 (leave a message). E-mail info@osaadventures.com. Web site: www.osaadventures.com

Aventuras Tropicales -- This tour operator, specializing primarily in kayak trips around the Sweet Gulf, has over 14 years of experience guiding tourists in the Osa Peninsula. All the guides speak English and have various levels of training in tourism, biology, or other related subjects. Tropical Adventures (their name in English) is a Costa Rican company operating in the Osa Peninsula. They feature ecotourist tours, environmental education, kayaking, boating trips, and rain forest hikes with specialized local guides. They make their own kayaks for their tours, which are hardy, seaworthy craft with storage compartments. Some are built for two, so you can paddle with a friend. Most trips are up the Platanares River, which is just down the road from their office. This trip is fascinating, passing through primeval mangrove forests vibrant with life. You can see not only an incredible variety of exotic rain forest and shore birds, but iguanas, monkeys, sloths, raccoons, coatis, and more. You can cross over to the beautiful, pristine Platanares Beach (see Lodgings section) and swim in the warm water. Other options are walking mangrove tours, snorkeling on living reefs, sport fishing, sunset dolphin excursions, and multi-day Corcovado expeditions. Some unique trips are kayaking to botanical gardens across the gulf, multi-day gulf kayak/camping trips, and combination tours of bird watching, snorkeling and kayaking. They have several different rain forest hikes and excursions to choose from, for single day to multiple day, both in Corcovado National Park and on private forest reserves. They even have special trips to Drake Bay and Caño Island. To see more of their offerings, go to www.aventurastropicales.com. Phone 735-5195 or fax 735-5692. E-mail kayak@racsa.co.cr.

Osa Sportfishing / Delfin Blanco Dolphin Tours -- These

two businesses, owned by the same couple and managed by an experienced North American captain, operate directly out of Puerto Jiménez. They share an office in town with Río Nuevo Lodge, next to Restaurant Carolina. Osa Sportfishing runs a 30-foot Stamas, fully equipped with a full tower, Rupp outriggers, downriggers, an enclosed head and all the modern electronics. The captains have U.S. Coastguard licenses, and will safely guide you to the happy fishing grounds where you can snag giant yellowfin tuna, massive marlin, sailfish, dorado, wahoo. Inshore jaunts go for roosterfish, snook, and giant snapper. The super wide beam of this boat greatly reduces the 'rolling effect' of the swells, so you'll be more comfortable than in most boats. The 28-knot cruising speed will get you to the fish in a hurry – more time to catch the big ones. Half-day trips are $550. You leave at 7am and return at around 12:30pm. Snacks and drinks are included. Full day trips run $750, include a full lunch and beer, cold drinks and snacks. These trips leave at the same time but get you back at around 3:30 – around double the fishing time. The good ship **Delfin Blanco** (White Dolphin) is a brand new custom-built vessel designed specifically for dolphin and whale watching on the Golfo Dulce. The 50-foot, double-decked boat has twin 200-horsepower Yamaha power plants – no lack of speed here. It is equipped with a fresh water shower for rinsing off after a salty swim, and an enclosed bathroom. Full 110 electric is installed, and it has a great stereo for serenading both those above and below the water line. It has all the recommended U.S. Coastguard safety equipment, so have no fear. The 400 square foot observation deck has tables and chairs for relaxing in the sun and breeze, and great elevation to help observe the wild sea life, which can include dolphins, whales, whale sharks, turtles, manta rays and even sea snakes. Inside, on the lower deck, the molded benches are cushioned for comfort. During the season there are two tours per day: The morning tour, from 8am till 12:30, which includes lunch and cold drinks, and takes you rambling around the Sweet Gulf seeking our intelligent neighbors of the sea. The sunset tour – or booze cruise, as some call it – includes snacks and cold drinks, with alcoholic beverages available. It leaves shore at around 3:30pm, and gets you back to town at 7pm. After interacting with the denizens of the sea, you can observe the magnificent bioluminescence on your way back to port as night falls. Either tour is $45pp. In the U.S. phone toll-free 877-FISH-OSA; in Costa Rica call 735-5675 or 823-3685. E-mail lozo@quest.net. See their web site at www.fishosa.com for more detailed information about both the sport fishing and dolphin tour offerings, and their combination tour and accommodation packages.

Changing Tide Diving and Boat Tours -- This new tour operator, founded by North American ex-pat Charlie Plummer and his
partner Bob Merriam, is the ***only*** professional dive operation in the
Golfo Dulce area. In addition, the boat tours — developed over the past
two years through careful research and experience — are very unique,
and something worth checking out. The diving tours focus on the PADI-
certified 'Discover Diving' program, in which you can depart your lodge
in the morning and, upon your return at the end of the day, claim to have
experienced scuba diving for the first time. Also offered are classes for
full PADI certification, for both basic and advanced students. The dive
instructor carries a US Coast Guard Boat Operators License and is a
master scuba diver trainer. The gear is all new and first quality, as are
the boats and motors. They have two custom-built 25-foot launches for
their diving and boat tours, both powered by 115-horsepower 4-stroke
outboards, much quieter and less polluting than the standard 2-stroke
engines. Each boat has a huge sun top and is equipped with a back-up
motor, VHF and cell phone, depth sounder, full safety gear, and fresh-
water rinse-off. They can each hold up to 7 people. The **'Touch The
Gulf'** tour is an up-close, intimate ride along the coastline of the pristine aquatic wonderland of the Golfo Dulce, one of only four salt water
fjords in the world. The boat travels slowly along the banks of the gulf,
introducing passengers to over 50 miles of incredibly diverse coastal
land and seascapes, including mangrove swamps, reefs, sandy beaches,
and rain forest. The boat can approach very close to the shore most of
the time (the trip is timed to coincide with the best tides), and cruises
at a speed that provides both a constant breeze and enough time to
check out the flora and fauna of the coastline. During the five-hour tour
you can see dense jungle, idyllic private beach homes, secluded lodges,
tall mangrove forests, and primeval estuaries. You may spot one of four
types of monkeys, many species of birds, or huge iguanas on shore, or
dolphins, turtles, rays, massive schools of fish, or even whales out on
the water. Lunch is taken at Playa Blanca, a nice sandy beach named
after the white coral that washes up on shore. Occasional stops are
made for swimming and stretching. The entire time you will be constantly entertained with insightful knowledge of the indigenous species, the history of the area, and anecdotal stories that may get the
boat rocking with laughter (Charlie is a quit wit). Many people have
claimed this tour to be 'the most fun thing I did on the Osa'. To find out
more about these tours, and prices, call 735-5669.

HIKING AND CAMPING

The best way to do the Osa is with a guide, by far. If your budget or independent style preclude this best option, see the two areas following this section. Like I mentioned earlier, most campers head to Corcovado or Cabo Matapalo, with Carate being another attractive option (see that section). Along with Drake Bay on the other side of the Osa, these are among the best spots on the <u>planet</u> to camp in and explore. No kidding. In the town of Puerto Jiménez itself, the only place I know that openly offers campsites and facilities is Cabinas Iguana-Iguana.

PUERTO JIMENEZ

1 Cabinas Iguana Iguana
2 Cabinas & Rest. Carolina
3 Cabinas Bosque Mar
4 Cabinas Marcelina
5 La Choza de Manglar
6 Rest. Il Guardino (Jardín)
7 Cabinas Agua Luna
8 Parrot Bay Village
9 Cabinas Eilyn
10 Crocodile Bay Lodge
11 Cabinas Jimenez

12 Osa Natural
13 Pollosa
14 Cabinas The Corner
15 Osa Sportfishing/Río Nuevo
16 Aventuras Tropicales
17 Rest. Jade Mar
18 The Epicenter
F SANSA office
T Corcovado Park Office
B Bank (Banco National)
S Bus Station
O Post Office
E Emergency Clinic
G Gas Station
† Church

— N —

DOS BRAZOS
LA PALMA
RINCÓN
IAH

GOLFO DULCE

PIER

SOCCER FIELD

MANGROVES

TO PLAYA PLATANARES

TO CABO MATAPALO & CARATE

AIRSTRIP

To 16 & 17

CABO MATAPALO

The area at the southern tip of the Osa Peninsula is an incredible experience in nature set in a tropical beachside environment. Four types of monkeys, scarlet macaws, toucans, coatis, raccoons, sloths and many other tropical species abound here, and are easily observable. Pumas and jaguarundis are occasionally spotted, and the 90-foot "King Louis" waterfall is only a short hike away. Well-maintained trails lead up from the beach area through the dense rain forest on the cliffs above, and the beaches themselves with their reefs and tide pools are very clean and picturesque, putting even many postcards to shame. Beachcombing, spear fishing, kayaking, and snorkeling are all excellent, and easily accessible.

To get to this special area, take the road leaving Pto. Jiménez from the southeast for about 30 minutes. After you reach the small school on your right and the hills begin to rise again in front of you, you will re-enter a rainforest environment on both sides of the road. After you cross a wide, rocky stream at the bottom of a steep gully, you will be only about one minute from the turn-off to the beach area, where many custom homes and the following accommodations are located. The road will take a sharp turn to the right and begin climbing — the turnoff is on your LEFT at that point, right at the curve. You will see a large white concrete gate and unoccupied guard house, which is the entrance to the road that winds through the small development. The collective taxi service that departs Jiménez at 6am daily (except Sundays) will drop you off here for about $3pp on its way to Carate, passing back through to Jiménez at about 9:15am. Private taxis are also available any time for about $20 one way.

Clandestina — This casual yet very comfortable lodge above the beach is definitely a first class destination. Sixty acres of private rain forest and fruit orchards with trails, a spring-fed pool below a canopy of trees, panoramic ocean views and international gourmet cuisine will make anyone forget about the rat race real quick. Set on a mild slope on the side of a verdant secluded hill about three minutes from the beach by foot, the three story main lodge is built right up next to the rain forest, looking out over a clearing to the sparkling Golfo Dulce and

Pacific Ocean beyond the tree tops. It has a large, tiled breezy terrace for lounging, dining and listening to music. A particularly nice feature is a garden dining deck which overlooks the spring fed pool and stream, and the extensive organic garden to augment the wholesome meals. The dining deck is made with varnished local hardwoods, an open-air structure that affords a nice shaded view, with comfortable tropical furniture for lounging. The lodge grounds have three private cabins, an open air barbecue in its own rancho with a swing hammock, and two other houses for the attentive staff. The atmosphere is laid back, with guests encouraged to relax and share their experiences between outings. Sportfishing, kayaking and surfing are popular activities here. The three private cabins have teak parquet floor, high vaulted ceilings, lots of window space, and their own private hardwood decks, with spectacular ocean views. All rooms are tastefully decorated with prints, tapestries and paintings. Each cabin has its own tiled bath with hot water showers. The meals are international fare, including scrumptios organic salads, fresh baked breads and muffins, and menu items from around the world, like vegetarian masterpieces to steak and potatoes au gratin to fresh catch of the day, all with exotic homemade sauces livening up the dishes. Homemade ice cream for dessert? No problem. **Rates:** $125pp full board, $100pp low season, with discounts available for children, large groups and long term stays. Fresh, natural drinks are included, and bar items are available. Email, cellular phone and laundry services are available to the guests. Many local tours are available, including guided hikes, ocean kayaking, sport fishing, and horseback riding. Call 381-8521 or 828-2516 direct, or email at osaclandestina@racsa.co.cr. Web site: www.osaclandestina.com.

Bosque del Cabo — Shangri La in Costa Rica? It is difficult to describe the beauty of this cliffside resort, a magnificent reserve of over 550 acres with primary rainforest interspersed with bubbling creeks, and trails for every ability. The manicured tropical landscaping around the lodge, sweeping ocean views from the romantic bungalows, incredibly abundant wildlife and magical ambiance make this "Forest of the Cape" a place to remember. Set 500 feet above the blue Pacific, with private trails leading down to secluded beaches and reefs on the Pacific side of the cape, the sense of a secluded paradise is overwhelming. The main lodge, recently expanded and renovated, houses the kitchen, dining and common lounge areas. It is open at the sides and furnished tropical-style with a touch of elegance. A freshwater pool is fed by a nearby stream and kept moving by a solar pump, and you have the choice of full sun or cool shade on the large wooden deck where you can take advantage of the poolside bar service. The elevation here makes Bosque del Cabo slightly cooler and breezier than the beach down below, and virtually bug-free. The ten thatched-palm-roof bungalows are spread out along the edge of the bluff, taking advantage of the breathtaking view while affording privacy. They are all built of tropical hardwoods, have private full baths with enclosed outside showers (a nice feature in this climate), and their own decks to soak in the ocean vista. The luxury bungalows have king-sized beds and other perks, while the standards have two double beds. All have mosquito netting, though this is really not necessary here. All bungalows have lights, fans and hot water, as the lodge has both solar and hydroelectric power year-round. Recently added are two cabins and a 2-bedroom house in the botanical gardens, with their own restaurant, bar and conference center. The food is excellent in the renovated and expanded main restaurant, with a tasty variety of local and international dishes to keep your palate satisfied. Basic bar drinks are available, too. Of course, many tours are available, with an emphasis on nature hikes on the near the property. For adventure, Bosque del Cabo has their own 110-foot canopy tree platform, reached by a breathtaking flight through the forest on a 250-foot zip cable, and a high 100-meter suspension bridge. Trips to Corcovado, kayaking and fishing can all be arranged as well. **Rates:** $140pp double std. per day, $155pp double luxury, full board. Bar drinks, including beer and sodas, are extra. There are also two nice rental houses available on the property (3-day minimum, ask for rates). Green season discounts. Call 735-5443 or telefax 735-5206, or try 381-4847; or e-mail: boscabo@racsa.co.cr. Definitely call or e-mail ahead for reservations, and/or visit their web site at www.bosquedelcabo.com. Taxi service to and from their lodge is available from Pto. Jimenez in their own late model LandRover Defenders.

Lapa Ríos – Perched high atop verdant ridges overlooking the gulf over 100 meters below, this top shelf ecotourism complex, an award-winning project for ecologically sensitive development, looks down onto a densely forested valley surrounded by 1,000 acres or pristine lowland tropical rainforest. After passing through a tiled entry with a thatched palm roof, you walk by the polished reception desk and into a huge soaring *rancho* supported by massive pillars of fallen (not cut) tropical hardwood. The central focus of the main lodge building is a spiral staircase that winds three stories up to an observation deck where you can take in the spectacular 360-degree view. On the main floor the attractive Lapalapa Bar offers any number of specialty tropical drinks. The open-air dining hall has ten bamboo tables with glass tops and padded chairs, and several more tables outside on the wooden deck. At the edge of a bluff near the central *rancho* is their large sculpted pool with surrounding furnished split-level deck affording breathtaking panoramic views of the Golfo Dulce and Pacific Ocean beyond. On excellent lighted gravel pathways over wooden bridges and lined with incredibly vibrant landscaping you walk to your cabin set on the edge of the ridge. Three sides are open to the cooling breezes (fully screened, of course). They have polished hardwood floors and detailing, and private furnished decks with small gardens and outside showers (moonlight bathing *au natural*). Under a soaring thatched palm roof, a central ceiling fan keeps the air moving while sumptuous details like varnished white cane trim, bamboo lounge furniture with floral cushions, his and her reading lamps, a polished hardwood desk, a coffee table with mugs, and two queen-sized beds with box spring mattresses reassure you that you are being well taken care of. The huge bathrooms boast huge mirrors over double sinks, hot water on tap, and tiled showers with garden views that could fit a whole family. On to the food. The menus are a mix of Costa Rican, international and tropical styles, with items like tomato and black olive linguini alongside smoked tuna salad for lunch, and entrees like coconut crusted fish filet and chicken relleno offered as dinner choices. There are 13 breakfast choices, over 14 lunch choices, and a rotating dinner menu with desserts that will blow your mind. To work off your meals, there are five separate trails through the property, all with their own theme (waterfalls, birding, medicinal plants, etc.). All the standard local tours, including treks into Corcovado National Park, are offered, usually with their own guides. *Rates:* Standard high season rates are $222pp double. Low season discounts. Lodging/transportation/tour packages available (honeymoon, too). All meals and taxes included. Fluent English is spoken by the staff. Reservations required. Call 735-5130, fax 735-5179. E-mail info@laparios.com. Web site: www.laparios.com.

Encanta La Vida Lodge — This adventure-oriented lodge was one of the first places built in the Matapalo area, originally designed for the exclusive use of its owner as a private jungle dream house. It is located about a half kilometer along the Matapalo road on the right hand side, with the several unique buildings set back over 100 meters at the end of a private driveway on 8-1/2 acres of mostly rainforest. Two three-story jungle houses, a cozy private cottage, a 'honeymoon suite', a large outdoor rancho with a thatched-palm roof, and the employees' house are all tucked up against a verdant hillside of towering rainforest filled with flora and fauna of dizzying variety. Monkeys come by daily for the bananas and plantains the Costa Rican staff sets out for them, frolicking in the trees right next to the accommodations. The lush landscaping, accented by large piles of volcanic rock, is augmented by a variety of fruit trees. The fully-furnished accommodations are very comfortable and attractive, and designed to maximize your enjoyment of the environment, with wildlife observation decks, lots of varnished hardwood, and the requisite hammocks. The Casona is the main lodge house, a three-story structure of concrete and varnished hardwoods that boasts its own bar, a big viewing deck, and 3 bedrooms and two full baths. It is highlighted by mosaic tile detail and decorated with local art and indigenous artifacts. The Pole House is a fully furnished rustic structure with two bedrooms and two baths on different levels, each with its own spacious deck, and a private bar. The 'Ranchito Room' has a typical thatched palm roof, the main structure consisting of concrete and exotic hardwoods. It is backed by the jungle and has views of the property and gardens, and is conveniently connected to the second floor of the main lodge. It offers a breezy space to enjoy with a raised double bed and private bathroom. The 'Honeymoon Cabina' is actually a small bungalow. It is very spacious with about 700 sq ft and has its own dining area, large rear and front decks with hammocks and chairs, and a private bar. The large tiled bathroom has hot water. It is set apart from the other buildings and surrounded by tropical gardens. In the main lodge there are refrigerators and a stereo, as well as fans and reading lights. All electricity is provided by ecologically sensitive – and silent — solar panels. The whole property can be rented out exclusively if you have a group of 10 or more. For the fisherman among you, they can arrange both 1/2 and full-day sportfishing trips, as well as all other local tours. Surfboards and boogie boards are available at the lodge. *Rates:* $75pp standard, $85pp for the honeymoon suite. Rate includes all meals in their large open-air dining *rancho*, which are a mix of fresh fish, meats, salads, pastas, and the typical Tico fare. Sodas and beer extra. Laundry is available by the staff (tips only). Call 735-5062 or 735-5546. E-mail encantaosa@racsa.co.cr or info@encantalavida.com. Web site: www.encantalavida.com

Casa Tortuga de Oro — How about your own private house on the beach? Tim Cowman's Casa Tortuga de Oro is available for those who prefer the freedom and privacy of their own personal retreat at reasonable prices. Located right on the low cliffs overlooking Backwash Bay near Matapalo Beach, this secluded getaway for a couple, group of friends or family will help create indelible memories of tropical fun. Right in front of the spacious house is a limited access private beach and fishing spot amid beautiful lava rock formations. The surfing of Backwash Bay is literally in your front yard, while it's wide sandy beach – ideal for sunbathing – is only steps away. There are lots of tide pools to explore, and the sound of the sea always accompanies your activities. The monkeys, coatis, scarlet macaws and iguanas will be the only ones sharing your little slice of paradise. With the emerald green waters of the outer gulf coast right out the back door, the peaceful yet abundant scenery lays the foundation for a perfect vacation. The 2-story, 2 bath house is built of beautiful tropical hardwoods and concrete, with rare purple heart wood the most prevalent material. Downstairs is the spacious kitchen, furnished living room, storage room and a full bath, with a small concrete deck out back. Stairs lead up to the top floor, which is one large room surrounded by a wide deck for living and lounging. Another full, tiled bath is upstairs. There is an outside shower as well for beach rinses. The house is solar powered for those little conveniences like lights, and fully equipped for cooking and dining, with a refrigerator and plenty of dishes. Up to six can sleep comfortably on the double, single and bunk beds. The house is fully screened, and the wood is all finished and oiled to bring out its natural beauty. There is a caretaker's house at the entrance, so 100% security is guaranteed. *Rates:* $95 double per day, $30 additional for each extra adult, $20 each children 8-12, under 8 free. Low season and long-term discounts. To reserve "Golden Turtle House", call Isabelle in Pto. Jiménez at 735-5062, fax 735-5043, or e-mail osatropi@racsa.co.cr. Check out Tim's Web site at www.costarica.com/tortuga

Matapalito -- This pair of 2-1/2 story beach houses are the ultimate in privacy in a beachside jungle environment. The 5-acre property is set between Backwash Bay and Matapalo Beach in the Cabo Matapalo community, on the ocean side of the sandy road. Secondary rainforest predominates, with conscientious landscaping and the rocky shoreline itself complementing the sylvan surroundings. The two similar and uniquely designed houses and the caretaker's quarters are set at quite a distance from one another (~250 feet), so you don't see any neighbors from where you're staying, and the primary noises are of the abundant wildlife, especially monkeys and scarlet macaws. There is 280 meters of private beach frontage, so having a little cove or cliff by the sea all to yourself is guaranteed. The houses themselves are built solidly of concrete and rare sandalwood, sanded and varnished beautifully. The first floor is open on two sides, with stairs up to the upper levels and a storage room on the narrower ends. The second floor, with sandalwood floors extending out to wide covered decks on both sides of the building, is the primary living quarters. It is very spacious, fully furnished, and also open to the views and breezes on two sides. The compact and efficient kitchenette is fully equipped with everything to whip up your own gourmet meals. Solar power provides the power for lighting, fans and small appliances. The third-story loft serves as the sleeping area with 2 separate rooms, one with a double bed and the other with two single beds. All bedding and towels are provided, as well as mosquito netting if necessary. The bathrooms have hot water showers for cleaning up in comfort. Available to guests is a nice grill for cooking up the day's catch, whether it be from the sea or the store. *Rates:* $95 double, $30 each additional person up to 7 total. Maid service is included, and there are discounts for groups and long stays. VISA cards accepted. Also available through Jorge and Isabelle are many local tours, arranged through their office in Puerto Jiménez. Call 735-5062 or fax 735-5043 to book any of the above, or e-mail osatropi@racsa.co.cr.

Ojo del Mar – Nestled between secondary forest and the shores of the Sweet Gulf among rugged natural splendor, this secluded beachfront bed & breakfast is a peaceful retreat ideal for melting stress off your being. The central Casa Grande is the focus of the property, which is lush with vibrant landscaping and dotted with interesting stone, concrete and wood sculptures and pillars for lanterns. The gardens are given much love and attention, and sandy stone-lined paths take you all around the shady property. Out near the beach, across an arching wooden bridge, one finds a wide yoga platform under tall almond and coconut trees full of scarlet macaws, complete with a massage table. The beach itself adjoins a small river mouth, and tide pools form nearby. Monkeys, toucans, parrots and other wildlife are common here. Back across the bridge is a wide lawn for lounging and socializing. The atmosphere is very laid back – peaceful relaxation is the rule. The main lodge is a high *rancho*, open all around with a long central table for talking and dining. There are lots of books to peruse, and nice music that blends with the sounds of Nature. The three cabins are hidden among the thick foliage, raised bamboo and wood structures accented with driftwood and handmade furniture. One has a wide deck with a hammock, a table with bench seat, a double bed downstairs with a separate loft with a single bed. The high roof and open front keep the heat away, and the views of the gardens are very serene. Another cabin is split-level in design, and has two double beds and bamboo walls. A third cabin was being built when I visited, constructed in the same rustic tropical style. All the cabins have private open-air garden showers, and they share two bathrooms nearby, home of a family of hummingbirds. The secluded beach house has two beds, double and single, under a its own large *rancho* near the shore. Besides just de-stressing and hanging out, you can participate in invigorating daily yoga sessions, led by the co-owner/manager Nico or other visiting yoga practitioners. Nico is a holistic doctor from Germany, studied in homeopathy, osteopathy and various therapeutic massage techniques. His massage services are available to guests. The lodge can arrange local tours, such as those offered by Everyday Adventures (see this section), or bird watching and horseback riding with a local Tico guide. A full breakfast is included with your stay, and lunch or dinner is available to guests, prepared by an international cook who is reportedly quite good. *Rates*: $30-$40pp (tax included), depending on the accommodation you choose. English, German and Spanish are spoken fluently. E-mail 2-3 days ahead of time at ojodelmar@yahoo.de. Web site: www.osaviva.com/lodgedetail.php?bus_id=10.

Kapu / Rancho Almendro -- This seaside jungle retreat set just above Matapalo Beach, right where the road turns closer to the shore, is ideal for those looking for a casual, laid back atmosphere surrounded by the sights and sounds of nature. Listen to the waves crash on the sand and white rock shore just 50 meters away while you lounge in a hammock amidst a unique tropical garden. The rainforest rises behind you up the cliffs while creatively designed landscaping, organized into unique garden clusters, stimulates your retina. The tall main rancho sits towards the front of the property with a view towards the surf, while the 2-story guest house overlooks the forest farther back, the tiled wading pool beckoning just a few steps away. Various jungle trails lead out from here. Fruit trees and pineapples are abundant, and the organic garden adds a healthy touch. The main rancho houses the kitchen, 2 bedrooms, a large bathroom, outside shower, and a very spacious split-level covered lounging and dining terrace with hammocks, chairs, tables and lanterns. White cane and hardwoods are prevalent in the construction. The two guest rooms in the main lodge have louvered windows for maximum air circulation, hanging beads as doors, and closets with screened shelves and hangars. The recently renovated and remodeled private guest house out back has two large rooms on two floors, and you can see the ocean from the second story deck. The downstairs room has a full kitchen with a washer, while the upstairs has a built-in writing desk and large deck with hammock and chairs. Louvers cover three sides of the rooms, and both have private bathrooms. The outside shower next to the wading pool is surrounded by lush foliage like the one at the rancho — very nice, private and spacious. Meals at Kapu are prepared personally by John, the North American manager. His years of experience as a 'gourmet jungle cook' will be at your disposal as he whips up exotic international dishes to satisfy your palate. He often leaves the lodge early to catch dinner out at the 'Matapalo Rock', armed with a spear gun or fishing pole. You're welcome to join him. Other activities here include ping pong, chess, badminton, volleyball and surfing (boards available to rent). More involved tours can be easily arranged (Everyday Adventures is right next door), including world class kayaking. Future plans include a barbecue pit, yoga platform, and tent platforms. **Rates:** $70pp includes 3 good meals. The house can be rented for $100 per night for up to 6 people, with optional meals, or for $85pp full board. Kayaking, horseback riding, fishing trips, etc. can all be arranged. Discounts for long stays and for groups. In the USA call (310) 839-4864. E-mail kapu@earthlink.net or johnhannegan@hotmail.com. Web site: www.home.earthlink.net/~kapu.

Other Lodgings: Finca Roca Dura, Casa Bambu, El Remanso

FOOD SERVICE

Restaurant La Buena Esperanza -- Owned and managed by a German woman now living in Costa Rica, this popular tropical eatery in Carbonera, just past the school and not far from the entrance to the Matapalo area, has a wide variety of snacks and meals available for the hungry traveler. Many locals stop here for a bite or a beer, and it is the *only* regular public restaurant in the area. The big, open-air restaurant and bar are built almost exclusively of shaped concrete, surrounded by lawns, colorful shrubs, ilang-ilang, flowers, fruit trees, and tall shade trees. There are some old surfboards hung above the long concrete bar, some with very catchy maxims written on them. The paints are bright and funky, with colorwashed mauve, light green, blue and orange. There are several wooden tables besides the bar stools, and a nice corner section of large cushioned concrete sofas that extend up and over a low wall to the outside. Great for lounging. There are potted plants and some very cool lights and decorations. The food is an eclectic mix of German, Costa Rican and American styles, with a discernible focus on vegetarian dishes. Fish, chicken and occasionally beef dishes are also available. The well-known bar has the whole assortment of domestic and imported liquors, and Martina (the owner) knows how to whip up a full range of cocktails. Prices range from $3 breakfasts to lunches and dinners for $4-8. The restaurant is open daily from 9am till 10pm, with the bar often open later, especially on weekends. Fluent English and German are spoken. The two rental cabins are set far apart from the restaurant. They are basically a duplex, but share a common covered lounging area instead of a wall. They are open-air concrete rooms, painted in mod colors like the restaurant, with a table and chairs in the central terrace. There is one raised double bed in each room, and a molded concrete corner sofa with thick cushions and lots of pillows. Other furnishings include a long wooden coffee table and concrete end tables, one with a lock box. The raised double beds have mosquito netting, as the room is completely open, though each has curtains for privacy. The private open-air showers are behind the rooms, while guests use the bathrooms at the restaurant. Rooms are $20pp, which includes breakfast. There is no contact information so . . . . just go!

TOURS

Everyday Adventures, a.k.a. Psycho Tours – The inimitable Andy Pruter and his girlfriend Terry are now running their fun and off-beat adventure tours right out of Cabo Matapalo in the heart of what many people consider to be one of the most beautiful spots on the planet. They now also offer overnight accommodations in a really cool little beach house just steps from the waves. Cabo Matapalo is a premier destination for the eco-tourist, with pristine rainforest and oceanside environments full of exotic wildlife like scarlet macaws and four kinds of monkeys. Andy has been offering quality guided hikes and kayak tours in the area for over nine years, and he continues to do so with the help of Terry, perpetually armed with his indefatigable up-beat attitude and engaging, quick-witted manner. No boring trips with this guy! Climb enormous strangler figs, rappel over a 100-foot waterfall or kayak to the tip of the Osa Peninsula and off the infamous Arch where the gulf meets the open Pacific. With the discovery of a huge new Ent-like tree (named Treebeard -- the other is Cathedral), there are now two old sentinels of the forest to climb. His tours are always interesting, educational, and stimulating. He uses high-quality equip-ment for maximum safety, and has more experience than most of the local guides. Originally from the USA, Andy can help you overcome your fears and immerse yourself in what may become the most excit-ing vacation of your life. The standard tour runs $45pp, which includes lunch. The beach cabin, equipped with solar-powered fans and lights, has a double and two single beds. Its kitchen has all the utensils, a cooler, and a propane stove. The wide living room faces the beach, with the bedrooms towards the back. Shower with hot water under the full moon surrounded by lush foliage, with enough room for a small party, after returning from the beach on the private path. For more information and rates for the accommodations (which are very reasonable), access their web site at www.psychotours.com, or e-mail them at trustyourguide@yahoo.com. Phone 353-8619.

HIKING AND CAMPING

This is a great place to experience. The beaches are fantastic for swimming and snorkeling, the wildlife is abundant — especially the scarlet macaws, squirrel monkeys and coatis — and the surfing, kayaking and fishing are world class. Hiking along the coast is an option. A spectacular waterfall, named 'King Louis', is just ten minutes or so from Matapalo Beach along the road and up a short trail. Awesome tide pools can be checked out at Carbonera Beach straight down from the entrance to this area, along with thousands of trippy hermit and sand crabs.

Camping is popular with visiting surfers on a low budget at Matapalo Beach, but if riding the waves is not your thing there are plenty of secluded beachfront spots for exploring, sunbathing or whatever. IF you have a respectful and cordial attitude towards the locals, they'll let you get water from their hoses. You may be able to buy some meals, too, if you don't want to walk back to La Buena Esperanza. Three things to remember here and everywhere you camp: Respect the land, respect the locals, and *pack your trash!* Other attitudes will simply not be tolerated. Thank you.

CARATE

The end of the road. When you arrive in Carate on the far western side of the Osa Peninsula, you are truly at the frontier of this captivating land, the wildest and most remote region on the Costa Rican mainland. The natural beauty of this area is indescribable, with verdant ridges full of monkeys and scarlet macaws cascading down to a wide black sand beach with nothing but driftwood and coconut shells on it for miles on end. This is the primary entry point to Corcovado National Park, where the airstrip and the main public road end at exactly the same spot at the Río Carate. The only services are provided by a small *pulpería* — there is no town. The Carate river is a great spot for exploring gold panning possibilities and visiting gold miners a little upriver, and the fishing right off the shore is fantastic. The huge lagoon down the beach is also great for fishing (especially for snook), and has abundant wildlife including crocodiles, caimans, iguanas and lots of aquatic waterfowl. For those heading into Corcovado, the park entrance at the La Leona station is only about 45 minutes away by foot.

The cooperative taxi that departs daily from in front of the old bus station in downtown Jiménez will get you there in about two hours. It leaves at 6am sharp every day except Sunday (about $6 per person), or a regular taxi will take you out at any time (about $50 for the trip, for as many as can fit). You can also book a chartered flight from anywhere in the country. No matter how you get there, the deserted sandy beaches with tall palms full of coconuts, almond trees full of scarlet macaws, unridden waves peeling offshore almost every day of the year, and endless acres of wild jungle looming above, will all be there waiting patiently for you.

LODGINGS

Terrapin Lodge – This rustic lodge nestled in the rainforest near the coast is a very natural, peaceful destination for those looking for a quiet place to immerse themselves in the environment. The private, secluded retreat boasts 32 hectares of both primary and secondary forest, with a 20-foot waterfall a short hike up one of the streams. You reach the main lodge about 350 meters after turning off the main road into Carate, just a kilometer or so before you get to the beach, which is always accessible. Sitting at the base of a steep-sided valley cloaked in rainforest, the wood construction shines as light passing through the skylights reflects off the varnished *cara tigre* and mangrove wood. The vaulted roof with finished wood and cane ceiling covers a spacious open deck with four large tables that serves as dining, lounging and socializing area. There is a hammock in one corner of the dining rancho, and some books and field guides. A new hydroelectric system provides 110-volt power for both the main lodge and the cabins. All but one of the cabins are up on a ridge above the property's narrow valley, and most have ocean views. The cabins are designed to afford guests the (accurate) feeling of being ensconced in a remote jungle, with half walls giving way to screening up to the roof. Except for the attached private bathrooms, all the construction is of hard and semi-hard local woods, and is beautifully finished. Each cabin has a wooden deck, hammocks, a large spacious room and skylights. Several have 'monster' ocean views. You can hear the surf crashing on the shore from here, which blends with the rainforest sounds to create quite an impressive natural symphony. There are two beds in each cabin, either double or single or a combination. Just a few dozen yards from the lodge building is a deep spring-fed pool with an accompanying *ranchito* with hammocks, chairs and a table. It's very cool and breezy, a great place to escape from the heat. There are frog ponds, too, to add to the tropical orchestral composition. The food is quality Tico fare, with some American foods such as pancakes, French fries, etc. Meat, chicken, fish and pasta dishes are all standard, especially fresh catches from the nearby lagoon or surf (they throw back the crocodiles, though). English is spoken by the staff. ***Rates:*** $75pp with all meals included. A free hike to the waterfall is included, and also free kayaking both on the lagoon and in the ocean, both of which are only a few minutes' walk away. Call 735-5182 or 735-5431. E-mail BArgyle@aol.com. Web site: www.terrapinlodge.com.

The Lookout Inn — Carate's premier beachfront hotel is an exotic, romantic luxury hideaway away from the crowds. Perched on the side of a verdant cliffside between black sand beaches and vibrant primary rainforest, the B&B-style inn boasts absolutely spectacular vistas of the coast and Pacific. Terry Conroy, the North American owner/operator, takes care of you with the help of his significant other Katya Bellanero. The colorfully decorated three private luxury rooms are all on the first floor, each having its own attractive tiled bath with hot water shower. The rooms are impeccably furnished and detailed, with beautiful carved doors and colorful murals, and all have lights, fans and 110-

volt outlets, powered by a massive solar system. In addition there are two private cabins hidden in the garden, with hanging lanterns, fans, reading lamps, private decks and nice baths with hot water showers. The spacious furnished deck in front of the rooms -- where breakfast is served under wide umbrella tables -- has fantastic views out over the pool and gardens to the Pacific. The second story has the owners' room, kitchen, covered deck, and lounging room with a stereo and extensive library, which includes all the relevant books on the local creatures of the Osa. The third floor observation deck is equipped with a telescope for spotting passing whales or dolphins. Scores of scarlet macaws can be viewed daily, as well as toucans, tanagers, and other exotic bird life. All four types of monkey live in the rainforest around the hotel and up on the ridge, and many visit daily looking for bananas. There are many trails in the forest for guests to hike, including the Jurassic Trail to a private waterfall deep in the jungle, all arrived at via the new 'Stairway To Heaven', 220 wooden steps that lead to the rainforest paradise of the upper ridge and the vaious loop trails. After a hike or tour, there is not only a fresh water pool to beat the heat but a spring-fed cool tub ensconced in the foliage to relax the muscles. The tub feeds two frog ponds, one with a fountain, home of the red-eyed tree frog in season (the lodge's mascot). Both the owner/chef and his excellent cook whip up a wide variety of dishes in Italian, Oriental, Southwestern US and Costa Rican styles. They even smoke cheeses, meats and seafood. He can also accommodate vegetarians. To wash it all down, Terry makes his own wines, and offers beer, mixed drinks and store-bought wines as well. Included with your stay is free use of kayaks, a canoe, fishing equipment, boogie boards, and many indoor games. Other available activities include horseback riding, guided tours to Corcovado, guided night tours of the nearby lagoon (particularly exciting), and Zodiac boat tours for fishing, surfing, or sight-seeing. *Rates:* $89pp full board, $59pp lodging only. Discounts for children. Laundry service is available. Call or fax direct 735-5431 or call 735-5062. E-mail (best) at: terryjconroy@yahoo.com, Web site: www.lookout-inn.com.

Luna Lodge — Picture this: The sun is setting over the Pacific behind a steep forested hill down the deep river valley that drops over 800 feet below your feet as you sip on your papaya juice and listen in on the symphony of jungle sounds that bursts into your consciousness as another perfect day in the rainforest comes to a close. This is reality on the 60-acres of tropical Xanadu that is Luna Lodge, Lana Wedmore's personal dream come true. Over 30 acres of exuberant rainforest, five year-round waterfalls, 100 + fruit trees, and a healthy organic vegetable garden are some of the highlights of this hilltop resort, where Lana's passion for conservation and education helps to provide an ideal environment for engulfing yourself in the rainforest environment. Scarlet macaws nest right by the lodge, endangered animals can often be spotted on the property, and the views are spectacular. Lana offers several luxurious bungalows and optional canvas tent lodgings spread out above the main building on a slope and accessed by nice stone paths. The main lodge houses a restaurant, store, and office, all nestled together under a soaring thatched-palm roof. In front of the *ranchón* is a large semicircular view deck suspended above the Carate River valley. All of the construction utilizes beautiful tropical hardwood harvested from trees naturally fallen on the property, white cane from the rivers, and sustainably harvested palm fronds. Luna Lodge also serves as a dynamic, health-oriented retreat center with its spectacular 1600 sq. ft. yoga platform, open year-round for groups seeking secluded, inspiring environments. The unique multi-sided cabins have private decks, 2 double beds, soaring *rancho* roofs of native palm leaves, and a full private bath with open-air shower and mini-garden enclosed by a low wall for your personal exclusive enjoyment. The top-quality tent lodgings are higher up the hill near the yoga platform. Among the many available activities are a short hike to a postcard perfect private waterfall and swimming hole only 5 minutes from the lodge, horseback riding, sea kayaking, surfing, bird watching, daily yoga, massage, fishing, gold panning, and more. A hike to a secluded 40-ft. waterfall a little deeper into the property is included, and many shorter trails wind their way around the property itself. Meals are prepared fresh and naturally, with homemade breads, organic fruits and veggies, and scrumptious salads highlighting the menu. Full bar service is available. ***Rates:*** Bungalow $125pp plus tax, tent cabin $85pp plus tax, which includes three meals and one tour to the waterfalls. Full bar service available (extra). Discounts are given if you mention this book when reserving your stay. VISA and M/C accepted. The restaurant is open to hungry travelers not staying at the lodge. Call or fax direct at 380-5036 or 358-5848. E-mail lana@lunalodge.com. Web site: www.lunalodge.com.

La Leona Eco-Lodge – Over 85 acres of beachfront and primary rainforest bordering Corcovado National Park beckon the hearty ecotourist for an unforgettable stay in the bosom of Nature. The towering trunks of old-growth rain forest tumble down the ridges to meet the sandy shore at this rustic lodge beyond all roads where you are much more likely to encounter a monkey and scarlet macaw than a telephone. A Costa Rican family created this ecologically sensitive tent camp in a dreamlike setting by the beach. Their friendly, open-hearted attitude have already won over many first-time visitors who rave about both the place and the hospitality in their guest book. Why go all the way into Corcovado? All the wildlife seen in the national park can be spotted here: all four types of monkeys, coatis, peccaries, wild cats, even the elusive tapir on occasion. Scarlet macaws and capuchin monkeys are abundant in the almond trees lining the shore. Well-maintained trails lead up onto the high ridges of the property where you can catch fantastic panoramic views of the coast from deep within the jungle, and visit the massive woody custodians of the forest. The birding is incredible, too, of course. The fine grey sand beach in front of the lodge, more than a mile from the end of the road in Carate but only steps from the La Leona station at the entrance to Corcovado National Park, is perfect for sun bathing, swimming, and boogie boarding. The twelve tents currently available are staggered along the grounds on wooden platforms above the sandy soil under tall shade trees, with gardens of flowering and ornamental shrubs in between. The tent cabins share four very nice bathrooms and showers, lighted at night and kept very clean and tidy. The tents themselves are made of a thick man-made material, with screened windows that zip down, plus a thick roof above. They each have two thick single mattresses, a small private deck, and two chairs. The lodge building itself, housing the kitchen, dining and lounging areas, is a nice concrete and hardwood structure with a magnificent mural painted by a famous local artist (see the cover of this book). Solar power provides lighting at night, along with romantic lanterns and candles. The food is a mix of Costa Rican and international styles, mostly fish, chicken and pasta dishes, with excellent sauces and professional presentation. The desserts are especially good. Exciting tours are available, like nighttime shrimping runs in the rivers and treks into the park with English-speaking guides, besides the lodge's own trails. Boogie board use is free for guests. **Rates:** $60pp includes all three meals and unlimited natural juice drinks. Lodging only is $15pp. Meals available separately for non-guests. Low season and group discounts. Telefax 735-5704 or 735-5705; e-mail laleona@racsa.co.cr, Web site: www.laleonaecolodge.com

Other Lodgings: Corcovado Tent Camp, Cabinas Carate, Carate Jungle Camp

HIKING AND CAMPING

As mentioned earlier, Carate is where most people start their trek into Corcovado National Park. Corcovado is by far the most popular hiking and camping destination in the Osa, from both here and Drake Bay on the other side. However, the above lodges have extensive areas of primary rainforest to explore, and additional suggestions for more local hiking that is among the best in the world. They can arrange guided park excursions, too. Luna Lodge will serve you a healthy, delicious meal with fresh organic fruit juices to non-guests for a reasonable price, and both The Lookout Inn and La Leona Eco-Lodge offer meals, too. The Lookout Inn also offers trail maps and access to a secluded private waterfall, boogie board and kayak rentals, and all their standard guided tours to day trippers.

Camping outside of the park is, as always, available on the miles-long beach, with ample shade under the tall palms and almond trees. Luna Lodge offers meals and will allow you to pitch your tent on a secluded site on the property for a nominal charge. The lodge is farther up the road along the Carate River and up above the valley, about 30 minutes by foot (see their description). There is also beach camping out in front of The Lookout Inn, which offers use of their facilities (bathrooms, showers and fresh water) for just a few dollars per camper per day. La Leona Eco-Lodge also will provide facilities for those camping in front of their lodge for a nominal charge.

THE EASTERN GOLFO DULCE COAST

The following places of interest to the traveler are located along the eastern and southern shores of the "Sweet Gulf". This picturesque area offers the opportunity of enjoying some of the best of Costa Rica's beaches and water activities, without the crowds and touristy atmosphere of the northern part of the country. The Golfo Dulce, as mentioned earlier, is the home of an incredible variety of sea life, including dolphins, whales, flying fish, sea birds of all types, and world-class game fish. Another feature of the area is access to the Osa Peninsula across the water, though this side of the gulf has thousands of acres of its own rain forest as well, including the Golfito Wildlife Refuge and the forests above Pavones and out at Punta Banco.

GOLFITO & VICINITY

Golfito gets its name from its location: inside a miniature San Francisco-style bay or gulf, accessible by water through a narrow channel from the Golfo Dulce. Golfito is described in one major guide book as a place "for travelers who love adventures in forlorn ports." This old banana port town, strung out along the shore between the steep forested hills of the Golfito National Wildlife Refuge and the gulf, is almost like two towns in one. The northern section has the airport, the *deposito libre* for duty-free shopping (very popular among the Ticos and foreign ex-pats living here), and the hospital, with the attractively landscaped US.-style housing and other buildings of the original United Fruit Company development. The central part of town holds the town center, with its many bars and restaurants, several hotels, a few marinas, the municipal dock, and other typical port town development spreading down towards the south along the water. The one main road takes you down the entire length of the seven-kilometer town.

Golfito can be reached by sea from Puerto Jiménez and Zancudo Beach, by land through Río Claro on the IAH, and directly by air via SANSA, NaturAir or other local airlines. Tours are generally to the rain forest above the town or to beaches outside of the small gulf, and taxi boats can be hired at the municipal dock in the central part of town. TRACOPA has a bus station here, with departures leaving San José from their Alfaro terminal. You can also catch TRACOPA buses from San Isidro, Palmar, Ciudad Neily and Paso Canoas. The two daily buses from Pto. Jiménez to Ciudad Neily will drop you off at Río Claro on the IAH, and from there you can catch another Golfito-bound bus for the 23-km. trip into Golfito, which is basically at the end of the road. By the way, if you plan on staying here during the months of October, November or December, make your reservations well in advance as the town fills up with Christmas shoppers at this time, just like Paso Canoas. Transportation within Golfito is excellent, with local buses passing through every spot in town every ten to fifteen minutes or so, and taxis to anywhere within the town limits costing less than a dollar (about 60 cents in 2004). Collective taxis to and from Río Claro are available for less than a dollar per person as well, cheap and quick if you're coming from or going to the IAH — they swing by the bus stop in Río Claro calling "Golfito, Golfito!". From Pto. Jiménez and Zancudo Beach, you can also catch the Golfo Dulce Express, which runs on Tuesdays, Thursdays and Fridays during the high season. A regular ferry to Golfito leaves Pto. Jiménez every morning at 6am.

LODGINGS

Lodgings in and around Golfito basically run from low to mid-range in both pricing and quality. Below are a few of the better ones.

La Purruja Lodge — About 4 kilometers before you arrive on the Golfito waterfront from the Inter-American Highway, in the tiny town of La Purruja (also known as Kilometer 7), two signs indicate the driveway leading to the absolutely enchanting setting of this small family-run hotel owned by a Swiss man and his Tica wife. The driveway off the main road leads you through low walls of multicolored tropical bushes, over a small stream winding through a patch of rainforest, and up a small hill to the two guest buildings and owners' residence. The property is beautifully tended with expansive areas of low-cut lawns, widely spaced trees and shrubs, and backed by another small stand of rainforest housing over 100 species of birds: ". . . the best bird watching area I found in all of Costa Rica" according to a natural history consultant studying here. From the upper rooms set among the greenbelt you look out over the parking area, residence, and trees below to the meadows and rainforest on the opposite hillside. Seclusion and quiet are two of the hotel's great assets. There is even an open-air *ranchito* that catches the breezes for lounging in the shade amongst the grass and foliage. You can observe exotic birds at close range visiting the bird feeder next to the *ranchito*. If it's too hot even in the shade, there is a new swimming pool and adjacent wading pool (2004) to escape the tropical heat. The spacious rooms all have double or single beds (or both), ceiling fans, full private tiled baths, night stands, full closets, curtains over large glass windows, and lots of space. The floors are tile, as is the large porch that runs in front of the rooms. The porch has lighting, a table and several chairs. There is a pool table and darts at the owners' house available to guests. During most of the year a boat is available for tours of the Golfo Dulce and Río Coto, or transportation to other places from Golfito, as is a 4wd car. All arrangements can be made from the lodge for tours or travel, as La Purruja Lodge has a phone, fax and Internet service. Laundry is available, too. English, Swiss and German are spoken by Walter, the Swiss owner, and some English is understood by his wife Rosie and daughter Susan. A special feature of this lodge is the availability of camping. There is a fully-equipped camp site on the property, set on lush green grass under mature teak trees by a stream bed, with table, benches, sink, toilet and shower. Both camper vehicles and tents are welcomed. **Rates:** $25 double, $30 triple per night which includes a full breakfast. Camping is only $2 per vehicle or tent per night. Breakfast and dinner are available from the owners upon request. They even do barbecues sometimes. Call or fax 775-1054 for reservations. E-mail w.rosenberg@gmx.net. Web site www.purruja.com.

Esquinas Rainforest Lodge – Part of a model project sponsored by the Austrian government combining development aid, nature conservation and rainforest research, this enchanting lodge welcomes all nature lovers to partake of the pristine beauty of unspoiled lowland rainforest in a relaxing and comfortable setting. 50 acres at the end of a verdant valley surrounded by the Piedras Blancas National Park is the setting for this, the only non-profit eco-lodge in Costa Rica. Neighboring the La Gamba Biological Station, the seclusion and proximity to nature are unsurpassed. A gentle brook runs by the grounds separating the lodge property from the park, as thousands of trees and ornamental shrubs dot the wide green lawns. There are lots of toucans and other exotic bird life, and monkeys and sloths are frequently seen in the trees around the lodge. There is a small fish and caiman pond, a large spring-fed pool, and small *ranchito* right over the brook with hammocks and lounge furniture. Lighted stone and gravel paths wind around the complex, with classic little wooden bridges over the small streams. Fortunately for its guests, the lodge does not believe that to be close to nature means to subject yourself to uncomfortable lodgings. Quite the contrary. The main lodge itself is a very spacious open-air *rancho* with nice tiled floors, plenty of attractive cushioned furniture (even rockers), an extensive library with field guides, a nice bar, a dining hall with linen tablecloths, and orchids hanging around the open perimeter. The construction is rustic but all varnished with really nice bamboo and cane detailing, and beautiful mural in the dining area. There are even souvenirs, handicrafts and skin care products available. Up in the loft is a TV and VCR. The fourteen rooms are equally well finished, very nice duplexes of wood and white cane. They all have queen-sized beds plus one or more single beds, night stands, ceiling fans, stained glass overhead lamps, and tiled floors. The fully tiled bath has a stone wall shower with hot water. The private porches have padded rocking chairs and glass tables. The food here is 'Tico gourmet', with lots of local fruit and produce, some of it grown organically on the property. They feature homemade breads and jams made from fruit grown on the property, and have their own chickens for eggs. Lunch and dinner are multi-course affairs. Guests can choose between self-guided walks of half an hour or so, or more strenuous guided hikes of several hours, most of which lead through untouched primary rainforest. Other tours available include horseback riding to the coast, waterfall treks, boat trips on the Golfo Dulce, kayaking, mountain biking, and even night tours. *Rates:* $125 single, $95pp double, $75pp triple. Low season, group, and child discounts. Many lodging/tour packages available. Call or fax 775-0901. E-mail esquinas@racsa.co.cr. Web site: www.esquinaslodge.com

Cabinas Buena Vista – This small business a few kilometers outside of Golfito on the main road is surprising in its deceptive feeling of seclusion. Partially hidden behind a thick hedge, the four guest rooms and owners' house are backed by a steep verdant ridge full of vibrant forest and running water. The property is actually over 50 acres, and has its own waterfall. The stream that runs down from the mountain is guided into an attractive rock cascade that drops into a swimming pool behind the rooms, surrounded by lush foliage for cooling off in peace as birds such as toucans and parrots cry in the canopy. Endangered squirrel monkeys come by on occasion as well, sometimes right into the house during certain fruit seasons. The continuous flow from the pool is channeled down to a fish pond near the entrance, where frogs live in their own little paradise, with lily pads to jump on and coy swimming below. The rest of the area around the buildings is nicely landscaped with ornamental shrubs, flowers, and green lawns. The rooms are lined up behind a nice white tiled corridor and concrete planter full of colorful shrubs and flowers. There are three spacious standard rooms, all with tiled floors and a fully tiled private bath with hot water showers. Amenities include a double and single bed, TV with cable and remote control on a mobile stand, both drawers and shelving, and a ceiling fan with a light under a porous ceiling for heat reduction. The big glass windows are screened, so at night you can open them to let the cool mountain breezes flow through your room. The corner room has two connected bedrooms, one with a big double bed and headboard plus a separate single bed with a shelf headboard and drawers. The other bedroom has another single bed with a shelf headboard, plus bunk beds. There is a huge window in the master bedroom and two large windows in the second bedroom. Continental breakfast is available to guests at $5 per couple. The German owner Peter (fluent in English as well) and his Tica wife Grace operate four of their own tours. One goes to the Río Esquinas (Piedras Blancas) National Park, which is an extension of Corcovado; another takes you to the Wilson Botanical Gardens; a third is a boat tour on the Golfo Dulce; and the fourth is a trip to Grace's parents' *finca*. You can also hike up to their own waterfall on the property. They will help arrange other tours if necessary. *Rates*: $25 double, $5 for the breakfast. $10 for a third person with breakfast. Phone 775-2065. E-mail petergolfito@hotmail.com. Web site: www.1costaricalink.com/eng/hotels/hotp/hotp-buenavista.htm.

Hotel El Gran Ceibo — At the extreme southern end of town, just as you come to the waterfront on the road into Golfito from Río Claro, this hotel with bilingual management stands on the south side of the road by a huge old ceibo tree. The local Golfito bus that travels up and down the length of the town every 20 minutes or so turns around right in front of their restaurant, the Restaurante El Ceibito. The hotel buildings, standing only about 100 ft. from the waterfront, house 27 clean and modern rooms, while a neighboring pasture abounds with bird life. The best feature of this hotel are its two swimming pools and associated deck and snack bar. The pool area was renovated recently with new showers, bathrooms, and tiling for the snack bar. The attractive office at the entrance has a TV, reception desk and lounge furniture. There are many exotic plants and trees around the buildings and walkways. Adjacent to the hotel is a marsh area where caimans breed, and monkeys come for breakfast nearly every day while toucans visit the papaya trees. All the hotel rooms have a porch or balcony out front, either in front of a greenbelt close to the pool or facing the courtyard in the two-story building, with lounge chairs to relax in. The rooms have floors of ceramic Spanish tile, are very clean and cool, and the furniture is beautifully finished with varnish. A nice touch to the décor is added by original local paintings on the walls. There are rooms with air condi-tioning, cable TV, and hot water available, as well as more basic rooms, all with private tiled baths. Comfort and economy is the emphasis here. The poolside coffee shop serves sodas and refreshments, as well as breakfasts. All the water comes from an artesian spring nearby. There is secure parking and 24-hour security. The restaurant serves a variety of dishes, both typical Tico and American fare, in a nice atmo-sphere near the water. Full bar service is also available. There is a phone & fax available for messages at the hotel. English is spoken by the bilingual Tica manager, Janet, who personally tends to the guests needs during their stay. All the local tours can be arranged by the manager. *Rates:* Prices are per <u>room</u>, and do not include taxes. They vary from $18 to $40 depending on the type of room and number of beds. Laundry service is available. Most major credit cards accepted. Call 775-0403 for reservations, fax 775-2303, or e-mail info@elgranceibo.com. Web site: www.elgranceibo.com.

Las Gaviotas Hotel — This hotel on the quiet side of town is owned and managed by a Costa Rican couple. It is located just north of the last Golfito bus stop, right between the road and gulf, with attrac-tive lawns and young coconut palms lining the sidewalk out front. This is a modern, international-style, fully self-contained hotel, with its own restaurant, bar, souvenir shop, and private pier, all well secluded from the road with high walls keeping the world outside at bay. The grounds are professionally landscaped and maintained with exotic plants and trees. The concrete and hardwood buildings housing the bungalows and rooms are off to one side, while the open-air restaurant and fully stocked sunken bar are right by the water. The restaurant has teak and rosewood tables and accents over an old-fashioned tile floor, with nice touches and hanging plants. Meals are served from 6am - 10:30pm, featuring Costa Rican and International fare that runs the gamut from Tico-style *casados* to fancy seafood dishes, with imported French, German, Spanish and South American wines to soothe the palate. Beer, liquors and cocktails are naturally available as well from the bar. Prices range from less than $6 for breakfast to a high of about $10 for a full dinner plate. The reception office and souvenir shop are right next to the restaurant, as well as an enclosed, air-conditioned phone room for either local or international calls. The large pool, wading pool and expansive furnished deck are just around the corner, also on the waterfront, with tables and chairs under cover nearby if the sun gets too much for you. On weekends there are poolside barbeque buffets, all-you-can-eat. There are three options in accommodations. The standard rooms are classic mid-range U.S. hotel style, all concrete, tile and wood, with either a double and single bed or 3 singles, all having real mattresses. The full tiled baths with hot-water showers are spacious and fully equipped (some with hair driers), and each room has a nightstand, desk, closet, ceiling fan and a small private tiled porch looking past the landscaped greenbelt out to the gulf. Very well-done and comfortable. The deluxe rooms have small refrigerators. ALL rooms have telephones, air conditioning and cable TV. The 2-bedroom, 2-bath bungalows are fully-furnished retreats with full kitchens, lots of space, and even bathtubs (a very rare luxury in these parts). *Rates:* $42 single or double standard, $48 triple; $54 deluxe room; and $84 for the bungalows. All major credit cards (and AmX) accepted. Fluent English is spoken. Fax, laundry, and tours are available. Las Gaviotas can arrange sportfishing excursions leaving from their own pier (see C-Tales in the TOURS section). Call 775-0062 or fax 775-0544 direct. E-mail lasgaviotas@hotmail.com or avicente@racsa.co.cr. Web site: www.resortlasgaviotas.com and www.sportfishing.co.cr.

Hotel Golfito – This centrally located commercial complex next to the gas station, with a hotel, internet café and souvenir store, was completely renovated in 2003 by the Costa Rican family that owns it. The hotel is on the second floor of the building, which stretches between the main road and the water of the gulf. You climb up metal stairs into the lobby and reception area, which has a nice lounge with couches, potted plants a television, and soft drinks for sale. After getting your key from a receptionist behind a glass partition, you walk down a tiled corridor with rooms on both sides. At the end of the corridor is a small balcony with chairs overlooking the municipal docks and the gulf and hills beyond. The rooms are nice and modern, with fans, night stands, luggage tables, tiled floors and large tiled showers in the private baths. The double and single beds have real spring mattresses with nice linen and bedspreads. The rooms with air conditioning have real hot water showers (not the 'suicide' type) and more space to move around. The internet café (**Internet Golfito On Line**) and souvenir and gift shop (**Artesanias**) are on the first floor, right in front of the paved parking lot. The internet has 10 very fast, modern computers, some with headsets and web cams. It's fully air conditioned for comfort, and there are games on the computers. The also offer the following services: Fax, printing, scanning, computer parts and supplies, cold drinks, and a nice bathroom. The place is tiled, clean, spacious, and cool. English is spoken by the staff. They build and manage web sites, too. Internet hours are 8am to 9pm daily. The souvenir shop next door has an incredible variety of items to check out, all while getting out of the heat in the air conditioned store. They have tons of stuff, from candles to chimes, bowls to balms, post cards to paintings. Hats, T-shirts, banana paper, pipes, macadamia nuts, chocolate covered coffee, handcrafted cutting boards, ceramic dolls, purses, painted masks, necklaces, key chains and mirrors can be found here. You can find something for everyone here – maybe even yourself. Hours are 8am to 4pm daily. Rates: Hotel rates are rock bottom (one of the best deals around) at $10 double standard, $14 double and $21 triple for the rooms with air conditioning. Phones: 775-0047 for the hotel, 775-2424 internet, and 775-1274 for the store. E-mail gol@bozape.com. Web site: gol.bozape.com.

Hotel Sierra Fishing Lodge — This modern hotel has recreated itself into a premier fishing lodge. Similar in style to a Red Lion or Holiday Inn, and appropriately located right next to the Golfito airport and not far from the gulf, Hotel Sierra has all the amenities that befit a full-service hotel. Situated on the ring road around the free port on the northern side of town, this 72-room hotel is by far the largest and most contemporary in the region. The property covers approximately 16 acres, though the buildings occupy only about 2 acres, with the Golfito Wildlife Refuge serving as a backdrop. As you enter there is a large parking lot and drive-up check-in area. The large reception area with couches, TV and potted plants has a real front desk with computerized reservation and billing. There are two pools surrounded by spacious lounge areas and some decorative flora, all enclosed within a courtyard created by two of the three 2-story guest buildings, and a nice turtle pond. The restaurant and bar area is a massive open space under an enormous vaulted ceiling. There are both tables with comfortable chairs and dining/lounging nooks with padded seating. The tables have double linen tablecloths, and the chairs are padded over shiny varnished hardwood. There is a long padded bar with a big TV, a huge chandelier, and lots of ceiling fans. Upstairs there is a separate lounge area with its own bar where the hotel hosts karaoke on most weekends. The menu covers a full range of typical Costa Rican and international dishes like spaghetti, chicken curry, steaks, and palm heart salad, and there is a good variety of classic tropical cocktails available at the bar.   Breakfast is a nice buffet with lots of fresh fruit and both American and international standards. Prices range from $2 to $8. The rooms are something right out of a good chain hotel from the States or Europe, with tiled floors and baths, air conditioning, a ceiling fan with lights, matching double beds, night stands with lamp, dresser drawers, cable TV with remote, a table with chairs, and a double set of light and dark curtains. The beds have mattresses and box springs, the large shower has a bench for seated bathing (or whatever), and there is hot water. They even supply an ice bucket, water pitcher and glasses! Basic English is spoken, so you can ask where to find the ice machines. Phone, fax and Internet services are available. The lodge specializes in sport fishing, having 10 boats of their own, from a 17-ft. Pro Line Sport to 6 26-ft. Pursuits. All the boats have the latest equipment, and all have heads. *Rates:* $45 single, $50 double. Low season and group discounts. VISA is accepted. Besides the sport fishing, the hotel can arrange many other local tours, including car rental. Call 775-0666 or 233-0997. E-mail hotelsierra@racsa.co.cr. Reservations are necessary on weekends. For more info (especially about the fishing) check out their web site at www.hotelsierra.com.

Golfo Dulce Lodge -- The Swiss owned and operated Golfo Dulce Lodge is surrounded by the undisturbed primary lowland rainforest of the newly established Piedras Blancas National Park, set right on the shore of the Golfo Dulce. Its own property encompasses over 300 hectares (750 acres) and was bought primarily to conserve the existing virgin rainforest habitat, and to set up a small place for nature and animal lovers to experience the magnificent world of an virtually untouched environment far from the maddening crowds. There is a network of established trails on the property for hiking, and an easily accessible observation platform on the edge of the primary rainforest for excellent birding or nature studies. More than 340 different species of birds have been observed and confirmed by specialists on the lodge property or in the adjacent park. The little complex of buildings is informally grouped together as a tiny village in a large landscaped garden right on the edge of the tropical rainforest near the beach. The vibrant garden has lots of tropical plants such as orchids, heliconias, and a variety of palm trees. The pineapple plants and fruit trees are regularly visited by groups of coatimundis, and monkeys cavort nearby in the trees. They have a spring-fed pool if the calm gulf isn't your style, and a little *ranchito* with hammocks to seriously chill out. The restaurant has a nice bamboo ceiling and a large, covered rooftop observation deck furnished with comfortable bamboo sofas and decorated with tropical plants. On the first floor guests enjoy European meals with local flavor and ingredients. There is also a cozy full-service bar. The pure, healthy water for the lodge is taken from a fresh spring high up in the rain forest. Many of the fruits and vegetables are grown on the property. Electricity is generated by a hydroelectric plant, with minimal ecological impact.

The standard rooms are housed in a concrete structure with comfortable bamboo furniture, ceiling fans, and a large, private veranda with a rocking chair to enjoy the surroundings. The five detached, spacious wooden bungalows serve as the deluxe accommodations, with all the features of the rooms plus a full private bath. The bungalows have much larger rooms and verandas. For activities, the platform can be reached within 20 minutes on a self-guided tour with an educational description of the most interesting plants growing along the path. They also have sea kayaks, light fishing tackle, and snorkeling equipment for guests. Proper tours offered here include various rain forest hikes with an English and German speaking guide, boat tours to mangrove swamps or snorkeling beaches, and trips to nearby botanical gardens. *Rates*: $105pp full board, plus a $20 boat transfer fee from Golfito (round trip). Low season and group discounts. Laundry service available. Phone 821-5398. E-mail info@golfodulcelodge.com. Web site: www.golfodulcelodge.com.

Other Lodgings: There are literally dozens of other small *cabinas* scattered around the central area and near the *depósito libre* in Golfito. Additional lodgings located outside of Golfito on the gulf, accessible only by boat, are Dolphin Quest, Caña Blanca, Sailfish Ranch, and Rainbow Adventures. Plus see below for the Playa Cacao area.

- - - - - - - - - - - - - -

PLAYA CACAO

This small waterfront area, across the bay from town and accessible by either road or boat (usually the latter), is a nice area to get away from it all yet still be just minutes away from everything. It reminds me a bit of a tropical Catalina Island setting, though much less developed, of course. There isn't much here as far as infrastructure, but I see that as a good thing. The most important things are here: forest with monkeys and birds, calm waters for swimming or boating, lawns and beaches for tanning or reading, and a very quiet, relaxed atmosphere. If you want to get there by car, you can drive around on the long road that begins behind the free port. If you go in the winter, however, be careful – it's a pretty rough road. You need great clearance and 4-wheel drive is recommended. Hiking or biking out is a nice option. Going by boat is much, much quicker and easier. Any taxi boat can get you there, but don't pay too much! Daytime rates are around $2.30pp round trip for two people. No matter how you get there, it should be worth the trip. See below for lodgings and dining options.

Cabinas Playa Cacao -- This charming little set of rustic bungalows on the bay are a great place to get away from town, yet be only
a few minutes away from all the conveniences. There are nice views of
Golfito, the wildlife refuge and the mountains across the water — especially at night — and the complex is backed by a nice patch of forest
where many monkeys, parrots, toucans, etc. can be seen. The landscaping utilizes colorful flora, and lighted concrete paths lead to the
rooms. You arrive at their own private dock, which is a nice place to
sunbathe, or try some fishing or diving at high tide. The little rancho
above the shore has hammocks, tables and chairs for guests, plus a
full kitchen where guests can cook their own meals. There are three
private bungalows on each side of the central path, nice roundish structures of part concrete, part cut wood and part bamboo, all having a
thatched palm roof. Classic. The big cane window shutter on one side
swings back, revealing a indoor-outdoor varnished wooden counter.
There are curtains on the several screened windows, and even around
the beds for more privacy. The double and singel beds themselves
have nice spring mattresses, and each bungalow is furnished with a
table and chairs as well. There is shelving for luggage, and a full private
bath. The bathrooms are really nice, with excellent stone and tile work
finishes. They even have decorative bamboo roofs over them. The
white stucco walls and red tile of the main room add nicely to the décor,
and the ceiling and floor fans keep things cool. Three of the bungalows
have their own kitchenettes. Food service is provided by the best cook
you can imagine – yourself! You don't have to do the shopping, though,
as the manager will take your order and have it brought out from town.
If you don't like that particular cook, you can dine down the beach at
the local restaurant (see next section). For activities, the place has
kayaks, a rowboat, and even an inflatable boat for lounging on the bay,
all free to guests. They even have waterskis, a unique set of equipment
in the southern zone. All the local tours can be arranged, as they have
a phone. ***Rates***: $35 double, $10 additional person. Laundry service
available. Call 382-1593 or 221-1169, fax 256-4850. E-mail
isabel@racsa.co.cr.

Siete Mares Bar y Restaurante --The Seven Seas Restaurant
and Bar is located on Playa Cacao just a hundred meters or so from
Cabinas Playa Cacao. The classic seaside restaurant is set well back
from the water behind a wide greenbelt, though they have some tables
under almond trees near the sea wall in the open for seaside dining or
drinking. The spacious open-air dining room has three sections. There
is a long terrace that wraps around to cover two sides. Inside there are

many additional tables, more protected from the elements. To one side of the restaurant are several concrete patio tables with umbrellas for enjoying the sun and breezes. You can see the nice bay view from anywhere, though, as the land is flat here and raised above ocean level. There is also seating on stools around the wide bar, complete with a polished hardwood counter. A powerful stereo and DirecTV provide entertainment, and there is a dart board and throwing area as well. Ceiling fans augment the natural breezes to keep things cool. The food, both typical Costa Rican fare and some 'fast food' items, is presented on a menu in both English and Spanish. English is spoken fluently here, too, as a North American woman and her bilingual husband are part of the family of owners. The food here is a bit better than most Tico-run restaurants, and definitely the best on Cocoa Beach. They have many appetizers or snacks to choose from, including five different dishes served with their delicious, locally famous *patacones* (twice fried green plantains – they're great). Fast food includes burgers and fries, and hot dogs. They have palm heart salad and several types of ceviches. For main courses, there are fish platters, fresh shrimp, steaks, and rice dishes. Full bar service, including a full cocktail menu, is available to quench your thirst. Prices are very reasonable, ranging from $3 – $5 for most plates. They also have a small store where you can pick up beachwear and supplies. Restaurant hours are from 10am till 6pm weekdays except Thursdays (closed), and 10am till 8pm on weekends. Breakfast can be served, but by prior arrangement only. Available for rent at the restaurant are kayaks and pedal-type paddle boats (hard to find in the southern zone). The same owners here run **Barrakuda Boat Tours**, which operates aquatic tours all over the Golfo Dulce. Options include trips to Puerto Jiménez, Zancudo Beach, and Casa Orquidea Botanical Gardens. A tour of Golfito's coastline (mangroves, isolated beaches, etc.) is offered, and a more extensive ring tour of the entire Golfo Dulce. Inshore fishing for snook, roosterfish, snapper and tuna is available at low rates. For more information on either the restaurant or tours, call 824-5058 or 825-7424. Ask for Logan or Sara.

TOURS AND OTHER SERVICES

C-Tales – This professional sportfishing charter business is operated out of Las Gaviotas Hotel on the south end of Golfito. Pacific sailfish, marlin, yellow fin tuna, dorado & other sport fish can be sought offshore, and inshore fishing has an abundance of snapper, roosterfish, grouper, snook & more. C-Tales charter guides use bait & switch techniques by trolling artificial baits. Conventional tackle is provided, though fly fishermen need to bring their own. They practice catch and release for big game sailfish & marlin. The option of bringing home dorado, tuna, snapper, and other big fish for cooking up back at port is up to the fishermen. They are members in good standing with the IGFA & other billfish foundations. The captain & mates speak English, and all have many years experience fishing the waters of the Pacific coast of Central America & Golfito. The captain, Chuck Tilton, is USCG licensed & certified. C-Tales utilizes a USCG equipped 1999 30' Island Hopper. This sport fishing vessel is rigged for tournament class deep-sea fishing. The equipment includes a fighting chair, transom door for your large marlin & tuna catch, outriggers, live well, the latest electronics, a full cabin and head, very good cover from the sun and a large open air salon. Their fishing tackle includes famous brand names like Penn International and Shimano (both heavy & light). Call 775-0062 or fax 775-0544. In the US call (561) 335-9425. E-mail ctilton2@bellsouth.net. Web site: www.c-tales.com

Transportes Marítimos Maricruz y Conejo – Located right on the waterfront between the central part of town (Pueblo Civil) and the big wharf towards the free port, this boat taxi and tour service owned by a Tico couple operates a total of *twelve* launches. The sizes range from little outboard motorboats for quick trips over to Playa Cacao, to massive covered tour boats with big engines for collective trips to Zancudo Beach. There are boats that seat two, four, eight, twelve or even thirty-five people (12 meters long with built-in seats). Trips include destinations such as Puerto Jiménez, Zancudo Beach, Punta Encanto, Playa Azul, Casa Orquidea, and the lodges out on the Golfo Dulce. They have a variety of tours on offer, including inshore fishing (only $15 an hour), mangrove swamps, snorkeling on coral reefs, and sunset turtle and dophin cruises. If independence is your thing, they rent kayaks, or small boats wth oars for only $6 to $10 for the whole day (depending on the size). You can park right next to their little hut by the boats, which is directly across the street from the huge black and white port markers on the ridge facing the mouth of the bay. To get there, head north from the gas station along the main road. You'll come to them about 700 meters (1/2 mile) after Samoa del Sur, just before the Hotel El Cerro. In case you're in need, they sell phone cards, too. If you can't find them, call 775-2329.

HIKING AND CAMPING

In Golfito the only serious hiking to be found is within the National Wildlife Refuge, though the road to Playa Cacao can be interesting, too.   If you go on your own to the park, there are several routes, the main one being up the road to the Las Torres radio tower, about 5 km. above the town. The road entrance is about 2 km. south of central Golfito across from the soccer field in the Pueblo Civil. Another route is via a steep trail across from the Samoa del Sur hotel and restaurant. The road that goes past the Free Zone on the northern end of town goes through the reserve all the way to near where Esquinas Rainforest Lodge is located.

The only camping area I found suitable is at La Purruja Lodge, which is absolutely ideal. Forget the beaches, since there aren't any. Playa Cacao has a beach, but it's not suitable for camping. You can't camp in the wildlife refuge, either. The Osa is the place to be for campers, though Pavones and especially Punta Banco are nice, too.

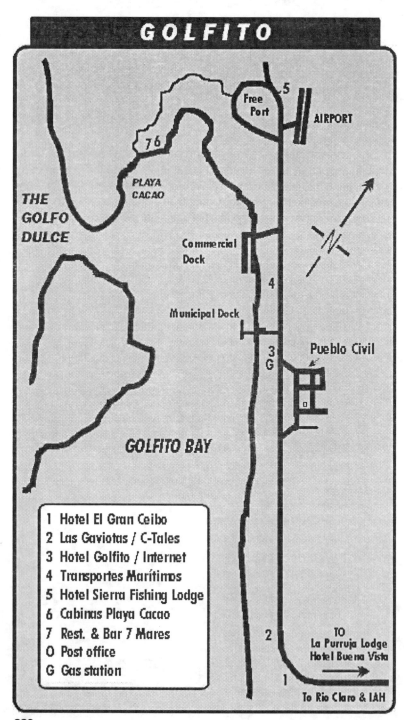

GOLFITO

THE
GOLFO
DULCE

Free Port

5

AIRPORT

7 6

PLAYA
CACAO

Commercial
Dock

4

Municipal Dock

3
G

Pueblo Civil

GOLFITO BAY

1 Hotel El Gran Ceibo
2 Las Gaviotas / C-Tales
3 Hotel Golfito / Internet
4 Transportes Marítimos
5 Hotel Sierra Fishing Lodge
6 Cabinas Playa Cacao
7 Rest. & Bar 7 Mares
O Post office
G Gas station

2

TO
La Purruja Lodge
Hotel Buena Vista

1

To Rio Claro & IAH

ZANCUDO BEACH

This lazy beachside community is stretched out along six kilometers of classic tropical coastline south of Golfito on the Golfo Dulce. The one main sandy road runs along the beach for the entire length of the area, only about 150 meters of land separating it from the shores of the gulf. The large private lots are little colorful slices of paradise, with tall coconut palms, almond trees, and dozens of other types of trees providing shade and fruit for the very attractively built homes and businesses. The beach here has the hard-to-get "Blue Flag" rating from the government, meaning it is kept more or less clean of trash, has many garbage cans, signs to warn and educate visitors, recourses for safety and policing, etc. The Río Sabalo opens up to the gulf about halfway through the area, making the eastern half of Zancudo a peninsula, meeting here with the Río Coto. Mangrove swamps dominate the waters on the river side of the isthmus, and makes boat transportation easy with several docks on the calm estuary. There is a little bit of rain forest reserve in some areas on the southern side of town, and the fishing is absolutely world class, with something like 50 world records held at one time or another by one fishing lodge alone here (see below). There are also several prime beach breaks for those seeking good, uncrowded waves. The atmosphere is very easy going, and the foreign expats, both North American and European, dominate the local scene. Remarkably, this beach and its laid-back town is yet to be fully discovered by foreign tourists, especially North Americans, though it has long been a popular place among the Ticos to weekend and vacation. Most foreign travelers, especially surfers, head directly to Pavones. Unbeknownst to them, Zancudo is a cut above in regards to lodgings and food — especially the latter, with among the best selection of good to great restaurants in the southern zone — and has much more space and more easy-going vibes. For surfers, the waves here are probably one of the best un-kept secrets in Costa Rica. Great surf, no crowds.

One can get to Zancudo by water or land, a boat being the quickest, most comfortable, and most scenic mode of arrival. There is a public collective taxi boat which leaves Golfito at the municipal dock every day at noon, and a boat shuttle service – the Golfo Dulce Express — operating between Zancudo, Golfito and Puerto Jiménez during the high season which can get you to Zancudo from either Golfito or Pto. Jiménez quickly and safely. Tickets for the Express to Zancudo must be purchased ahead of time at either Samoa del Sur in Golfito or Café Net El Sol in Pto. Jiménez. It runs on Tuesdays, Thursdays and Fridays. A bus leaves Golfito every day around 2-3 pm (and 10am during high season) from the street in front of the municipal dock. There is also a bus leaving Ciudad Neily at 1:30pm for the Zancudo/Pavones area, all buses stopping in Conte for transfers. There is a sign marking the turnoff for Zancudo (to the right) 2 kilometers after you take the turnoff from Conte towards the coast. Once you get to Zancudo Beach, all the places below are located either right on or just across the road from the beach, so access to everything that Zancudo has to offer is readily available to all. Beach bikes were made for this type of place.

Socially, there are a few things happening here. There are two discos that host dances on weekends primarily during the high season, one on each side of town. There is a monthly open-air market where indigenous goods are sold, on the beach behind El Coquito. Naturally, there are several bars to drink and hang out at (see below for a couple of them).

LODGINGS

Zancudo Beach Club– This private beachfront hideaway has been developed into a reasonably priced top-notch retreat for all. Since waves break here almost every day of the year, this particular spot is ideal for surfers, but anybody in love with the sea, sand and sun will like it here, especially the open-air second-story bar and restaurant. The property is right on the beach and very close to a small river mouth about 4 km. south of the center of town (the first public lodgings on the left as you drive in), comprising about 25 acres at the very edge of local development — very quiet and secluded. The area around the buildings is well landscaped with small tropical plants and shrubs, and concrete walkways help you through the sandy soil. They have around 15 acres of their own virgin forest across the road for jungle hikes, with a mangrove swamp, two types of monkeys, many bird species, and other flora and fauna. The two-story restaurant is beautifully finished with hardwood floors, bar and furniture, and has a great view of the waves and gulf. Gary and Debbie, the owners, have multitudes of cassettes and CD's to accompany your drinking and dining. Entrees include locally famous steaks, Mexican fajitas, fresh fish filets, curry shrimp, pastas, chicken, salads, rice dishes, and other Tico and international dishes, all dinners being multi-course and priced reasonably for the high quality at from $6-12. Breakfast is great, too. The open and attractive bar has beer, wine and national and international liquors, and cocktails of almost any type. Special weekly events include their very popular pizza night – made fresh in their wood-fired brick oven – and Tuesday night movie nights, when they set up their DVD player with a projector and surround sound and offer a bar & grille menu – plus pop-corn, of course – and show blockbuster Hollywood films. The attractive cabins are raised above the sand with their own large decks for sunset viewing. They all have private tiled baths with decorative palms, two fans, three beds, and hammocks. Louvers, nightstands, reading lamps, tables and chairs, solar hot water, refrigerators, microwaves and coffee makers make these cabins the most complete for the independent traveler in the area. A new option here is a very spacious and private villa, fully furnished and set on the second floor of a concrete and hard-wood building with its own tiled porch looking right out to the ocean. It has sliding glass windows, a hot water shower, a small fridge and mi-crowave, and is very handsomely finished and decorated. *Rates:* Cab-ins are $60/day double, while the suite goes for $75/day for up to 3 people. Weekly, monthly and low season discounts available. Laun-dry, transportation, phone, fax, and internet available, and local tours (see their popular horseback tour in the TOURS section). Call 776-0087, fax 776-0052, or e-mail zbc@costarica.net. Web site: www.zancudobeachclub.com.

Cabinas, Restaurante y Bar Tranquilo— Just a few meters towards town from Zancudo Beach Club, this Tica-run business offers very comfortable rooms and an attractive bar and restaurant at afford-able prices. The property runs from the road through forest and man-groves to the estuary behind, though the two buildings are located right off the road. The main two-story structure houses the restaurant and kitchen below and four rooms above, with a separate adjacent building of one story with two more rooms and the shared bathroom facilities. The restaurant serves all three meal starting at around 5:30am. The service is friendly and personal. Fish, shrimp, rice and beans, meats, spaghetti, and home-made wheat bread are among the selections on the Spanish/English menu. Beer, wine and basic mixed drinks are available. The decor is very attractive, with varnished hardwood furniture and detailing mixed with varnished mangrove roots partially covering the three open walls of the restaurant. All the rooms here have a table, chair and shelving, and the rooms upstairs share a large deck with a big table and chairs for looking out over the road to the gulf, along with hammocks for really serious relaxing. The two rooms in the adjacent building are larger and have both a double and single bed each. Laundry is available, as is a telefax. English is understood. A nice Toyota Hi-Lux pick-up is available for transport to anywhere in the area, including Pavones and Punta Banco. They will take you to Golfito, too, by land, or basically anywhere you want to go. *Rates:* $10 double. Call 776-0131, or fax 776-0143.

Latitude 8 Lodge— This comfortable and laid back beachside lodge offers fully equipped luxury cabins on the sand. The immaculately-cared-for property lies between the road and shore, tall coconut palms and almond trees providing lots of shade. Ornamental bushes and flowering plants add color to the grounds as you walk across concrete stepping stones, and many types of fruit trees such as lemon, lime, almond, orange, and cashew give the property a garden-like atmosphere. Just a few steps away through a 'coconut belt' is the wide sandy beach where surfing, boogie boarding and shell collecting among the driftwood is all excellent. Added in 2003 is a spacious dining rancho with full kitchen facilities and a barbecue, available to guests for either self-cooking or for pre-arranged dinners served by the owners. The lodge was taken over by the current North American owners in 2001, and they completely renovated the buildings and grounds. In the two main cabins they added air conditioning, tiled shower rooms, and totally refurbished the beautiful original hardwoods. The cabins are set several feet above the sand on stilts, steps leading up to a private furnished hardwood porch with a view over the grounds towards the sea. Walking through the front door you enter a large living space under open beam vaulted ceilings of polished hardwood. The big double bed has a nice firm mattress and twin reading lights overhead, and there are two twin beds as well in one of the cabins. A central ceiling fan with lights keeps the air moving, and if you open the wooden shutters of the large screened windows the breezes can pass right through. If you want to get even cooler, you can adjust the optional air conditioning to suit yourself. The full kitchenette has long hardwood counters, a large refrigerator, a stove, and even a coffee maker and bottled water dispenser. There is a walk-in closet area with plenty of shelving, and the bathroom is exceptional: a huge mirror, a hand painted decorative sink, and nice thick towels. Hot water is piped in to both the sink and shower. The shower itself has its own big room attached to the cabin. You go down tiled steps into a private shower area big enough for an entire family to bathe in. It's excellent. The overall effect is one of warmth and comfort. They also have a very clean cabin without air conditioning that is a bit smaller than the others, and this one is available for rent as well. *Rates:* $50 double standard, or $60 double with A/C. $45 double for the smaller cabin. $10 each additional person. Weekly, monthly and green season rates. Laundry and phone service available. Surfboards are available to rent, and boogie board use is free. Transportation and tours are also available. They offer their own sportfishing charters as well, with Penn International fishing equipment or similar top quality fishing tackle provided, as well as a US Coast Guard licensed captain. Phone 776-0168, e-mail don@8-above-the-equator.com, web site: www.latitude8lodge.com

Cabinas, Bar and Restaurant Sol y Mar — This full service resort, with its own public restaurant and bar, is set up to be your tropical beachside "home away from home". The North American owners have established their 10-year-old getaway as one of the major centers of local and tourist activities in the area. The property stretches along 180 meters of beach front. The rental house, private cabins, and bar/restaurant face the ocean, just 50 meters from the shoreline. The Sol y Mar's volleyball court plays host to weekly horseshoe tournaments and frequent volleyball games. The restaurant and bar are a popular hangout for tourists and local expatriates alike. The buildings are ensconced in a tropical garden setting, with tall coconut palms shading the open-air bar and restaurant with its tall thatched-palm roof. Free equipment is provided to guests for paddle ball, volleyball, boogie boarding, badminton, and horseshoes. Both DirecTV and a book exchange program are available for those with more sedentary pursuits in mind. The restaurant serves all three meals from 7am-9pm, with a *real* breakfast menu, including French toast, home fries, and an omelet you can create yourself! They bake their own breads and desserts, and offer nightly specials. They have a wide variety of standard international dishes of excellent quality, including Mexican food, and an extensive sandwich menu. There is a trained chef working in the kitchen at night who prepares lots of 'surf and turf' dishes and other international specialties, focused mainly on seafood. The popular bar is open till late every night. They also have a nice little store set up next to the restaurant with beach clothes, t-shirts, colorful imported Asian clothes (like sarongs), handicrafts, local guide books and other sundry items. There are five private, screened cabins and a 3-story house at Sol y

Mar. Each cabin is equipped with electricity, fans, hot water showers, and screened windows with shutters. All of the cabins have been renovated with private verandas, tiled floors, unique showers, and translucent bathroom roofs. The fully equipped, secluded and fully screened split-level house can sleep up to about 4 people comfortably, and is designed for both maximum air flow and privacy between the four levels and two decks. Laundry and phone services are available. **Rates:** The cabins go for $20-39 per night double. Third person is $5. Discounts for weekly and monthly rentals. Lower rates apply from June-December. The house rents monthly for $700. Camp sites and facilities are available for only $2pp per night, or $3pp if you need a tent. VISA is accepted for the rooms and reservations only, at a small charge. Call 776-0014 for reservations. E-mail solymar@zancudo.com. Web site: www.zancudo.com.

Cabinas Los Cocos — Just a hundred meters or so down the road towards central Zancudo you come to Susan and Andrew Robertson's cabins by the sea. The large property has 200 meters of coconut grove beach front, and is set up to accommodate those seeking a tranquil and comfortable base from which to explore the area's many natural treasures. The landscaping is exquisitely organized, and walkways lined with coconut shells guide you through palms, bamboo, flowers and almond trees as you stroll to your private cabin. The owners' house is a good distance from the cabins, ensuring privacy. Only a few steps away is the long sandy beach, lined with coconut and almond trees for miles in either direction. Each cabin is its own self-contained unit, with a fully-equipped kitchen and private bath. They are all screened and have mosquito netting as well. Two of the cabins are quaintly restored banana company houses. They were moved to Zancudo from Golfito and reconstructed to give the ambiance of bygone days. They each have a double and single bed. The other cabins are built more in the typical style, with a palm frond roof and gorgeous hardwood floors, one sleeping up to four with a double bed downstairs and a second double bed in a spacious loft, the other newer one more cozy with just one double bed. They all have tables and chairs on a private deck with a hammock, and desk space for those who'd still like to get a little work done. Laundry service is available. Susan and Andrew also have two boats for their other business, Zancudo Boat Tours. They not only provide transportation to and from Golfito and Puerto Jiménez, but also offer a wide range of tours of the area. There are also kayaks for rent right on the property, for either ocean or river journeys. They offer a special kayak trip where they will drive you to the insertion point on a shady, exotic river channel. After 2 hours on the river, they'll pick you up and take you back to your room. See the TOURS section for more details on the variety of tours they offer. **Rates:** The 'banana' cabins are $55/night, while the 'rancho' cabins are $60/night, both plus tax. Green season rates (June-November) are 20% lower. Weekly rates subtract 10%. Contact info: 776-0012 telefax; e-mail loscocos@racsa.co.cr or loscocos@loscocos.com. Web site: www.loscocos.com.

Cabinas BM -- This collection of rooms and cabins right on the beach near central Zancudo is a great place to rent out for beach party weekends, which many do, or for independent travelers that like to cook for themselves and have their own private space while they explore the area. There is a nice white wooden fence along the road with its own little roof, and a wide entry gate. There is plenty of parking between the buildings on either side of the driveway/parking lot. There are three one-story structures on the left, and a two-story rental on the right, next to the owners' house. The first rental is a 2-bedroom *casita*, built of concrete and fiberboard with varnished wood trim. It has two fully enclosed bedrooms, one with bunk beds and the other with a double bed (ideal for a family), both with ceiling fans. The fully equipped kitchen has a refrigerator/freezer, gas stove, coffee maker, and rice cooker. The private bath has tiled floors and a hot-water shower with sliding glass doors. Next to this there is a studio *rancho* cabin with a double bed and two singles. The closest rental to the beach is another little house, with a wide patio out front with a padded couch and chair, plus a table with chairs. The full kitchen opens up on the beach side like a bar to serve people on the side patio. The largest rental across from these is a fully furnished two-story house, with a kitchen, bathroom and outside covered patio downstairs, and a spacious sleeping room and balcony upstairs. This house also a small private room downstairs with one double bed and a private bath. The downstairs patio has a large TV for guests, and the balcony has a great view of the beach. Also available to guests of any of the rentals is a common open-air *rancho* with a thatched palm roof, set near the shore with hammocks and concrete patio furniture. If you'd rather camp out, they rent huge tents with 7-foot ceilings that fit up to eight people, and there are separate bath facilities for these people and day trippers to share. They have a portable barbecue grill available to guests wanting to cook outside. Every rental has its own television with remote control, so you won't miss any soap operas or soccer games. **Rates**: Per unit rates are $20 for the small studio, $35 for any of the one-story *casitas*, and $47 for the two-story house. Group rates available for renting the whole place. Bring your own food and toys. Phone 776-0045.

Roy's Zancudo Lodge – With over 50 world records held at one time or another by guests of this famous beachside lodge, one can't go wrong here if fishing is on your itinerary. Over the last 20 years Roy Ventura and his wife Dunia have fine-tuned their luxury accommodations to maximize the comfort of their guests. The 12 rooms and 4 bungalows are surrounded by professionally landscaped grounds right by the shore. The large pool has exceptional tile work both inside and out on the spacious deck, with a covered Jacuzzi tub to boot. There is a manicured green lawn with patio furniture under tall almond trees and coconut palms, and the bananas and bird feeders attract many exotic species. From the open-air bar and restaurant, with beautifully finished hardwoods and double linen tablecloths, one can gaze across the lush grounds to the open gulf beyond. The rooms are housed in an independent two-story building behind a colorful garden. Each air-conditioned room is equipped with two queen sized beds with box springs and thick mattresses, a large TV with remote control, reading lights, a couch, a writing desk, dresser drawers with a huge mirror, a dressing *room* with a full-length mirror and a big closet, an exquisitely tiled full bath with built-in hair drier and a large beveled mirror (hot water showers, of course), and a mini-refrigerator full of drinks. There is even a telephone. They are without doubt some of the nicest rooms in the southern zone. The four private bungalows are equally well furnished and finished, with additional features like a kitchenette with breakfast bar, a living room, and a wide private wooden deck with bench seats. Extra amenities include vaulted hardwood ceilings and polished hardwood floors. They are well separated from both the restaurant and the standard rooms. The breakfast here is buffet style, lunch is usually taken on the boats, and dinner is an extravagant buffet, with two types of vegetables, salads, pastas, meats, chicken, seafood, and dessert. The head cook has many years of experience in North American and European cooking styles. Examples of lunch and dinner courses are filet mignon, tenderloin brochette, chicken cordon bleu, and of course daily seafood dishes like seared tuna, grilled mahi-mahi, etc., etc. Food *and bar* service is all you can eat and drink, and they can mix up almost anything you can throw at them – 95% of their guests are fishermen. Standard services include daily laundry and internet. English is spoken fluently by the staff. If you'd like to do something besides fish, other tours can be arranged. **Rates**: $115pp for lodging and meals only (open bar included). 3-day all-inclusive fishing packages start at $2,295pp double occupancy. The fleet is made up of fully equipped 25-ft. center console boats with 115hp four-stroke engines, and top quality deep sea tackle. Lighter fly tackle provided by request. Phone toll-free USA 877-529-

6980, 776-0008 in Costa Rica. E-mail fishroys@racsa.co.cr. Web site: www.royszancudolodge.com.

Other Lodgings: Arena Alta Sportfishing (see TOURS section), Macondo Hotel and Restaurant (see below), Palmera de Oro, Coloso Del Mar, Cabinas Sussy, Cabinas Tío Froilan, Cabinas Río Mar, Cabinas Los Ranchitos.

FOOD SERVICE

La Puerta Negra – Alberto, from Genoa in northern Italy, brings his culinary skills to the southern zone in the form of a small Italian open-air restaurant nestled behind a two-story house off the road on the beach side of Zancudo. Across from Ricardo's pulpería you can sample exceptional Italian fare in a relaxed, secluded atmosphere. Appetizers of fried calamari or bruschetta start you off before the distinctive flavors of northern Italy are presented in the main courses with sauces such as armando, pomodoro, and puttanesca among the choices for your pasta dishes. Every night there are blackboard specials, usually seafood, one of which (the jumbo shrimp) both impressed me and filled me up. He uses as many of his own garden-fresh herbs as possible. There are six different types of pizza, and Alberto will prepare your custom pizza order with a smile. Each pizza is prepared fresh to order. The pizza is classic Italian thin crust, with the special mozzarela-like cheese made by a local Tico family, much better than the store-bought cheeses. Every meal is served with a crispy green salad and homemade bread, with extra virgin olive oil and wine vinegar right on your table, Italian style. Cloth napkins and bread baskets with linen cloths add a classy touch to the atmosphere, and there is always good music to dine by. There is a decent wine list -- including imported Italian wines -- to choose from to help you digest the rich meals. He offers the classic Italian dessert Tiramisu, and rich espresso coffee drinks to perk you up if the wine slows you down too much. The professional, friendly service by the owner helps you calm your nerves after a hectic day of vacationing, and if that's not enough Alberto has four guitars for impromptu jam sessions (he loves it). Enjoy! Prices for standard dishes go from $6-7, with specials running up to $15 or so. Open 6pm to 10pm every day but Monday. English, Italian and Spanish all spoken fluently. Check out his pizza nights. Basic bar service is available, including beers and some hard liquor. Phone 776-0181.

Macondo Italian Restaurant and Hotel — This very attractive, well-established Italian restaurant, boasts two second-story dining decks in a large building set far back from the road, and a friendly Italian chef to serve you there. Up among the trees you can sample home-made pastas, a wide variety of sauces, and fresh breads right out of their own brick oven. Table seating is on covered hardwood balconies, with twisting varnished mangrove roots decorating the balustrade. Italian, English, German and Spanish are all spoken, so no worries about getting your order mixed up. Light music accompanies your meal, which can be preceded by homemade antipasto, garlic bread, salad, or bruschetta (Italian toast with toppings). Daniele, the owner and chef, makes most of his own cheese and sausage, too, just to ensure the quality of their pizzas which they usually make once a week (ask which night). They'll deliver, too. The ample portions of the rich main courses and home-made desserts will leave you satisfied as you digest your meal while sipping on a cappuccino (they have their own espresso machine). The prices are very reasonable, among the lowest of the formal restaurants in town. Almost all the main courses go for only $4-5 each, including the fish filet and beef tenderloin platters. Most appetizers are a very affordable $1-2. Restaurant hours are 12pm-3pm and 5:30pm-9:30pm. There are also several spacious rooms available for overnight guests, very nice mid-priced rooms near the center of town. Besides the excellent restaurant on the second floor, they also have a wonderful 10-meter L-shaped pool with a tiled terrace for lounging, surrounded by palm trees and tall foliage, and furnished with lounge chairs, a bathroom and a shower. There are four rooms downstairs and two upstairs, all with private baths with hot water showers (gas heated), and two with acir conditioning. The upstairs rooms are surrounded by an expanded hardwood deck, while the downstairs rooms boast a wide, covered patio out front, both facing the pool. The downstairs rooms have beautifully tiled floors and baths, powerful ceiling fans that you can adjust from your bed, hardwood bed frames with headboards and varnished hardwood nightstands, a writing table, a full armoire, and glass windows that swing open. All the rooms have big double and/or queen beds with firm box springs mattresses, and nice linen bedding with thick terrycloth towels for the bathrooms. The upstairs lounge next to the restaurant has a TV, VCR, and a nice stereo, all available to guests. Rates run from $35 double. Call direct 776-0157.

Soda & Cabinas Katherine – This little business owned by "Memo" and Nuvia about 300 meters south of the public dock offers classic Tico food and inexpensive lodgings. The beef, pork, and chicken dishes are complemented by lots of fresh seafood brought in by the locals. The cook learned to . . . well, cook, at a local resort run by North Americans, and so has a bit more talent than the average Costa

Rican, and knows foreign tastes. Spaghettis, nachos and shrimp platters are the specialties, with ceviches and *casados* available as well. The prices are naturally on the low end, from $1.50 to $4.00 generally, with jumbo shrimp topping the expense chart at around $9. Open from 6am-8pm daily, take-out is available. The *soda* is in a small ranchito with thatched-palm roof right on the main road. Classic. The rooms for rent are basic in style with upgrades: ceiling fans, tiled showers, and curtained glass windows. They installed air conditioning in 2004, and planned to have televisions in every room. Nothing special in construction or design — made of concrete block, with patios, ceilings and private baths — except for DirecTV in every room. The two duplexes are set well off the road, and the owners have a private canal leading to the river in the back. Room rates are $23 double with A/C, negotiable in low season and for groups and longer stays. Memo also has a motorboat for hire, offering water taxi service, fishing trips, and local tours. The inshore fishing gives you the chance to hook up snook, snapper, barracuda, rooster fish, and several other exciting species at a fraction of the cost of the more professional outfits in the area. He can taxi you to Golfito, Puerto Jimenez, or anywhere in the gulf you'd like to go. Call 776-0124.

Other Dining Options: Zancudo Beach Club, Restaurante Tranquilo, Coloso del Mar, Cabinas Sol y Mar, El Sushi Bar at Arena Alta, Estero Mar, Mar y Sol, and a few other small eateries concentrated in the central part of town, plus one on the south side next to the *minimercado*.

TOURS AND OTHER SERVICES

Although still basically undiscovered by international surfers -- they all just go to Pavones -- there are some really good waves here. If the lodge you are staying at doesn't have any, and you don't have your own, surfboards can be rented at the Tres Amigos mini-mart at the extreme southern end of town. A local surfer has a little eatery next door, too, so you can probably get some details about the breaks, etc. For regular tour operators, please keep reading.

Arena Alta Sportfishing — The Golfo Dulce and its surrounding waters are the premier fishing grounds in all of Costa Rica. Great offshore fishing is found within a 45 minute cruise. Inshore and river fishing are within a stones throw of the Arena Alta dock. Fish aboard fast 28 ft. Magee Anglers, fully rigged, with tournament grade tackle, state-of-the-art electronics and operated by bilingual captains and mates.

These center-consoled fishing machines are powered by twin Johnson 130 hp outboards and all have enclosed marine heads on board. Their engines are no more than four years old and are routinely serviced by an on site-mechanic to ensure that they are always in top shape and running strong. There is also a back up boat at dock at all times to guarantee that they can provide our guests with uninterrupted fishing excursions. The on-board electronics are state of the art and include GPS, fish finder (to 3,000 feet!), rear-facing transducer, depth finder, and radios to enable the captains to communicate and locate schools more readily. They only use Penn International II rods and reels. Arena Alta is the only sportfishing company specializing in multiday excursions to Quepos, CR and Hannibal's Bank, Panama, fishing where none have gone before. They guarantee that you will catch fish during the months December through May. If you don't hook a Sailfish on a charter of three days or more, you can return for the same package next year for *free*. Their standard packages include airport transfers, one night of lodging in San Jose, round trip airfare San Jose-Golfito, transfers from Golfito to Zancudo, lodging in Zancudo, all meals, all beverages at camp, boat, captain, mate, bait, lunch and beverages on boat, fishing licenses, and all taxes. For anglers taking a day off from fishing and non-fishing guests, Alta Arena provides plenty of additional outdoor activity. Additional tours offered directly by them are water skiing, snorkeling, dolphin watching tours, surf trips to Pavones, and horseback riding. They can also arrange many other local tours, like jungle treks and visits to botanical gardens on the gulf. Call 776-0115, fax 776-0117 or email info@costaricasailfish.com for rates and/or more info. Best to check out their web site at www.costaricasailfish.com to get a better visual idea of what they offer.

Raedar's Marina, owned and operated by Arena Alta Sportfishing, is a full service marina located on the Rio Coto Colorado in central Playa Zancudo. It is the only dock-side gas reseller in the Golfo Dulce. They offer slip and moorage rentals at reasonable rates. In recognition of the fact that 90% of the visitors to Zancudo arrive by boat, and may have need of local ground transportation, Raedar's marina also rents electric golf carts. These provide quiet, eco-friendly transportation in a beach village setting. You can also rent beach bikes (also perfect for this environment), kayaks, boogie boards and snorkeling gear. Book any number of tours here, even your lodgings if you're not staying at Arena Alta. Just a few steps from the pier you can find both restaurant service and accommodations, described below. There is even a gift shop with things like cigars, souvenirs, local handicrafts, flyfishing flies, kites, beach stuff, etc. The internet café provides rapid, state-of-the-art online access.

El Sushi Bar is the only one of it's kind in southern Costa Rica. It recently had a beautiful new ceramic and mosaic tile floor installed by a local artist, with a mermaid and fish plus a terra cotta border pattern. Very nice. The restaurant opens from 5:00am to 10:00am serving breakfast to Arena Alta fishing clients, and opens to the general public from 11:30am to 9:00pm for lunch and dinner. True to the name, they specialize in sushi. An "Island Oasis" frozen drink preparation machine highlights the bar to keep glasses brimming with Margaritas, and they have real draft beer. Local Tico fare is also available at reasonable prices. The specialties are both typical and 'Latin sushi', but many other meals are available like fresh seafood (naturally) and pasta dishes. The menu changes with what's available, and they do unusual events like Friday fondue nights. A big satellite TV and great stereo help maintain the festive atmosphere. The open-air space is highlighted by excellent murals on the supporting columns, polished rustic hardwood furniture and beams, and a lofty thatched palm roof.

Arena Alta's accommodations are luxury private rooms and bungalows surrounded by lush, well-crafted landscaping. A miniature putting green was planned near the rooms. They are located off to one side of the office and restaurant, and built solidly of concrete to keep the cool air in and the noise out. The spacious rooms have a queen sized bed plus two doubles, night stands, and a writing table. The large glass windows are mirrored on the outside to provide both coolness and privacy. The rooms have good air conditioning as well. The fully tiled baths have hot water on tap, and nice sliding glass doors on the shower. There is a common concrete porch out front for the three rooms to share, complete with lounge furniture. The detailing of varnished hardwoods adds a touch of tropical class. The deluxe bungalow s are set apart from the rooms, and have a high roof plus a ceiling to minimize the internal temperature, along with air conditioning. The two queen sized 4-poster beds are unique in the area, and the private covered patio out back looking out to the local soccer field is nice. The bungalows are fully furnished, plus have a ceiling fan with lights, a refrigerator, a coffee maker, and even one of them has a big TV with DirecTV satellite service. Rates are $60 nightly for the rooms, $80 for the bungalows. English, German and Spanish are spoken fluently. 5% discount if you mention this book when reserving your stay. Call 776-0115, fax 776-0117 or email info@costaricasailfish.com for reservations.

Beach Club Horseback Tour – This adventurous morning tour run by Zancudo Beach Club takes you from the verdant local countryside through the towering jungle and onto the wide sandy beaches of the Zancudo area. After an early morning coffee service you are taken to the Beach Club's private ranch where you'll saddle up on one of the dozen horses bought specifically for these tours. All level of riders can be accommodated, and the owner herself accompanies you on the trip. The tour takes you up onto high ridges with fantastic panoramic views and down into valleys teeming with wildlife. Monkeys, coatis, and an incredible variety of birds (including many rare species) can be spotted along the way. After finally descending to the beach for open-ended frolicking in the sand, you return at a comfortable pace to the ranch. Upon your return to Zancudo Beach Club, you are served a full breakfast in their upstairs dining room overlooking the gulf. The tour begins at 6:00am and returns to the club at 10:30. Cost is $50 per person, which includes all transportation and food service. Debbie, the North American co-owner of Zancudo Beach Club, usually leads the tours herself. For more information call 776-0087.

Zancudo Boat Tours – Operated out of Cabinas Los Cocos, Susan and Andrew offer several local tours that represent some of the amazing variety of activities that one can enjoy in the Golfo Dulce area. They have two of their own boats, as well as six sea kayaks. The more popular tours include a Río Coto River tour which takes you up a tranquil river and estuary bordered by virgin jungle and myriad wildlife, including crocodiles and monkeys. For the kayak tour, they will take you with their boat to a gorgeous shaded and canopied canal, where you can paddle silently by primeval scenes that haven't changed for eons. Or you can simply take the kayaks out on your own on the placid Golfo Dulce and explore the coastline at your leisure. A very colorful tour is offered to the Casa Orquideas Botanical Garden. For twenty years the owners, a couple from North America, have been landscaping, collecting, and cultivating scores of plants and trees from all over the tropical world. Zancudo Boat Tours will take you to their garden and on their tour of the ornamental and agricultural gardens. Both to and from Casa Orquidea – located across the gulf – you can see dolphins (and sometimes whales) playing in the warm waters. Snorkeling on a brain coral reef can be combined with this tour as well. Basic water transport to and from Golfito, Puerto Jiménez, and other points around the Sweet Gulf can also be arranged. Water taxi rates are $12.50pp from Golfito to Zancudo Beach, with a 2-person minimum; Pto. Jiménez to Zancudo costs $15pp, with a 3-person minimum. Call 776-0012 or check out their web site for current rates and bookings. E-mail loscocos@racsa.co.cr or loscocos@loscocos.com. Web site: www.loscocos.com.

Other tour options: See the lodgings section, as some places offer their own tours (like sport fishing).

HIKING AND CAMPING

Hiking — well, there isn't much, really, unless you consider beachcombing as falling into that category. There is good biking along the road, but really nothing else outside of the bit of forest at the southern end of town, which is probably your best bet (see above under Zancudo Beach Club). A scenic and vigorous hike is possible from here to the town of Pilón, which connects with the road to Pavones. It's about two hours south along the curving beach, so if you're headed that way and don't feel like getting on a bus at 5am (when the local bus departs for Golfito and Ciudad Neily), this is a great option. I've done it myself. The bus into Pavones passes Pilón at about 11:45am. Low tide is best. For more adventurous options, check the tours section above.

Camping you can do on the beach, but the only place I found offering facilities to campers is Sol y Mar (a great spot, especially for their restaurant and bar). I'm sure another place along the beach would take your dollars for using their facilities, but nobody else advertises it. On the extreme south side of the Zancudo strip, La Jungla Bar offers free access and camping on the beach in front of their property -- with the hope you visit them, of course. I'm sure if you ate and/or drank there, they would let you take a shower and fill up your bottles. Realistically speaking, camping is better in Pavones, with Punta Banco being the best for both camping and independent hiking along this stretch of coastline.

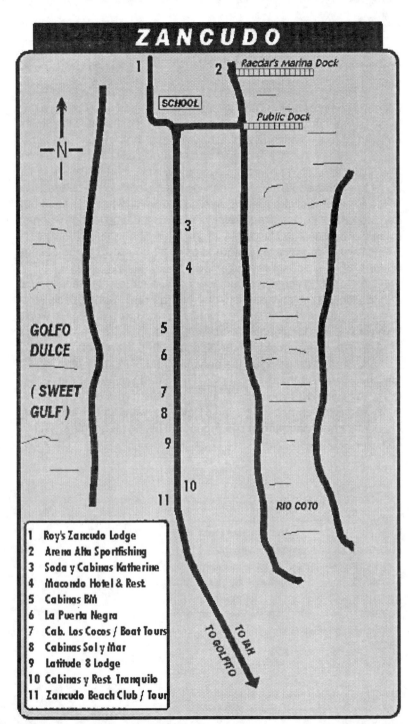

ZANCUDO

Raedar's Marina Dock

SCHOOL

Public Dock

N

GOLFO
DULCE

(SWEET
GULF)

RÍO COTO

TO IAH
TO GOLFITO

1 Roy's Zancudo Lodge
2 Arena Alta Sportfishing
3 Soda y Cabinas Katherine
4 Macondo Hotel & Rest.
5 Cabinas BM
6 La Puerta Negra
7 Cab. Los Cocos / Boat Tours
8 Cabinas Sol y Mar
9 Latitude 8 Lodge
10 Cabinas y Rest. Tranquilo
11 Zancudo Beach Club / Tour

PAVONES AND VICINITY

This small community on the southwestern frontier of Costa Rica, officially known as Río Claro de Pavones, is not just a place to ride one of the longest waves in the world, but also a little-known getaway for those with more subdued and relaxing activities in mind. This area is just as safe and hospitable to tourists as any other part of Costa Rica, if not more so in some regards, and offers much potential for visitors of all predilections. Ride the local rhythms and all will flow well.

The scenery here is spectacular. The coastal hills slide steeply down to wide sandy beaches and rocky tide pools, where large snook and other tasty game fish can be caught right from shore, while the rain forest life gets up close and personal in this sparsely populated area. There are even some scarlet macaws here now, as the area is getting repopulated -- excellent!

The road to get here branches off 2 kilometers west of Conte (there is a sign), and the same buses that take you to Zancudo Beach can bring you to the center of Pavones. The bus in leaves Golfito from the parking lot of the municipal pier at 10am and 2 or 3pm daily (If you take the later bus in, get off where the road T's to the left by the beach and walk straight about 200 yards to the soccer field area. The first daily bus will take you right to the soccer field). Taxi boats can also get you there from Golfito or Pto. Jiménez. The early bus out leaves from Banco at 5:00am daily, passing through Pavones about 1/2-hour later (you have to catch it on the main road). The midday bus out leaves at 12:30 from central Pavones by the soccer field.

Important note: If you're going to stay in the Pavones / Pta. Banco area for long, make sure to bring both cash and gas (if you have a car). At the time this was written, nobody in this area accepted credit cards or travelers checks. Cash is the rule. You don't want to get stuck here without it.

LODGINGS

Vista Dulce -- This small set of B&B-style lodgings is set high above the surf on the very edge of the town, but within easy walking distance of all facilities, including Nature's (the waves). Built by North Americans with quality materials, there are two contiguous rooms in a duplex next to the private driveway, and a one-bedroom house up higher on the side of the hill. The grounds are very nicely landscaped, with lots of mature shrubs and flowering bushes, like ginger and heliconias. There are also lots of fruit trees like papaya and banana, plus pineapple in the garden. At the upper end of the property, up a long set of steps lined with nice ornamentals, sits the Lookout Deck, a small *ranchito* platform built on posts where one can enjoy the fantastic 'sweet view' of the sunsets over the gulf and Osa Peninsula. The house has an open tiled terrace for dining, lounging, etc., with a fully equipped kitchen. The bedroom and tiled bath is located towards the back of the house, with the hill backing the whole structure. The views over the town and out to the gulf are excellent, and it is very breezy and relaxing. The duplex is divided into the 'Surf Bunks' and the 'Rainforest Suite'. The former has two sets of bunk beds, one twin and one double. It is equipped with surfboard racks, and has a private bath with hot water shower. The Rainforest Suite has queen and twin beds and its own private bath. Both rooms have fans and security storage, as does the house. With house rental comes the use of a washer and drier. All construction is of concrete and local finished and varnished hardwoods, with nice features like arched windows and fully tiled and polished floors. **Rates**: $30 double, $15 per extra person per night. An optional breakfast is a possibility here, prepared by one of your bilingual hosts. Phone 381-4063, 838-7294, or 827-4868. E-mail pavoneslocal@racsa.co.cr. Web site: www.vistadulce-pavones.com.

Mira Olas -- These secluded cabins above the town offer private accommodations with kitchens close to a river with crystalline swimming holes, only a short walk to the waves of Pavones. Eleven acres of lushly landscaped and planted grounds are tucked away at the end of a private road. There are hundreds of fruit trees, whose produce is available to guests, a lots of flowering shrubs and bushes, amid wide grassy lawns that climb the hill up to thick forest where three types of monkeys, sloths, anteaters, coatis, and exotic birds can be observed. The views are fantastic across the gulf and over to the Osa Peninsula. Blue morpho butterflies can be seen daily, especially in the mornings – they love the fallen fruit. There is a semi-private trail that goes along the river to the main surf break (the surfing owners use this often). Water comes from their own pure spring up the mountain. There is one two-story rustic cabin for rent, and a deluxe cabin on the other side of the owners' house, both very secluded and partially hidden by thick foliage. The rustic cabin has two floors, the first having the covered outside shower, bathroom, entry and storage room. The upstairs has one bedroom and a spacious living room, which has a single bed for an extra guest. The construction is all wood, with round beams and a loft ceiling. There is shelving, a fan, curtains, and woven grass mats on the hardwood floor. Furnishings include a large wooden table and single bed, while the kitchenette has a sink, small fridge, and gas stove. The bedroom has a double bed and shuttered windows, which open to nice views of the lush surroundings. The deluxe cabin is a very nice open-air one-story affair propped up on stilts on a higher part of the property. A concrete path leads up from the parking area. You walk by the outside shower under the cabin, then on to the entrance on one side. The main room opens out to the private covered deck with a nice view of the gulf, and there is a separate loft up a ladder with two single beds. The main bedroom, with a double bed, table and nice chairs, can be screened off for privacy. The tiled bathroom has a large shower, big mirror and pedestal sink. This cabin also has a fully equipped kitchen, located next to the living room area. The deluxe cabin is nicely finished with varnished hardwoods. Rates: $25 double for the rustic cabin, $35 double for the deluxe cabin. Weekly and monthly rates available. Kids under 12 free. Taxes included. The owners Paul and Lily can arrange many area tours, including a trek to the Conte-Burica Indian Reservation. Phone 393-7742. E-mail miraolas@hotmail.com. Web site: www.miraolas.com.

Hotel Maureen — Located right across the road from the cantina and soccer field in the central area, set back from the road with wide lawns and tropical shrubs, these rooms are well located for all activities. They are arguably the closest decent rooms to the waves (not counting the cantina, which I don't really recommend), and have a great view from one side. The flowers, plants and trees in front of and to the side of the second-story cabinas add nice colors to the small group of buildings owned by a local Tico family, which includes a small store, surf and gift shop, and wholesome eatery (see food section). Basic meals are available in the restaurant next to the *pulpería* downstairs from the hotel rooms, where typical Tico food can be had. A very short walk takes you to the world-famous 'lefts' of Pavones, and to the local watering hole on the shore. If you need a new surfboard, a balsa-board surf 'factory' was scheduled to be opened in 2005 next to the hotel. As far as the rooms go, all the 5-by-3-meter rooms are finished in the beautiful Christopher Columbus (*cristobal*) wood. They are pretty spacious for budget accommodations. They have wooden racks for surfboards (or whatever) and thick, firm mattresses in most rooms. Most of the beds are bunk beds, with some single beds as well. There are four shared full baths for a total of six rooms, and two large sinks. Several of the rooms have their own deck facing the beach, which are both secure and private. Parking is on site, and laundry service is available. The rooms fit up to four people. *Rates:* $7pp. Discounts for groups or long stays. Special package rates for lodging and meals. Travelers checks are accepted. Alexis can arrange the use of a 15-ft. boat with a 40hp outboard for $20 per person for fishing, surfing or touring.

Cabinas Willy Willis -- This newer set of rooms, set back from the road across the street from the soccer field, are conveniently located for all activities, just a few steps from the waves, cantina, eateries, and bus stop. There is a well-stocked store at the entrance to the 4-plex, owned by the same people. The four rooms are lined up next to each other behind a private parking area with grass and ornamental plants like red ginger. There is a wide tiled, covered patio in front of the rooms with a table and some chairs for relaxing. Between the rooms and the store there is a big tiled concrete table, and some chimes and hanging carved fish for decorations. The rooms are very secure, with barred windows and good locks. The construction is solid concrete block, with tiled floors and showers. They are spacious, with louvered glass windows to reduce any outside noise, and curtains for privacy. They have double and single beds with wood headboards. All the rooms have both air conditioning and a fan for maximum comfort, very rare in these parts, especially at these room rates. The store has all the basics: cold drinks, vegetables, fruits, bread, and all cooking staples. Other items like pots and pans, skin and beauty supplies and batteries can be bought here, as well as candy, snack foods and bathroom supplies. Good security is provided for rental cars. The owner can arrange boat tours around the gulf, including boat taxi service to the waves at Cabo Matapalo and Punta Burica. Fishing trips can be arranged as well at around $100 a trip for several people. *Rates*: $20pp. Low season discounts. Phone 770-8221 (public phone at restaurant).

Cabinas Carol — 50 meters up from the beach road past the soccer field, set apart amid tall shade trees and stone-lined paths, yet less than two minutes' walk from the shore, this set of lodgings offers both convenience and quietude with plenty of space to move around.

There are two huge mango trees on the property, which is fully landscaped with lots of hibiscus, heliconias, palms, and other ornamental and flowering plants. Besides the mangos, there are orange, avocado and banana trees. Tucked away on its large lot near the end of the short road up from the beach area, the Kiwi (New Zealand) owner Carol has created a casual and comfortable environment for both surfers and non-surfers alike. The main guest building sits on one side of the property with its back to a wide greenbelt. The open-air kitchen and dining area are just 20 yards away, and there is ample parking space in the grass and gravel yard. There are several hammocks hung under large shade trees next to the rooms, and the atmosphere is very relaxing. An outside shower rinses the sand off. The two downstairs rooms in the original guest lodgings have all tiled floors and a tiled porch and bench out front. A unique feature is a large round window in the front wall and a whole wall of screening on one side — lots of air circulation. Double curtains of floral patterns and white lace maintain your privacy. Shelving is built in for clothes and such, and there is lots of space to move around. The oversized private baths are open in the back to a private rock and tropical plant garden, and furnished with a sink, mirrored cabinet, and spacious shower. They are fully tiled and totally private, and a really nice feature of these accommodations. The upstairs rooms have varnished hardwood floors and balcony, also a huge bathroom and shower (minus the garden), nice curtains and lots of space. There are four newer rooms in a separate 2-storey building as well. They are smaller and share bath facilities. They also have tiled floors downstairs and hardwood floors upstairs, and have a porch (downstairs, both front and back) and balcony (upstairs). New shared bathroom facilities were constructed in 2004, with superior stone and tile work, surrounded by a high bamboo wall. One shower has hot water (the guests with private baths can bath here if they like). English is spoken fluently. The open-air kitchen has all the facilities for doing your own cooking, with two large picnic tables for dining. Use of the kitchen is available to guests, who share it with the staff. Also available is the use of a huge bank safe for storing valuables (remember, this is an all-cash town). *Rates:* $8 per person, or $10pp with kitchen priveleges. All local tours can be arranged. E-mail carolssurftour@yahoo.co.uk, or call 827-3394.

Cabinas Cazaolas -- Just a little further up the road, about 100 meters above the soccer field on the left, a wide green lawn lined with colorful shrubs and flowers leads to the "Wavehunter" cabinas. The lot has been expanded and enclosed with a high fence for security, and there is always somebody there to keep an eye on things. There is plenty of room to park a rental car on the grassy front yard. The rooms are located on the second floor of a modest building, the first floor being the owners' home. A varnished hardwood staircase leads up from the front patio of the house to the rooms above. There is a central porch furnished with a large table and bench for reading (there are a bunch of magazines and some books), socializing, etc. There are four standard rooms, two on each side of the enclosed porch, all built of native woods. They have foam mattresses on the primarily single beds (one room has a double), large screened windows with wood shutters, and a small table. Two rooms look out over a wide grassy field behind the building with lots of birds in the trees beyond, the other two over the front yard, and one has views towards the beach. There is also a covered deck right next to the rooms, adding more lounging space. One toilet and one spacious shower (big enough for two) are shared by those in the standard rooms. A separate room off the common area has beautiful teak floors and a tiled private bath. Next to the large concrete storage room downstairs, a kitchen was added for those wanting to cook for themselves. It has a 3-burner stove, double sink, dishes and a dining table. The bodega -- available for guests -- has a surf rack inside, and is always kept locked. The family lives right there on the first floor, so there is 24-hour security every day of the year. **Rates:** $10pp with private bath, $8pp shared bath. Low season rates negotiable. Laundry is available, and a boat for tours or transportation (Cabo Matapalo). A family member also acts as a guide for jungle treks (some English spoken). Fans are available only upon request. Open 24 hours for late arrivals. Call 826-3693, or e-mail jeskivel@costarricense.cr

Casa Domingo (Sunday House) -- This secluded resort perched high above the shore on its own private ridge is the pinnacle of comfort and class in the Pavones area. Greg and Heidi, your North American hosts from the Eastern seaboard of the U.S., have worked diligently for the last several years to make their top shelf accommodations one of the finest destinations in Costa Rica. The sweeping views of the gulf, Osa Peninsula and Pacific Ocean from the expansive deck are breathtaking, your reward after making the short drive or walk up the resort's private road bordered by wide lawns and fruit trees. The 15-acre property climbs up the front of a hill, peaks high above the flatlands that border the shoreline, and continues over to the other side with its own rain forest filled with abundant bird life, sloths and monkeys. There is a wide path that leads from the one main lodge just below the peak right into the heart of the tall tropical hardwoods. The elevation and openness of the resort allows for almost constant sea breezes and almost zero bugs. One large building houses everything in grand tropical style, with a 20-foot cathedral ceiling in the lounge and dining area. A wide patio runs the entire length of the front of the lodge, with plenty of room for groups of almost any size. The decor is rich tropical style, with varnished bamboo furniture sporting cushions with colorful rain forest patterns. The floor is ceramic tile, as well as the spacious private baths. There is track lighting in the lounge area for nighttime activities, as well as satellite TV. One of the really pleasant surprises here — unique among all the places in this handbook — is real *walk-in closets* in the four guest rooms! Nice touch. The very private rooms, which do not share a wall with any others, have either 2 double beds or 2 doubles and a single (children are welcome). Natural fruit drinks are limitless, but bring your own sodas or alcohol (there is a separate refrigerator for guests). Laundry is free, as is use of the marine radio if needed. Boat trips, taxis, and especially horseback riding can all be easily arranged, as well as trips to a Guyamí Indian reservation. **Rates:** $25 per person + tax, which includes a full breakfast. By car, look for their sign and turnoff on the left along the beach road about a mile past the town of Pavones. Follow this about 200 meters to the upper road, make a right, and the road will take you about 100 meters farther to Casa Domingo's front door. Phone 820-4709, e-mail heidi@casa-domingo.com. Web site: www.casa-domingo.com.

Sunset Lodge -- This luxury rental home and cabin high in the hills over the Pavones area outside of town offers upscale accommodations with fantastic ocean views. The lodgings are backed by tall secondary rain forest, alive with monkeys, coatis, other mammals and lots of birds, including scarlet macaws. Surrounding the buildings are well-landscaped grounds of wide lawns and colorful ornamental shrubs. The cabin is set a little higher than the house about 50 feet away. Its two stories are constructed primarily with purple heart wood and *cristobal* woods, two of the most beautiful and rare to be found in Costa Rica. The first floor has bathrooms, while the upstairs has the living area. There are decks on both the ocean and mountain sides, with a king sized bed inside. The air conditioned studio has two closets with drawers, fan, refrigerator, a dining nook with dishes, and a fully tiled bath with hot water on tap. A lighted concrete path leads to the two-bedroom house, which is fully air conditioned (each bedroom has its own unit) and lavishly equipped and decorated. The views are breathtaking of the mouth of the Golfo Dulce and the Osa Peninsula from the long wood and white cane deck hanging over the hillside, where you can also see a nice point break. Despite the altitude, you can hear the surf pounding the shore far below. Here is a partial list of the amenities: DirecTV, DVD player, sliding glass windows, cushioned bamboo furniture, a fully equipped kitchen with bar and padded bamboo stools, several hammocks, and lots of framed local artwork on the varnished hardwood walls. The two spacious and well-furnished bedrooms share a central tiled bathroom with sliding glass doors on the hot water shower and bathtub. If you don't want to clean up after yourself, full maid and laundry service is available. The lodgings are also equipped with radios for communication. *Rates*: $100 per night single, $15 each additional person up to six. $50 double for the cabin only. Call 827-4868. E-mail pavoneslocal@racsa.co.cr. Web site: www.pavoneslocal.com.

Other Lodgings – Cabinas Aleri, Cabinas Mendoza, Cabinas Mendoza Victor, Esquina del Mar, La Piña, La Ponderosa, Cabinas Sharon.

FOOD SERVICE

Café de la Suerte -- This small wholesome eatery is located right near the beach across from the soccer field, in the little complex next to Hotel Maureen. It has an L-shaped dining patio with bench seating facing both the soccer field and the waves of the famous point break – there is a view either side. The dining counter is fully tiled, and the area is kept very clean and tidy. There is always some good music emanating from the large kitchen, where a young couple and their one employee take care of customers. The focus here is on freshly prepared vegetarian foods, and killer smoothies. Breakfast drinks include freshly squeezed orange juice and a full range of espresso drinks. If it's too hot for regular coffee, they have iced coffee, and iced tea as well. Fresh carrot juice? No problem. Other juices available are mango, pineapple, papaya, star fruit and more. They can mix up any combination you like, too. Fresh fruit smoothies can be made with additional ingredients like honey, chocolate, raisins, peanut butter, bee pollen, and fresh ginger. Food items, posted on their chalkboard and changing slightly depending on available ingredients, include omelets and great sandwiches. Pesto and cheese, guacamole, hummus, and egg sandwiches are featured. The most popular food here are the snacks, though. These are not your regular snacks, however: fudge brownies, incredible 'power bars' (popular with the surfers), and freshly baked cakes and cookies. They make their own fresh breads, too, which you can buy as loaves for picnics or whatever. There are daily breakfast and lunch specials, like quiche, burritos, lasagna, and salads. Fluent English is spoken by the owners and staff, and they can fill you in if some area info is what you need. In addition to the café, they rent a small room with a private patio and full bath around the corner, in the same building. It has air conditioning and hot water, and can fit up to four people. Restaurant hours are flexible depending on the season, but they are usually open from fairly early in the morning till dusk.

Other Dining Options: There is restaurant service at the cantina. Hotel Maureen has a restaurant on the first floor of its building. There is a popular *soda* where the public phone is administrated.

TOURS AND OTHER SERVICES

Pavones Local -- Primarily a real estate business, this conveniently located office offers free tourist information and accommodations in the Pavones area. They also promote forestry projects, and encourage planting threatened local hardwoods. You can stop in for some fresh fruit or a cold drink and get information about lodgings, tours, and local culture. They have many of their own places to rent (they are property managers), which is good if you are looking for a private house or cabin to stay in, versus a hotel or lodge. The following are two examples of rental homes that they manage: A large 2 bedroom house with two queen sized beds with orthopedic mattresses and an air-conditioned office. A long private drive leads up to a fully furnished house with a beautiful panoramic view of the gulf. There is a fully equipped kitchen, hot water, and a clothes washer is available, as well as daily maid and laundry service. This very secure rental goes for $250 per week, or $800 per month. Another rental, the 'Casa Sueño Del Sur', is a cabin built of local hardwoods, fully screened, and perched on a lush hillside overlooking the Golfo Dulce. The private cabin sleeps four in one large bedroom. It rents for $40 a night, or $450 a month. The office is located on the east side of the main road into Pavones (on the left as you come in), just before the cantina and soccer field, and set back from the road about 50 feet. There is a sign. Phone 827-4868. E-mailpavoneslocal@racsa.co.cr. Web site: www.pavoneslocal.com.

Chen Taiji International Tropical Tours — Taiji (also written Tai Chi) has been considered a cultural treasure in China for centuries, a classical martial art and healing system for cultivating superior health, long life, and peace of mind. Taiji is an art, science, and philosophy that all people can enjoy and benefit from, regardless of age or physical ability. Taiji has gained enormous popularity worldwide because of its unique nature and inherent abilities to build health from the inside out, heal chronic health problems, manage stress, and reverse many of the so-called "normal" processes of aging. Now you can learn this ancient "internal" martial art in a tropical setting in Costa Rica. Dr. Bob Bacher, founder and director of Chen Taiji International (CTI), has been studying and teaching Taiji and other martial arts, yoga, and meditation on a full-time basis since 1969. He is a Doctor of Chiropractic with over 20 years clinical experience in the health and healing profession. Dr. Bacher studied Chen Style Taiji extensively in Chen Village, China, under the strict guidance of Grandmaster Wang Xi'an, 19th generation lineage holder and one of the highest skilled Taiji masters alive today. Dr. Bacher is one of the few westerners officially authorized by Master Wang to teach the Chen Style Taiji system. He is the author of two Taiji books, and he teaches workshops, retreats, and training camps internationally. He brings his teachings to Pavones as part of an all-inclusive package set near the shores of the Golfo Dulce. The complete vacation and retreat packages include: Roundtrip airfare (optional) from Miami to San Jose, Costa Rica; roundtrip ground transportation within Costa Rica; accommodations in Pavones; 3 meals per day; and daily Taiji classes. Other activities, such as diving, snorkeling, surfing lessons, horseback riding, rain forest tours, etc. are available and can be arranged. For more information about his retreats in Pavones, call (305) 931-0918 (USA). E-mail chentaijiinternational@yahoo.com. Web site: www.chentaijiinternational.com.

HIKING AND CAMPING

Beachcombing and walkng along the road out towards Punta Banco are about the only hiking opportunities in the Pavones area, unless you go on an organized tour. You can camp on any of the beaches in the area, of course, and there are some really nice spots. However, nobody that I've run across openly offers facilities for campers. You might have better luck -- and fewer neighbors -- in Punta Banco (see next section). Warning: During Christmas and Easter weeks, this area is *packed* with Tico campers. It's best to avoid them.

PAVONES

GOLFO DULCE

—N—

TO GOLFITO & TO IAH

3

C

4 5

6 7 8

SOCCER FIELD

RIO CLARO

TO BANCO

1

2

9

1 Vista Dulce	6 Cab. Willys Willis
2 Cab. Mira Olas	7 Cabinas Carol
3 Pavones Local	8 Cabinas Caza Olas
4 Hotel Maureen	9 Casa Domingo
5 Café de La Suerte	C Cantina

PUNTA BANCO

Punta Banco beckons you with its lush and isolated setting, literally at the end of the road about 6 km. southwest of Pavones on the Pacific. This is an enchanting area, with tons of dense rainforest just minutes away, and a tranquil beachfront atmosphere that puts the emphasis on relaxation and *pura vida*. An indigenous reservation and settlement is a short hike up into the mountains, and beachcombers will be completely in their element with miles of unpopulated shoreline to explore. Several species of turtle come on shore to lay their eggs from around August through December, though they are always around in the water just offshore. Surfers are welcome, especially those wanting to get away from the crowds of Pavones. There are several good breaks here. Personally, this is one of my favorite spots.

To get here, basically you just stay on the coastal road (or bus) till you get to the end. The small village of Banco itself with its obligatory soccer field is only a kilometer or so from the end of the road. The only bus that goes all the way to Banco from the outside is the afternoon run, the morning run stopping in Pavones for lunch before its return to Golfito. The same bus departs daily at 5am from Rancho Burica.

LODGINGS

Rancho Burica — If its seclusion, sand and surf that you want, this beachside jungle outpost is for you. Built up against a high ridge cloaked in primary and secondary rainforest with several hiking trails, and also right on the beach with tide pools and peeling waves at your doorstep, this is a fantastic place. The road to the indigenous reserve starts here at the end of the main public road about 8 km. south of Pavones (which is where the bus spends the night), and there is a year-round waterfall and stream literally a few steps away from the cabins. Beautiful tropical fish and even moray eels can be seen in the reef right out front. There are wide lawns, pineapple plants, tropical flowers, tall palms and other attractive foliage among the lavish landscaping, and high observation benches on the beach. Squirrel monkeys frolic in the palms by the shore. One of the most attractive aspects of this place is the ownership, a group of young Dutch sportspeople who fell in love with the spot on a visit in 1998 and ended up buying it within a few months. They are here primarily to enjoy the rainforest, surf, etc. themselves, and so making money off tourism is at best a secondary consideration (which is why their rates stay so low). They participate in the turtle protection program for this area, helping to save the local hatcheries so future generations can enjoy our fellow sea creatures as well. The lodgings are made up of separate cabins of various styles, one being a large *rancho* with thatched-palm roof. Most are one or two-story wooden structures, having 1 double and 1 single bed, with a total of 7 rooms in 5 cabins plus the *rancho* closest to the beach. All have lights and electrical outlets. Some have decks with ocean views, and all except the one private cabin and the *rancho* share communal baths (only 2 rooms for each bath, so it's not bad). You may be able to arrange rental of the large *rancho*, which has its own private bath, can hold up to six people, and is cooler and more private than the cabins. They added a nice barbecue near the shore in 2004 for cooking up fresh fish and other great foods, and expanded the kitchen and dining room as well to accommodate their increasing numbers of guests. ***Rates:*** $8pp for the lower rooms with shared baths, $12pp for the upper rooms with shared baths, and $15pp for the separate cabin with the private bath. Negotiate for the *rancho*. Discounts for groups and long stays. English, Dutch, French, German and Spanish are spoken. Breakfast and dinner are available at the guest-only private restaurant. They have snorkeling gear available. They have their own boat for sea-bound tours like fishing or surfing. Horseback riding can also be arranged on the beach or up to the indigenous reservation. Since they have no radio or phone, just show up, or e-mail them ahead of time if you get the chance at info@ranchoburica.com. Web site: www.ranchoburica.com.

Tiskita Jungle Lodge — This lodge is one of the few upper end options in this part of the southern zone, a long-established and somewhat famous destination for those who want a comprehensive, all-inclusive resort experience in a rainforest setting. The original farmhouse of the 550-acre property, which started as a tropical fruit farm more than twenty years ago and still boasts over 100 species of exotic fruit trees, is the center of activity high above the coast, while the 8 large cabins are spread out nearby. There is a free form pool surrounded by greenbelt on top of a small rise near the main lodge with an outstanding view of the coast and Pacific. The wide road and trails are kept clean and clear, with a mix of natural and landscaped foliage blending with patches of fruit orchard in the more open spaces. The main lodge itself is a lofty *rancho* with an office, the dining area, and a lounge area with comfortable furniture, all finished in both rough cut and cleanly finished varnished woods. Just a few steps away is a bar for the guests with an absolutely beautiful hardwood ping pong table. There are several types of cabins, all very comfortable. They are all fully screened, have 2-3 rooms each built of hardwood from the property, nightstands, nice lamps, shelving, fans, and wonderful covered private bathrooms with tile floors and attractive stone walls. The majority have wide verandas out front with furniture and hammocks, and most have outside reading lamps, too. A couple of the rooms have fully enclosed bathrooms. Most are right up near the edge of the forest surrounded by manicured green lawns, decorative shrubs and myriads of fruit trees. Most have nice views, too, some spectacular. Three types of monkeys play in both the primary and reforested secondary forest of the reserve, as well as all the other jungle wildlife. Meals here are buffet style, with home-cooked local fare of great variety, most of the fruit coming right off the *finca*, and much of the rest from the ocean down the mountain. There is also full bar service for guests. Since this lodge is managed by the owners, the attention and service are exemplary, and both they and their guides are bilingual. Also nice are the bird list (over 275 species have been recorded here — birders love this place), fruit tree list, and detailed trail map for independent exploration of the rainforest. **Rates:** Non-package rates during high season are $145 single, $240 double, and $315 triple, with children under 12 $60. All full board (except for bar drinks). The 2-7 day packages are better. Low season discounts. All include guided walk with trained naturalist. Laundry available. Tours include Corcovado excursions, horseback riding, and *panga* fishing. Contact info: Phone 296-8125, fax 296-8133, e-mail tiskita@racsa.co.cr, Web site: www.tiskita-lodge.co.cr. Reservations are basically mandatory.

Sotavento Plantanal – *Where the forest meets the surf under the South Wind . . . . .* Local expat Harry and his partner Leo offer two furnished houses, Poinsettia House and Vista Grande, up on the forest-cloaked mountain above Punta Banco. They are both perched about 100 feet above sea level on 100 acres of private land with magnificent views out over the Pacific Ocean and private hiking trails through the jungle. Poinsettia House sits smack up against dense rainforest, where three types of monkeys cruise by, as well as lots of other animals, birds and butterflies. It's a large 2-story structure, built completely of local hardwoods, with 2 bedrooms and a tiled bath with a spacious shower with hot water on tap. The wide windows have hinged wooden shutters, there is lots of lighting, plenty of closet space and even two safe trunks with locks. There are four double beds in all, each with its own mosquito netting. The fully equipped kitchen has a fridge, toaster oven, stove, stainless steel sink, all the dishes and utensils, etc. There is a large dining table, L-shaped couch for watching DirecTV on the large color television, and a desk. Both the upstairs and downstairs have wide wooden decks. Vista Grande has an even more spectacular view up the coastline to the east, over to the Osa Peninsula to the north, and out to the open ocean to the west and south. Also two stories, this one offers 4 double beds in two furnished bedrooms, more closet space, and an extra 1/2 bath. The equally large windows let in a bit more breeze up here. There is bar seating on really cool stools made of cut chunks of logs to augment the large dining table next to the kitchen, which is also fully equipped. These houses are ideal for those desiring a little more privacy, and for groups of up to 8 people who want to share an adventure together in a secluded environment, yet with all the conveniences and direct access to their own patch of rainforest. A couple of additional benefits of Sotavento Plantanal are the availability of three horses and a surfboard for rent, and free use of boogie boards. You can even watch surfboards being made in a special workshop down near the beach, as the resident manager is an experienced surfboard shaper. Also, fresh organic black pepper is grown right on the property, and is available for use and sale. Rates: Poinsettia House - $60 per night for up to 6 people; Vista Grande - $80 per night for up to 8 people. $10 per person extra over respective limit of 6 or 8, up to 8 or 10. If you rent for a week, you get a day free. If you rent a month, you get a week free. E-mail in advance at flowmaster@sotaventoplantanal.com or flowmasterha@yahoo.com. Web site: www.sotaventoplantanal.com.

Casa Punta Banco – This secluded private house on 265 acres of verdant ridges above the Pacific shore is available to rent on a weekly or monthly basis. Both the isolation and privacy are unique, and nature lovers couldn't ask for a more pristine and enchanting environment. Most of the property is virgin primary rainforest, the rest composed of three exotic fruit orchards originally planted by the homesteader of the property in the 1970's, the same man who constructed the rambling 6-bedroom house. There are bananas, several types of coconut, lemons, limes, oranges, star fruit, lei chi fruit, guava, papaya, water apple, custard apple, and many other varieties of fruits, some hard to name. The bird life here is fantastic, with dozens of rare species among the exotic fauna like parrots, hummingbirds, toucans, hawks, trogons, wood rails, and countless sea birds on the coast. One of the most impressive treasures of this property is the voluminous 40-foot waterfall, one of the most impressive I've ever seen, surrounded by rainforest and looking out to the ocean. Around five minutes by foot along the beach after the end of the road at Punta Banco, you come across the wide road leading up to the house. After a few more minutes' walk up the ridge you come to an open-air wooden house 250 feet above the sea with six bedrooms, two bathrooms, a fully equipped kitchen and plenty of living space. There is a small lawn out front surrounded by ornamental bushes and fruit trees, where monkeys come almost daily to pick up a snack that the owners hang for them. The views are spectacular, capturing the mouth of the Golfo Dulce, the Osa Peninsula, and the open Pacific. The house itself is a combination of the original rustic homesteader style and more recent remodeling. The living areas on both floors are very open and breezy, especially the kitchen and dining areas on the first floor, which look out to the view. The two smaller bedrooms -- recently refurbished with glass block, closets and better ventilation -- are downstairs off the main living area, which is nicely furnished with cushioned hardwood seating. The downstairs bath has a sunken bath- tub with a seat – plenty of room for two – surrounded by a tiled sitting area and overhead shower. It is open at the top with a view to the ocean and rainforest. Upstairs you find four more bedrooms, all separated by a hallway with no shared walls. The two front bedrooms have big double doors opening onto a wide furnished deck with the panoramic views spread out at your feet and a powerful telescope to appreciate the details. The huge upstairs bath has a massive double shower (two shower heads) with classy glass block walls. It's all tiled, of course, with large mirrors. Power is provided 24 hours a day via a solar system with a generator backup. *Rates:* $1,200 per week double, $100/week each additional person. Car rental is available. Call 388-1395 in Costa Rica. E-mail DSJean@aol.com. Web site: www.costaricacpb.com

The Yoga Farm – This new yoga retreat perched above the end of the road (at Rancho Burica) was just finished in 2004. The mission here is to create a conscious spiritual center based on the practice of Yoga in all its various forms, and to assist in the develop- ment of a more conscious global community. Daily yoga practice on their huge covered platform is part of what this place is all about, nor- mally led by the owner or another visiting instructor. Circular breathing and occasionally Reiki can be learned here, too. They have a very extensive organic garden and fruit trees, and strive to make the retreat self-sustaining as much as possible. They use composting, and ex- tensive permaculture techniques. The main retreat house, almost fin- ished when I visited, is a massive two-story structure designed to ac- commodated the activities of a small community. The first floor, fin- ished with stone and concrete floors, houses the two dormitory rooms and one private room, four collective bathrooms, and two beautiful and unique fully tiled showers with incredible tile work, long bench seating, and hand-held shower heads. The second floor is dedicated primarily to the yoga studio. It has a sanded and varnished variegated tongue-in- groove hardwood floor. The beams are varnished hardwood, all under a vaulted ceiling with skylights. There is a small bathroom here, a massage table, and an amazing panoramic view of the forest and Pacific Ocean for awesome sunset yoga sessions to the sound of crashing surf below. The main house has solar power and – I almost forgot – a fully enclosed sauna downstairs with glass block windows. On a lower level of the property is a small *rancho* with a thatched palm roof that serves primarily as the dining commons. It has a large fully equipped kitchen and prep area, plus a dining table and chairs. There is a loft as well for extra guests, and some hammocks for lounging. Additional lodging can be found in the 'Tree House', a open bamboo structure built on two live mango trees growing on a steep slope on the side of the hill. Robinson Crusoe style, the platform has a tarp to keep the rain out. Meals here are vegetarian, with occasional organically raised meat. More and more of the ingredients come from the organic garden and fruit trees. ***Rates***: $15pp includes 3 meals and yoga instruction (Monday thru Friday). English, French and Spanish spoken. Lunch available to non-guests. Several tours can be arranged, including overnight hikes to the local Indian reservation, and horseback riding. To get there, just go to the end of the road (and bus route) at Rancho Burica, and keep climbing the steep 'road' up the mountain. There is a gate with a sign about 10 minutes up the hill, just before the stream. E-mail yogafarmcostarica@yahoo.com. Web site: www.geocities.com/yogafarmcostarica.

Cabinas & Soda Patricio – Three small buildings are spread out among lawns and mature landscaping of fruit trees, ornamental plants and flowering bushes represent maybe the nicest low budget accommodations in town. Set back from the road in central Banco with a wall of vegetation as protection from the negligible traffic, these rooms are clean, private and quiet. Two of the buildings are two stories, both unique, with rooms upstairs and a room downstairs. Both have very spacious balconies or porches and lounging areas, and are decently furnished. They all have private baths. The single story private cabin is exceptional, with tiled floors and bath, 3 large shuttered windows, and a queen sized 4-poster canopy bed made of varnished hardwood – a rare treat in this area for sure. It also has a tiled porch with chairs. The associated *soda* is a good place to eat, open on two sides with a nicely tiled floor and large tables, all with chairs of polished purple heart wood. The food is typical Tico – no fixed menu, so you need to know what you want – with big portions, excellent service, and really low prices (I was impressed). The owner Patricio speaks pretty good English. Dining hours are 7am-9pm daily. The small general store has lots of basic food staples available, plus the typical assortment of bath items and general household supplies. ***Rates:*** $7pp,

$5pp low season. Group discounts. Laundry, transportation, and tours available, especially horseback riding as they have their own horses. You have your choice of horseback riding tours, cruising just around the area and paying by the hour, or going on an extensive adventurous trek up to the local indigenous reservation, and returning along the shore (or vice-versa, depending on the tide). The rooms are located right next to Pulpería La Cuevita (same owner) just south of the wooden bridge and across from the northeast corner of the soccer field. Ask for Patricio. Call 770-8221 for reservations if you like.

Other Lodgings: There are several houses for rent in the area, including those of Sotavento Plantanal.

FOOD SERVICE

See the *cabinas* described above.

HIKING AND CAMPING

Hiking is fantastic here in both the mountains and along the beach down to Punta Burica and into Panama (though you may not want to go *that* far). Tiskita has lots of trails on their extensive property, but you'll have to hunt down Peter, the co-owner, to see if you can hike them and for how much (if you are not already a guest there). Your best bet is the trek through the dense rainforest up to the Guaymí Indian reservation. I was told there are about 3000 inhabitants living in and near their village, the highest concentration of indigenous people in the Golfo Dulce/Osa area. It would be best to have a guide bring you, as it is private property. The trail starts where the road ends at Rancho Burica. By far the most attractive, hospitable and convenient spot to camp is at Bar Marea Alta. Camping is on a wide grassy lawn, or under the trees in back where squirrel monkeys sleep, and you can use the bathroom and shower facilities. The surf is right across the road, and there is lots of space and privacy. Ask at the bar for rates. You can still camp anywhere on or above the beach, too, and ask about use of someone´s facilities. Rancho Burica might be an option.

MOUNTAINS, COFFEE AND FRIENDSHIP

High in the mountains above the humid plains and relatively diminutive hills of the coastal areas of the far south lies the cooler, very different land of the Coto Brus Valley, which lies between the southern ridges of the Talamanca Mountains and the northern peaks of the Fila Costeña, which rise to over 11,000 feet. If you want to escape the heat for a while, and check out vast coffee plantations and quaint mountain domiciles, this area is a nice place to visit. Three major attractions for foreigners are located here: the most abundant coffee region in Costa Rica, the Wilson Botanical Garden, and La Amistad International Park. The Wilson Botanical Garden is part of a roughly 632-acre forest reserve and biological station run by the Organization of Tropical Studies that acts as a center for research and scientific training, as well as for public education. The gardens and surrounding reserve are a cornucopia of delights for both naturalists and birders, with over 7000 species of flora and over 330 indigenous and migrant bird species spotted on the property (see LODGINGS and HIKING sections). Friendship International Park (La Amistad) is a gigantic biosphere preserve of almost 194,000 hectares (480,000 acres) that is situated on both sides of the border with Panama. Together with Chirripó National Park, the Hitoy-Cerere Biological Reserve, Las Tablas and Barbilla Protective Zones, Las Cruces Biological Station (where the Wilson Botanical Garden is located), and a handful of indigenous reservations, it forms the 600,000-hectare Amistad Biosphere Reserve, a UNESCO World Heritage Site, comprising the largest biological reserve in Central America. La Amistad has no less than eight 'life zones' and protects the country's largest concentration of tapirs, jaguars, harpy eagles, ocelots, and many other endangered species, as well as several important watersheds.

This area is famous for its rich, delicious coffee, and you can even buy some fresh from the *tostadora* (roaster) in the hamlet of Coto Brus near the town of Sabalito, or at a store in Sabalito itself. There are lots of working coffee plantations around, and you'll see many coffee loading shacks along the roads. Another reason people come here, both Ticos and foreigners alike, is for the climate. It's nice and warm during the day, but not nearly as humid or hot as the lowlands, and it gets deliciously *cool* at night, enough to throw on some sweats or a real jacket.

SAN VITO

San Vito is the major commercial center for this area, the county seat and the heart and soul of the local culture. It sits on a rise at around 3,200 feet looking out over the Coto Brus Valley. Originally founded by Italian immigrants in the early 1950's, who came with not much more than a spirit of adventure and a few WWII jeeps, you can still hear some Italian being spoken, see some of their European genetic heritage (especially the blue and green eyes) and, of course, eat some real Italian food. Other than the nearby naturalist attractions mentioned above, and a private park near San Vito, there is really not much to see or do in the town. One interesting place to check out, though, is the small tourist/historical/cultural center across the intersection from the small central park on the upper end of town. They have old photos of some of the original immigrants and the nascent town to check out. It's free. Another place you may find interesting is the new disco, located west of the gas station on the road heading out of town.

The road up to San Vito from Ciudad Neily is alone worth the trip, as you can see for at least 100 miles on a clear day as you ascend the switchback paved road up the side of the mountains that tower above the flatlands below. I spotted the Osa Peninsula and Sweet Gulf from those lofty heights. Just be extremely careful on this twisting road, especially when it's wet, if you are driving yourself. Go slowly and watch for hairpin turns – there are no warning signs. Regarding buses, there are no less than seven that leave daily for San Vito from Ciudad Neily, at 6, 9, and 11am, 12:30, 1:30, 3 and 5pm. Some go direct, others pass through the *campo* over gravel roads. Both TRACOPA and a company called Empresa Alfaro in San José have daily routes directly to and from San Vito. There is also an airstrip that serves this area. Internet service can be found in the lower part of central San Vito.

LODGINGS

There are several inexpensive places to stay in San Vito, designed primarily for Ticos, as this is not really a big tourist destination. There is only one North American-style hotel in the town (see below), and for that reason many foreign visitors stay at the Wilson Botanical Garden six kilometers outside of town, which is more like a comfortable naturalist resort combined with a working research station (also reviewed below). One thing to note: you definitely do not need fans here in these mountains, either for the temperature or the bugs. All the accommodations provide thick blankets for the relatively cool nights.

Dos Locos Canadienses – This funky little place halfway up the mountain to San Vito is touted by the Canadian owners as "the alternative to Jaco Beach. The real Costa Rica, in the *campo*." Primarily a popular local bar and restaurant, they have some basic rooms, too, for those who want to spend a little time soaking up the atmosphere and meeting some local ex-pats. Dances happen occasionally, sometimes spontaneously, and local Ticos often come around to play their guitar. The rooms are attached to the house via a separate wing off the carport. One room has a big double bed with a private bath. The other has two big double beds, with the bath facilities shared. Outside the rooms are a sink and laundry facilities. These are social style accommodations, where one can wrap with Al and his wife Pierrette in the restaurant and bar, which has been recently renovated. They now have full restaurant service available for all three meals from 1pm till around 2am, featuring an international menu specializing in specialty hamburgers, Italian and French cuisine. The restaurant can accommodate groups of up to 30 diners. One of the special features here is that the owners have a friend with a "600-foot waterfall" on his private property nearby, rarely seen by tourists. I didn't have a chance to check it out, but plan to some day. There is a phone available. They are located right on the main road between Ciudad Neily and San Vito, just above Agua Buena. Just tell the bus or taxi driver where you're going, or watch for their sign if you're driving. They are known locally (and affectionately) as Papa Loco and Mama Loca, in case you need to ask somebody. English, Spanish and French are spoken fluently. *Rates:* Around $5.50 for the room with shared bath, and $7 for the room with private bath. Many local tours can be arranged here to private properties that few tourists get to see. Tours include horseback riding, hiking and even camping, on preserved properties with primary jungle and even caverns. Call 734-0245, or fax 734-0286.

Wilson Botanical Garden – Located in Las Cruces just 6 km. outside of San Vito, and operated by the Organization for Tropical Studies, this combination biological research station, botanical garden and visitor center treats natural science professors and foreign tourists equally well, offering high levels of friendly attention and comfort in a relaxed and stimulating environment. The small complex of buildings is nestled among the 25 acres of gardens that Robert and Catherine Wilson developed and made famous. Over ten kilometers of trails wind through the garden and forest reserve, all well-marked and maintained for year-round enjoyment. Twelve spacious guest rooms are available to travelers. The rooms are housed as duplexes, arranged along a small ridge next to the dining hall, with nice concrete pathways and ample night lighting to find your way around. The lodge-style rooms are modern accommodations with thick concrete walls, varnished hardwood floors and vaulted ceilings. The rooms are amply furnished with a long writing desk, dresser drawers, desk chair, bamboo night tables, night lamps, a bamboo padded chair, framed prints, and even a telephone and laptop hookup for internet service. They provide an ice bucket and water glasses as well. The single beds have nice hardwood frames, tall headboards and firm mattresses. Extra blankets are provided if necessary. The back wall, constructed of huge glass panes in wooden frames, leads out to the private furnished deck overlooking the lush gardens, which is perfect for bird and animal observation. The fully tiled bath has warm water showers, a large mirror, and several thick towels. Dining is family style at long hardwood tables in the huge modern dining room. Students and researchers mix with tourists and guides in a spacious, friendly setting. The food is a mix of Costa Rican and international styles, with a focus on fresh fruit and vegetables. Fish, chicken, pasta or meat courses are served at lunch and dinner. Large urns of coffee and hot water are set out for self service hot beverages. Fruit drinks are placed on the tables in pitchers at every meal. Special diets are accommodated with prior notice. Next to the dining hall is a conference room with a TV, videos, and a large library with many books on the local flora and fauna (and some novels, too). Outside of the hall is a large wooden deck for birding, socializing or just relaxing in the sun. ***Rates:*** $70 single, $125 double full board including tax. Discounts for children 5-12. Accommodations for students, researchers, or families are also available. Guided tours are available at $10pp. An extensive gift shop has many useful items. English is spoken by all the guides and most of the other staff. Call 240-6696 for more information or reservations. Fax 240-6783. Call 773-4004 weekends. E-mail nathist@ots.ac.cr, web site www.ots.ac.cr.

Hotel El Ceibo – This North American-style hotel has 40 nicely finished rooms to choose from. Two concrete buildings house the rooms, one two-story, the other one-story. Located around 70 meters from the major downtown intersection (at the park) in San Vito, the hotel makes its own private cul de sac away from the crowds. The complex has secondary forest on three sides, with lots of birds sounding off in the mornings and evenings. Almost all the rooms are all equipped with a full closet, a vanity, a desk, a night stand with lamp, a TV with cable, and two wood framed beds with headboards and thick, firm mattresses. They all have tiled floors and baths with hot water on tap in the showers. Some of the larger rooms have both a double and two single beds, though most have either a double or two singles. Some rooms on the second floor have small balconies overlooking a verdant gully. The large restaurant has an extremely high cathedral ceiling over an expansive area with many tables, and even a huge brick fireplace with an oven inside. The double linen tablecloths and varnished hardwood detailing add a touch of class, while the comfortable lounge area with a cushy sofa and chairs provides a nice place to watch TV, read a magazine or chat. The restaurant is open from 6:45am to 10pm daily, and offers a full range of Costa Rican and Italian dishes at very reasonable prices, with the average being only $3-$3.50 per plate (sandwiches are only $1.50). Specialties include homemade lasagna and caneloni, but they have soups, salads, and sandwiches as well. Filet mignon, roast beef, fried chicken, fish filets, jumbo shrimp, rice dishes, and spaghetti with various sauces are also offered. The menu is in both English and Spanish for easy reading. Full bar service is available, with various imported wines, both national and international liquors, and multinational beers. They can make regular cocktails, plus the classic frozen tropical cocktails like piña coladas and daiquiris. Italian and a little English is spoken. *Rates:* $18 single, $28 double, $36 triple. Group discounts available. Telephone and fax service available. Call 773-3025, fax 773-5025. E-mail apapilic@racsa.co.cr.

Hotel y Restaurante Rino — Right in the center of town, yet enclosed within a small commercial center, is this 12-room hotel with several nice features and a small new restaurant that is worth the visit. The rooms are on the second story of a courtyard-style indoor commercial center off the main road in town climbing up to the small central park, and the street noise really doesn't penetrate much, especially inside the well-insulated rooms. The Alpizar family owns and runs both the hotel and the commercial center, which bears their name. A tiled corridor runs the length of the circle around the courtyard below, and there is a small lounge area on the street side with a table, chairs and a bench. The restaurant is located at the back of the center on the first floor, near the hotel office and stairs that go up to most of the rooms. It was built in 2003 with high-quality finishing of nice ceramic tile. It has tiled bar seating, plus several nice tables. The food is typical Costa Rican, all made fresh to order and all at among the lowest prices in the entire country. Really! They have great sanwiches for only about 75 cents, and their full lunch and dinner plates run about $2! How about a natural drink for under 25 cents. Amazing. And the quality is excellent. The co-owner herself works in the kitchen most of the time, and the place is kept absolutely immaculate. The commodious rooms all have secure thick wooden doors, tiled floors and baths, full closets, tables and chairs, nice bed covers, 1-4 beds with orthopedic mattresses and real headboards, thick concrete walls for quiet and privacy, varnished hardwood ceilings, and big glass windows with double curtains. The capacious bathrooms are really special, many with European-style *bidets* of all things. The baths have large mirrors and hot water from tap in the great showers. All of the rooms also have cable TV with HBO, Cinemax, CNN, etc.. Two new extra large rooms were added on the back of the second floor in 2003. They have two big double beds with padded headboards, cushioned lounge chairs, huge bathrooms with extra large showers, and air conditioning. Private secure parking is available behind the center by the owners' house. There is always staff available 24 hours a day in case of emergencies. *Rates:* $10pp + tax standard, $32 + tax for the air conditioned rooms. Group discounts. VISA, MasterCard, AmX, Unicard accepted. Phone and fax available. Call or fax 773-3071 direct for reservations.

    Cabinas Las Mirlas – Located about half a kilometer east of downtown San Vito on the road to Sabalito, these small private cabins are a budget option in a convenient yet secluded environment. The 10 cabins, mostly built of wood with some concrete, are set along a gravel road on the edge of a gully looking out over a park-like setting with fruit trees, tall pines, ornamental shrubs and other local tree and plant species. For being so close to the center of town, one feels almost in the country due to the tall trees and seclusion of the location. You can park right next to your cabin if you have a car, and the owner lives at the entrance to the short private road so there is good 24-hour security. The first cabin is about 50 meters off the main road out of sight of passersby, and the gravel road has almost zero traffic as it is a dead end. The rooms all have twin and single beds with wooden frames and headboards, a large sink and counter, a desk with a chair, large mirrors, and nice curtains over glass windows with louvers. Several rooms even have a good sized color TV with remote control. The private baths have warm water showers and thick towels and soap are provided. The cabins are spaced widely apart to allow for excellent privacy. There is a small eatery on the street with a standard range of typical dishes at good prices. **_Rates:_** Around $9 single, $12 double with a TV, and a little cheaper without one. These are arguably the least expensive of the decent lodgings in the area (though not the best), so if you're on a really tight budget but don't want to stay in a dump, these will do fine. Group discounts available. Laundry service available by the owners and staff.

Other Lodgings: See La Riviera in the next section. Low budget accommodations include Cabinas Las Huacas, Hotel Pittier, Cabinas Las Cascadas, and Hotel Colono.

FOOD SERVICE

Pizzeria y Restaurante Liliana — Real homemade pasta? Real Italian-style pizza? Italian hospitality? You got it, right in central San Vito in this very attractive restaurant just north of the park. Owner Dona Liliana Sorte is one of the original Italian immigrants who came here to help found the town in the 50's, opening the restaurant around 23 years later. The family atmosphere attracts many regular locals, who bring the entire family to eat the famous pizza here and socialize with other San Viteños. You will _not_ find Tico food at this restaurant (although here now for over 44 years, Doña Liliana is still "all Italian at heart", she tells me), just excellent Italian fare at extremely reasonable prices. The specialty here is pizza, of which there are several types including anchovy, chicken, vegetarian, neopolitan, plus all the standards. The tomato sauce is homemade from scratch — no canned junk here, by God! The menu is in English and Spanish, so you won't have any trouble ordering the homemade ravioli, cannelloni or fettuccine dishes. There is also spaghetti and macaroni, with your choice of several Italian sauces. The homemade lasagna is also a popular specialty here, as well as the Italian-style baked chicken. Additional menu items include hamburgers, French fries, salads, and sandwiches. They have all the typical refreshments, plus basic bar service including imported liquors and beers. The prices range from only about $1.50 for a sandwich to a maximum of around $6 — quite a bargain. The average dinner plate is only around $4.50. All this can be enjoyed inside the large restaurant (no smoking allowed) where there is a bar, large TV, and lots of nice table seating. Outside on the covered patio _al fresco_ is another option for dining, where you feel the mountain breezes while surrounded by potted plants, shrubs, flowers and trees. This is a great place to dine in the summer. There is a bit of a view here past the nicely done balustrade, and another TV in the patio, too. Regular hours are 10:30am - 10pm, and they can cater parties any time. VISA is accepted. Call 773-3080. Take-out is available.

Restaurante y Cabinas La Riviera -- Located just above the central intersection in San Vito, this nice 'double' restaurant and set of rooms has two environments and styles to choose from. The front part of the restaurant is a modern diner, with colorful formica tables both outside on the terrace by the sidewalk and inside, where music videos are usually playing on the TV. Live shrubs in concrete planters add a little greenery. The menu in this part of the restaurant revolves around fast food items such as burritos, hamburgers, hot dogs, nachos, fried chicken and French fries. They also offer three different ceviches, breakfasts, several salads, soups, and spaghettis. Costa Rican rice dishes, fish filet, steaks, and seafood can also be ordered. A very attractive feature is a real espresso machine, rare in this town. The spacious back restaurant, very popular with the locals for intimate dining, is separated by a thick glass sliding door at the end of a hallway. It has varnished hardwood floors, lots of nice wooden tables, and soft Latin music for a more subdued, romantic atmosphere. It is very private, and the lights are dimmed. This side of the building is elevated, and the large plate glass windows look out over a gully with tall trees and shrubs. The menu here focuses on traditional Costa Rican fare, plus many international dishes, as well as anything from the diner out front. Lots of seafood is always available, and they have daily lunch and dinner specials. Full bar service is available in the back restaurant. Prices range from around $2.25 to $6.50 max for full plates. Both restaurants are open from 6:00am till 10:30pm daily. Take-out is available, and English is spoken. The six rooms ($15pp) are in a separate section of the building. They are very spacious, with one double and one single bed with real spring mattresses and thick blankets. Amenities include glass windows with thick curtains, and fully tiled baths with hot water showers. The same owners also have a slightly larger and nicer hotel in Sabalito ($25pp), 25 meters east of the park in town, with a parking lot, cable TV, and a discotheque. Many tours are offered here, such as excursions to La Amistad International Park. Daily or multi-day tours are available, on foot or horseback. Trips to natural hot springs are arranged as well. Tour prices start at around $30 per person. For more information, all 773-3295 or 784-0305. E-mail riviera@costarricense.cr.

Other Dining Options: Restaurante Jimar, and at least a

dozen other small restaurants, *sodas* and bakeries around town.

TOURS

Finca Cántaros — This private nature reserve 2.5 km south of San Vito on the main road is a unique landscape restoration project. Formerly coffee plantations and cattle pasture, the 25-acre private residence and nature reserve has been landscaped and reforested since 1994, with an ancient lake that is unique in the area. There are lovely short walks including a forest loop and garden trails. Numerous picnic tables are found on the grounds and there are benches for relaxing by the lake. Walk along the finca's gravel road and arrive at a dramatic lookout spot of San Vito and the Talamanca Mountains. Archeological and biological evidence indicate the 1-hectare lake is over 3000 years old. The lake is most full and attractive during the wet season from September through December; however, aquatic birds may be seen all year long, undisturbed by civilization.   There is a nice *rancho* and barbecue area where one can relax with friends, equipped with bathroom facilities. Visitors' purchases from the Cántaros craft store and the small admission fee to the reserve help to maintain the property and keep the reading/play room open to neighborhood children to aid in their education and development. Contributions of children's books and games in Spanish are welcome to further this noble mission. The *finca* is open daily except Mondays from December 1st through April 30th, and then three days per week the rest of the year. If the door is closed, knock to see if there is someone there. Admission is around $1.25 per person, children under 6 are free. The *rancho* and barbecue area seats up to 24 people, and is rentable for parties and/or meetings. They welcome feedback from your experiences here at ghewson-hull@calacademy.org. Phone 773-3760 (Spanish). They are located right on the main road into San Vito from Ciudad Neily, on the east side, shortly before you arrive in town. There is parking right off the road next to the store.

HIKING AND CAMPING

The best hiking will be found in the Wilson Botanical Garden in Las Cruces — which are right on the road to Ciudad Neily about 6 km. south of San Vito — and La Amistad International Park. The gardens are absolutely stunning, and well worth a visit (see LODGINGS section as well). The immaculately maintained paths meander through park-like grounds, giving the visitor ample opportunity to view tropical flora from all over the world in peace and comfort. They have over 7000 species of plants and trees, and a rich diversity of wildlife including agoutis, armadillos, kinkajous, otters and monkeys. The office provides trail maps, and all the trails and even the trees and plants are marked and named for easy reference. Birders are especially thrilled at the magnificent abundance of rare and beautiful species (over 330) inhabiting various ecosystems, including forest dwellers, migrants and even aquatic fowl in a local marsh. The entrance fee is $6 for adults. They will serve lunch and/or dinner to day guests for $9pp. They're open from 8am to 4pm every day but Monday.

La Amistad International Park is huge, and it is recommended that you go in with a guide, as the trails are difficult, isolated and often hard to find. Buses leave San Vito at 10:30am and 3pm daily for Las Tablas, which is probably the easiest of the four avenues of access to the park for those without 4WD vehicles, and there is camping at the ranger station there. The park headquarters is in Progreso, about 30 km. northeast of San Vito. From there you can hike to the Las Tablas station about 10 km. in. There are no facilities within the park, though, only at the stations. More information is available through the Amistad Biosphere Reserve office in San Isidro, at 771-3155. You can ask at CIPROTUR in San Isidro, too (see that section).

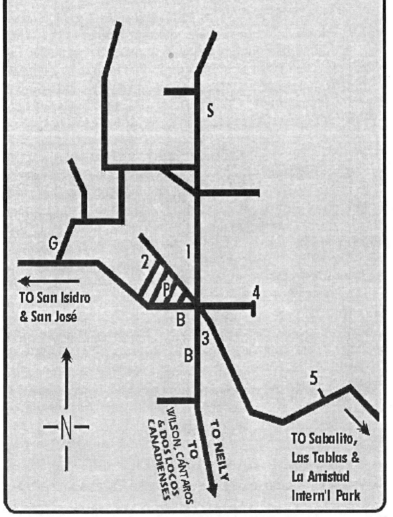

SAN VITO

1 Hotel Rino
2 Restaurante Liliana
3 Rest. & Hotel La Riviera
4 Hotel El Ceibo
5 Cabinas Las Mirlas

G Gas Station
P Park
B Bus Stop
S Bus Station

S

G

1

2

P

4

B

3

B

5

TO San Isidro
& San José

—N—

TO WILSON, CÁNTAROS
& DOS LOCOS
CANADIENSES

TO NEILY

TO Sabalito,
Las Tablas &
La Amistad
Intern'l Park

THE INTER-AMERICAN HIGHWAY

The Inter-American Highway (IAH) is the primary corridor of transportation through the southern zone on land. The highway heads southeast from Palmar almost directly to the border with Panama at Paso Canoas. There are many facilities along the way, and the following towns, though not really tourist-oriented, are good rest stops along this stretch of road.

RÍO CLARO

Located 59 kilometers southeast of Palmar, this junction with the road to Golfito is a major traffic hub. There are many stores right along the highway, a gas station, public pay phones and taxi service. You will know you are there when you see the flashing yellow lights over the highway at a curbed intersection with islands and a large gas station on the southwest corner.

CIUDAD NEILY

This town on the IAH, 15 km. southeast of Río Claro and 18 km. northwest of Panama, is the second largest commercial and transportation center in the southern zone next to San Isidro. It lies on the west bank of the Río Corredores, which is the name of the county as well. It is bordered on the south by vast banana and palm plantations and lots of other agriculture and pastures on the pan-flat lowlands, while the Fila Costeña mountains rise precipitously from behind the town to its north, heading up to the Coto Brus Valley and San Vito. There is really nothing here for tourists, with the exception of the bus terminal on the northeast end of town (towards the mountains) for those traveling in this manner.

PASO CANOAS

The border. Borders are a special place, and Costa Rica's with Panama is no exception. Like Tijuana in the U.S., this is where thousands of locals go to do much of their shopping, though here the 'locals' comprise virtually the entire country of Costa Rica. Easter week and the last three months of the year are a zoo here — avoid this area at all costs if you can. The only reason to come here is if you are going into Panama. There is nothing here but cheap hotels, broken sidewalks and maybe a few good shopping bargains (but not souvenirs). If you are going to Panama, at least you can get a meal and a room for the night if you need it. Otherwise, it's not worth a second thought. You should be staying in Costa Rica anyway!

SOME TICO SPANISH

Although you may be familiar with the Spanish language, Ticos have their own special dialect, like all Latin American countries. Some of the usage here can be very different from, say, Mexican or Puerto Rican Spanish, enough to cause you some confusion even if you are fluent in another dialect. This short section is here to help you deal with these differences, give you a few words and phrases in case you need them quick, and also be able to utter some appropriate *'dichos'* (sayings, or slang phrases). Some words and phrases you may not find defined elsewhere. I hope it helps . . . .

TICO SPANISH	AMERICAN ENGLISH
Buenas!	—Basic greeting, leaving out 'días' or 'tardes'
Adiós!	—'Goodbye', but often used as 'Hello' in passing
Pura Vida!	—Literally 'Pure Life', a happy, all-is-well statement
Buena Nota!	—'Right on!' or 'That's great!'
Qué dicha!	—'What good luck!' or 'Fantastic!'
Con mucho gusto	—You're welcome, more hearty than 'De nada'
Con permiso	—'Excuse me' ('Perdón' if you bump into someone)
Está bien	—'It's OK'. They use OK a lot, too.
Finca	—Ranch, farm, or both. Any large property.
El campo	—The countryside
Quebrada	—Stream or brook
Carro	—Car. (They don't use 'coche' here.)
Pick-up	—Pick-up truck. (What else?)
La bomba	—Common word for gas station (vs. gasolinera)
Llanta ponchada	—Flat tire
Repuestos	—Parts (for cars, machines)
Hay paso?	—'Is there passage', or Can I get through?
No funciona	—'It doesn't work'
Se falló	—'It failed'. More slang? Try 'Se hodió'.
Más para allá	—Farther
Más pa'cá	—Closer (Más para acá contracted)
Cuanto cuesta?	—'How much does it cost?'
Condón	—Condom. 'Preservativo' also used.
Paño	—Bath towel (They rarely use 'toalla')
La lancha	—Ferry boat or launch
Panga	—A small motorboat
Tickete	—Ticket. They don't use 'boleto' much.
Rancho/ito	—Traditional structure, usu. with thatched-palm roof
Soda	—Small eatery (restaurant or diner)
Casado	—'Married', or standard combo plate in restaurants
Gaseosa	—Soft drink (carbonated soda)

TICO SPANISH	AMERICAN ENGLISH
'Fresco (Refresco)	—Cold, non-alcoholic drink
'Fresco natural	—Natural fruit or powdered drink
Boca	—Snack. Look for the 'boca' bars.
Para llevar	—Carry-out (food)
Agua dulce	—Drink made with pure natural cane sugar
A la plancha	—Sautéed
Al ajillo	—Sautéed In garlic
A la parrilla	—Grilled
A su gusto	—To your liking
Hongos	—Mushrooms (also fungus)
Servicio sanitario	—Their polite term for toilet
Cabina	—A room, esp. in a small hotel or motel
Hay campo?	—Is there room (space)?
Fresco	—Cool, as in air temperature
No importa	—It's not important, doesn't matter
Lo que sea	—Whatever
No me digas!	—'Don't tell me!', meaning 'No way!' (slang)
De verdad?	—Really?!
Hágame el favor!	—'Do me the favor', but often 'Give me a break!'
Déjeme pensarlo	—Let me think about it
Así es la vida	—That's life
Cuidado!	—Careful!
Ojo!	—Watch out! (literally 'eye')
Ya!	—Already / Done! / Now! – take your pick (pr. 'yah')
Ya voy!	—I'm coming!
Ya me voy	—I'm leaving now (perfectly logical, right?)
Con toda la pata	—I've got it all (together). Hard to translate.
Gato/a	—Cat, of course, but also man/woman with light-colored eyes (blue, green, gray)

NOTES